NICARAGUA: WHAT DIFFERENCE COULD A REVOLUTION MAKE?

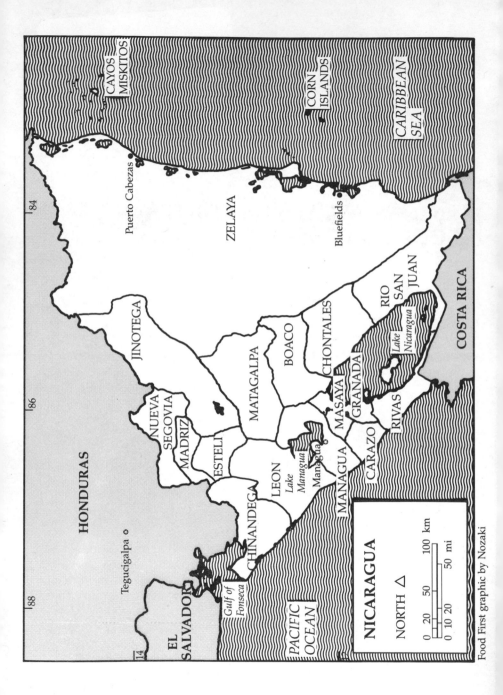

Food First graphic by Nozaki

NICARAGUA: WHAT DIFFERENCE COULD A REVOLUTION MAKE?

Food and Farming in the New Nicaragua

By Joseph Collins,
with Frances Moore Lappé and Nick Allen (first edition)
Paul Rice (second and third editions)

A Food First Book
Grove Press, Inc., New York

First edition published in 1982 by
Institute for Food and Development Policy
San Francisco

First Grove Press Edition 1986
First Printing 1986
ISBN: 0-394-55625-9
Library of Congress Catalog Card Number: 86-45424

First Evergreen Edition 1986
First Printing 1986
ISBN: 0-8021-3067-4 (pbk.)
Library of Congress Catalog Card Number: 86-45424

ABOUT FOOD FIRST

FOOD FIRST is a nonprofit research and education center, which, since its founding in 1975, has been dedicated to identifying the root causes of hunger in the United States and around the world. Financed by thousands of members, with modest support from foundations and churches, FOOD FIRST speaks with a strong, independent voice, free of ideological formulas and vested interests.

In over 60 countries and in 20 languages, FOOD FIRST provides a wide array of educational tools—books, articles, slide shows, films, and curricula for elementary schools and high schools—to lay the groundwork for a more democratically controlled food system that will meet the needs of all.

For more information write to:

FOOD FIRST
Institute for Food and Development Policy
1885 Mission Street
San Francisco, CA 94103
USA

Printed in the United States of America
A Food First Book/Published by GROVE PRESS, INC.

5   4   3

TABLE OF CONTENTS

LIST OF TABLES

Our special thanks to *Lance Lindblom and the Board of Directors of the J. Roderick MacArthur Foundation,* whose support made possible the publication of this book.

Acknowledgments

I AM GREATLY INDEBTED TO THE SANDINISTA government officials for the unwavering trust in me they have demonstrated over the past three years. Even after I told them I had decided to write about my experiences, they never showed the slightest hesitation about making themselves and their internal research—as well as the Nicaraguan countryside—available to me. Their candor is exceptional for government officials anywhere. At the same time they have never tried to control or even monitor what I was writing.

Special thanks must go to Jaime Wheelock, Minister of Agricultural Development and Agrarian Reform; Salvador Mayorga, Director General of the Agrarian Reform; and numerous other officials of the ministry, especially Robert Gutierrez, Pedro Blandon, Alvaro Reyes, and Ivan Garcia.

Also, I wish to acknowledge the invaluable cooperation of CIERA, the Nicaraguan government's agrarian reform research center. So many there have been helpful for so long that I hesitate to name anyone in particular for inevitably I will leave some out who deserve to be thanked by name. But I am deeply indebted to a CIERA staff member and old friend, Peter Marchetti, S.J., who remained always ready to help right up until the final fact-checking phone call. I would like also to thank CIERA director Orlando Nuñez S. and staff members Pascal Serres, Michel Merlet, Peter Utting, David Kaimowitz, and Eduardo Baumeister.

I am also indebted to many other institutions and individuals in Nicaragua, notably Xabier Gorostiaga, S.J., the Ministry of Planning, the Instituto Historico Centroamericano, the ATC, the UNAG, Sean Swezey, INIES, John Weeks, Elizabeth Dore, and hundreds of campesinos and farm workers who have so forthrightly told me what they think. Also Felipe Paz, Margaret Randall, the Maryknoll Sisters, the Jesuit Fathers, residents of Ciudad Sandino and several other barrios, Peter Shiras, Arnold Weissberg, Matilde Zimmerman, and Tommie Sue Montgomery.

Thanks also to those living outside Nicaragua whose writing has been so useful: Solon Barraclough, E. V. K. Fitzgerald, Joseph Thome, Jacques Chonchol, David Baytleman, Eugene Havens, Carmen Diana Deere, Philippe Bourgois, Jaime Biderman, Valerie Landau, Gustavo Esteva, Larry Simon, Michael Scott, Alejandro Schetmann, and George Black. While I have greatly benefited from their willingness to share their work, they are without responsibility for the use I have made of it.

This book would not have been possible without the Institute for Food and Development Policy. Therefore I want to thank the several thousand Friends of the Institute whose contributions make the work of the Institute possible, as well as the foundations and individuals who have helped us. In particular, I wish to express our appreciation for the J. Roderick MacArthur Foundation, whose support for this project was vital to its completion. Frances Moore Lappé and Nick Allen provided invaluable conceptual and editorial help.

Every time I attempt to write the acknowledgments for a new book, I admonish myself for not keeping a notebook noting those who help as the project goes along. Once again, I have failed. My omission is compounded by the fact that this book has been a three-year effort and there are so many to thank, so many whom I will recall only after this page goes to press. To all of them, my gratitude and my apologies.

Joseph Collins

Acknowledgments

FOR THE SECOND EDITION

First of all, I wish to express special thanks to Paul Rice for brilliant and dedicated assistance in Nicaragua. Together we carried out much of the field work for this edition and tracked down the data for the Tables. Paul wrote up our research on food production and distribution for the first drafts of chapters 20 through 23. Without his collaboration and companionship, the undertaking would have been much more formidable and much less joyful.

Also, I am especially grateful to Larry Rosenthal for his consistently solid editorial contribution. He is a master at curbing excesses.

Special thanks also to John Lear and David Wiltsie, interns at the Institute for Food and Development Policy, and to Craig Gallup for their cheerful assistance (despite long and irregular hours) in the final stages of manuscript preparation.

The manuscript benefited from comments and suggestions from Institute colleagues Nick Allen, Medea Benjamin, Kevin Danaher, Gretta Goldenman, Steve Goldfield, and Frances Lappé; from Betsy Cohn, Carmen Diana Deere, Mary Dugan, Richard Garfield, Saul Landau, and Jamera Rone in the United States; and from Laura Enriquez, Valpy Fitzgerald, Ivan Garcia, David Kaimowitz, Peter Marchetti, Doug Murray, Peter Rosset, Michael Zalkin, and Peter Utting in Nicaragua.

I also wish to acknowledge valuable interviews and conversations in Nicaragua with Robert Ambrose, Carlos Barrios, Eduardo Baumeister, Tomas Borge, Judy Butler, Julio Castillo, Miguel D'Escoto, Xabier Gorostiaga, Arturo Grisby, Marvin

Ortega, Dionisio Marenco, Salvador Mayorga, Michel Merlet, Orlando Núñez, Pascal Serres, Sean Swezey, Isidro Tellez, and Jaime Wheelock, as well as numerous campesinos, farmworkers, growers and ranchers, farm managers, shopkeepers, market vendors, and many other Nicaraguans.

This book would not have been possible without the Institute for Food and Development Policy. Therefore I want to thank the 20,000 individual and group supporters of the Institute. Their contributions, small and large, make the work of the Institute possible, along with the support from a number of foundations and religious grantors.

I want to thank the Publication Department of the Institute for Food and Development Policy, which has overseen this book's publication. Finally, my special thanks to Keith Wood who tamed my computer and to housemate David Fitzgerald who remained once again unflappable during even the most frenzied moments this book was being created in our home.

Joseph Collins

Word to the Reader

Why a New Edition

In the fall of 1982 I completed the first edition of *What Difference Could a Revolution Make? Food and Farming in the New Nicaragua.* Since then I have made several working visits a year to the ever-changing Nicaragua.

Each time I come home to the United States, I am immediately upset by media "coverage" of the Nicaraguan revolution. Arriving at the Miami, New Orleans, or Dallas airport, I pick up a newspaper and read an article on the country I had left only a few hours before. Often I can hardly believe it was the same country.

Going down to Nicaragua, I would sometimes bring newspaper and magazine articles on Nicaragua to American and other English-speaking friends working there; invariably they would be shocked by the images created. Similarly, Nicaraguan campesinos and farmworkers often ask me what is being said in the United States about their revolution. When I explain that my compatriots are being told that the Nicaraguan revolution is repressive and totalitarian and that the Sandinista-led government is a pawn of the Soviet Union and Castro's Cuba, they either think I am joking or respond as did one old peasant woman: "The American people must be the most misinformed people on earth."

Since the first edition I have often had the impression of a stepped-up "disinformation" campaign on Nicaragua emanating from Washington. Orchestrated or not, the U.S. commercial media, with exceptions rare enough to be individually memorable, have not helped those outside Nicaragua develop even a sense of the achievements—or the true short-comings—of the revolution. Repeatedly, the bases of media attacks on Nicaragua turn out to be administration handouts and (always unidentified) "Western diplomatic sources."

Since the completion of the first edition of this book, the Reagan administration and Congress have dramatically escalated their military and economic warfare against Nicaragua:

—The U.S. Congress has approved at least $73.5 million for the twelve thousand "contras"—many of whom were officers in Somoza's National Guard and who are directed by the CIA in their efforts to overthrow the Nicaraguan government. Undoubtedly, additional funding has been channeled through CIA and Pentagon budgets to this illegal, "covert" war. According to the *New York Times* (November 8, 1983), the CIA has organized a "network" of former U.S. intelligence and military personnel to supply aircraft, weapons and paramilitary support to the contras.

—The U.S. armed forces have engaged in several joint maneuvers, unprecedented in size and duration, with the Honduran armed forces. Some maneuvers have simulated naval blockades and full-scale invasions of Nicaragua. In late 1984, more than one thousand U.S. military advisors were stationed in Honduras. U.S. military aid to Honduras under the Reagan administration has been increased more than 20 times.

—The Pentagon has constructed eight airfields in Honduras to assist the contras and prepare for what it calls "extended deployment of U.S. combat forces."

—In October 1983, the contras launched an attack on Corinto, Nicaragua's most important port, from a CIA ship offshore. A few months later U.S. military personnel took part in the mining of Nicaraguan harbors. This CIA operation was rightly termed an "act of war" by conservative Republican Senator Barry Goldwater.

—U.S. pilots have repeatedly flown reconnaissance missions over Nicaragua. Since just before Nicaragua's elections, supersonic spy planes breaking the sound barrier have been causing booms that simulate bombings—clearly a form of psychological warfare.

—The CIA has recruited seven-man ranger squads to enter Nicaragua to carry out terrorist assassinations and sabotage (CBS News, April 11, 1983). The CIA has distributed manuals to the contras advocating and giving instructions on how to carry out assassinations, kidnappings, and economic sabotage.

—Having cut off U.S. economic aid to Nicaragua, the Reagan administration has pressured Western European and other governments to do likewise. Veto power and political leverage within international financial institutions such as the World Bank have been employed to block virtually all loans to Nicaragua.

—In May 1983 the Reagan administration virtually eliminated Nicaragua's share in the U.S. preferential price for imported sugar (often several times the world-market price).

Warfare by the most powerful nation in the world against one of the world's smallest and weakest nations has had an overwhelming impact on the Nicaragua I wrote about in the first edition. Even among those outside Nicaragua who are sympathetic to the Nicaraguan people's efforts to determine their own destiny, there is scant appreciation of the grave toll being exacted by the policies of the United States and other countries following the beat of Washington's drums. This lack of awareness confronts me every time I am speaking in the United States, Canada, and Europe and am asked whether I think the United States will "intervene" in Nicaragua. For, as every Nicaraguan knows, the United States has long been intervening against the revolution, indeed, prosecuting a very real, if undeclared, war on Nicaragua.

When I completed the first edition, I had no future edition

in mind. It has never been my intention to chronicle the Nicaraguan revolution. But continual outrage at the dangerous distortions in the media and in Washington, as well as alarm and frustration that so few truly appreciate the consequences of my government's policies, moved me to write this thoroughly updated account of a revolution that is still very much alive.

What the New Edition Is and Is Not

The research for this new edition got under way in May 1984 following several working stays in Nicaragua since completing the first edition. Fortunately for me, Paul Rice agreed to assist me. Paul, a Yale graduate in economics, draws on his rich experience during the summer of 1982 living on a peasant cooperative in northern Nicaragua. Since June 1983, Paul has been working in Managua at the nongovernmental Nicaraguan Institute for Economic and Social Research (INIES), which is associated with our Institute for Food and Development Policy in San Francisco. We worked together in Nicaragua in May, June, September, and early November 1984.

This new edition is not a revision of the original edition. None of the existing chapters were changed (I resisted all temptations to appear more foresighted!). In my opinion, these chapters still provide material unavailable elsewhere for understanding the Sandinista revolution today. I did drop the final chapter of the original edition, "Reflections," which has been replaced by a "Postscript" written with Frances Moore Lappé, cofounder of the Institute and my long-time colleague.

The new edition supplements the original with ten fresh chapters. As in the original edition, these chapters invite the reader to take an open-minded look at Nicaragua through what I have elsewhere called the "food window"—examining the differences in life in the countryside and in the national food and nutritional situation being made by the revolution. We look at the achievements as well as the shortcomings, the mistakes, and the obstacles.

In addition to the new chapters, *Nicaragua: What Difference Could a Revolution Make?* includes several new statistical tables and complete updates of those from the earlier edition. The chronology of Nicaragua's political history and our Resource Guide have also been updated. Finally, we have added a map of Nicaragua, a list of acronyms, a new cover, and a slightly modified title.

* * *

The peasant woman I quote before went on to tell me: "Someday your people will come to understand our struggle." My only hope is that the labor of many to make this book helps prove her correct.

Joseph Collins
January 15, 1985

Note to the Third Edition

This new Food First / Grove edition provided the opportunity to further update *Nicaragua: What Difference Could a Revolution Make?* With the assistance of Paul Rice, I have added a chapter tracking major developments into 1986. Also updated, as much as possible, are the statistical tables as well as the chronology of Nicaragua's political history and the Resource Guide.

I wish to thank Peggy Lauer for her proofreading assistance on this edition, and also María Eder, M.D. for checking Spanish usage.

Joseph Collins
February 15, 1986

PART ONE

ONE

"NICARAGUA IS A SCHOOL"

IN AUGUST 1979, THE INSTITUTE FOR FOOD AND Development Policy received a long distance call from Managua. On the other end of the line was an official in Nicaragua's Ministry of Planning. He asked for Joe Collins. "We are putting together an advisory panel of people with experience in problems of agrarian reform and food policy. Would you be willing to come down for a working session to discuss Nicaragua's policies? An international church group will pay your way."

That was the beginning of my unique opportunity to learn firsthand about the process of change set off by the Sandinista-led popular insurrection, which had overthrown the Somoza dictatorship just a month earlier. During the three years since that phone call, I have visited Nicaragua ten times as an unpaid advisor on food and farming policies. In late 1981, Institute cofounder Frances Moore Lappé, editor Nick Allen, and I began working together to analyze the changes under way in the Nicaraguan countryside as well as in the national food situation. This book is the result.

The more we learned about Nicaragua, the more we felt North Americans were being deprived of an opportunity to see Nicaragua through the eyes of Nicaraguans themselves. So in early 1982 Frances and I went to Nicaragua together,

1

and interviewed Nicaraguans in all walks of life. This collaboration resulted in our book *Now We Can Speak: A Journey through the New Nicaragua*, a companion to this one.

We've entitled this opening chapter "Nicaragua Is a School" for several reasons. First, you hear often this phrase— *"Nicaragua es una escuela"*—from Nicaraguans because it describes how they feel about the process of change they're engaged in. For us, it has a special meaning.

For many years we have sought to understand the roots of hunger throughout the world. Through our work at the Institute for Food and Development Policy we've learned that a society's food and farming policies are a powerful lens through which to evaluate the priorities, sympathies, values, and effectiveness of any country's leadership. This is especially true in most third-world countries, which, like Nicaragua, are overwhelmingly agricultural.

In this book we will ask you to join us in seeing Nicaragua through "food glasses." Doing so makes it possible to see behind the newspaper accounts, which too often transmit only the U.S. government's one-dimensional portrayal of Nicaragua's geopolitical role in the East-West conflict. Focusing on food and farming, we are able to report more broadly on how the lives of the Nicaraguan people are being affected by the country's new economic and social policies.

What has struck us about Nicaragua's new leadership is its clear common purpose: to build a new country based on what many Nicaraguans call "the logic of the majority." For too long, they believe, Nicaragua has operated according to the "logic of the minority," meaning that decisions were made in the interests of, and usually by, the wealthiest 10 percent of the population. As a consequence, the majority of Nicaraguans had been made among the poorest people in Latin America. The incidence of malnutrition had doubled in the ten years before 1975, crippling the lives of almost 60 percent of children under 4 years of age. By the time of the insurrection, 60 percent of rural people had been deprived of land they needed to feed themselves. Just 1 percent of landowners— a mere 1,600 people—had usurped almost half the land.

The success of the war against the dictatorship and the disintegration of the old system of exploitation, the new government argues, means that now the needs of the majority—

Nicaragua's poor—should come first. But while the "logic of the majority" provides a direction to guide the country's new leaders, it does not tell them which road to take or which vehicles are best suited for the trip. That they must learn by analyzing their experiences as they go along and by studying the experiences of other peoples.

The Nicaraguan leadership confronts seemingly impossible trade-offs as well as many unknowns and unforeseen consequences in pursuing policies guided by the "logic of the majority." Nowhere is this more true than in food and farming.

The first trade-off is obvious: By definition, redistribution of privately owned land means that some will gain, while others—the minority who control most of the land—will lose. Inevitably, those who have to give up some of their land will not be happy.

But the trade-off is more complex than simply trading the privileges of the rich for the rights of the poor. While the "logic of the majority" might superficially be interpreted as requiring the expropriation and rapid subdivision of big estates, the Nicaraguan leadership has not seen it that way. If export crop production on the large estates were undermined, the entire society—of which the poor are the majority—would suffer. So the Sandinista leadership has resisted the redistribution of any land that is being used productively.

For this reason a sense of justice, as well as a desire to respond to the demands of the landless, has had to be traded-off against the need to keep up production of export crops, essential to obtain the foreign currency necessary to import what Nicaragua can't produce itself.

A related trade-off confronted the Sandinistas. If they responded to the demands of the poor for land to grow their own food, then how would they be able to attract enough workers to help harvest the export crops? After all, when people can feed themselves from their own land, what's to assure that they'll still be willing to do the backbreaking work of picking cotton for ten hours a day?

How have the Nicaraguans wrestled with such painful trade-offs? This question, which has intrigued us for the last three years, is at the heart of this book.

While we have been intrigued, we have also been impressed. In three years we have witnessed this Pennsylvaniasize nation of 2.5 million people make remarkable advances, especially remarkable because they have been achieved at a time when conditions of life are worsening in most other countries in Central America and the rest of the third world. Since the beginning of Nicaragua's revolution:

—Over 40,000 landless rural families have received access to land on which to grow food for the first time.

—Production of basic food crops—corn, beans, rice, sorghum—is up. Land grants to the rural poor, lowered land rents, generous government farm credit, and better prices have enabled poor farmers to increase their production of the country's food staples. Corn and bean productions have climbed 10 and 45 percent respectively, while rice production has doubled compared to 1977–78 (a representative Somoza year).

—Export crop production is also up—coffee by 10 and sugar by 20 percent compared to 1977–78.

—Consumption of basic foods has soared. Corn consumption is up by a third, beans by 40 percent, and rice by 30 percent since 1978, the last year before the war.

—Food self-sufficiency is at hand. Following excellent 1982 harvests, imports of major staples have either been eliminated or substantially reduced. Nicaragua will soon be exporting rice and possibly beans.

—Infant death has been reduced. The infant mortality rate, perhaps the best measure of family nutrition and availability of health services for the poor, has been cut by one-third. An anti-malaria campaign has reduced the incidence of malaria by one-third. Over 1 million Nicaraguans have been immunized against polio, measles, and tetanus, diseases that continue to kill millions of people throughout the third world.

—Illiteracy has been dramatically reduced. A volunteer-based national campaign has cut illiteracy from over half the population to less than one-seventh. Over 1 million Nicaraguans—40 percent of the entire population—are involved in some kind of formal schooling. Over 1,200 new schools have been constructed, 95 percent of them in the countryside.

We have focused on these achievements because, since most did not require huge sums of money, they could in theory be accomplished in other third-world countries where control over economic resources in a few hands has impoverished the majority. That they were achieved in Nicaragua testifies to two things: first, the value of basing government policy on the "logic of the majority"; second, the broad support for the new government's policies, especially among the poor rural majority. This support is evident not only in widespread voluntary participation, but also in the initiative of tens of thousands of Nicaraguans without which many of these advances would have been impossible. These gains become even more impressive in light of the multiple obstacles we discuss below.

What Makes Nicaragua Different?

Nicaragua's ability to grapple with seemingly impossible trade-offs, to learn from previous revolutions, and to stay on course in the face of threats from its more powerful neighbors, especially the United States, shows this revolution is different from many other revolutionary movements. What makes Nicaragua different? And what can we learn?

To begin to answer these questions, let's return to the beginning, to my invitation to help advise the men and women formulating Nicaragua's food and farming policies. Among those invited to join the informal advisory group were people who had participated in developing agrarian reform in both the Christian Democrat and Popular Unity governments in Chile, those with expertise in food and farming in post-colonial Africa, and others like me who had been studying agrarian reform in many different societies. The very fact that Nicaragua's new leaders chose to gather such advisory panels—not only for food and farming but also for education, health, etc. —tells something about their openness.

Working in Nicaragua has given me a close look at other qualities of Nicaragua's young new leaders. First of all, I have learned they are serious people! Our meetings often began early in the morning and lasted late into the night. The Nicaraguans did not ask the foreigners what to do. Nor did they tell us what they were going to do and lobby for an endorsement. Rather, they often presented us "experts" with a number of options along with the relevant data (such as it was). They wanted those more experienced than they to help shine a light down the road each policy might take their country. What are the consequences we might not foresee, they asked us.

In itself, this approach told us a lot. It revealed qualities we have come to recognize again and again in our dealings with Nicaraguan leaders. They do not tend to be doctrinaire. They do not attempt to plug in rigid, preconceived, ideological formulas. They continue to adapt their policies in light of their experiences.

In working with the leaders in the agrarian reform, I have witnessed a genuine humility rooted in honesty. Over and over again, I've heard them admit, "We just don't know the answer"—or say, "Yes, we've made a mistake."

I've also come to appreciate their pragmatism. Realistically, the Nicaraguans concluded that their shortage of experienced leaders meant they had to rely on the knowledge and help of others. It also meant working toward a policy they call "national unity," that is, trying to maintain support for a program of reconstruction among both the capitalist producers and the peasants. *Business Latin America*, a weekly for managers of multinational corporations, summed up a recent survey of Nicaragua: "Despite increasing reports of bitter conflict between the Sandinista government and the private sector in Nicaragua, the great majority of international companies surveyed by *BLA* describe their relations with the government as good, or at least reasonable.... 'People in the Ministry of Economy are pragmatic,' one executive explained."

Another striking feature of the Nicaraguan revolution is the extent of voluntarism. While I was in Managua in February 1982, for example, 70,000 volunteers were giving up a Sunday to participate in a polio vaccination campaign. The Sandinistas' approach to controlling malaria, a disease of epidemic proportions in Nicaragua, reveals the unique potential of voluntary action. Instead of spraying DDT in an effort to kill the mosquito vectors, they opted for the safer and ultimately more effective *simultaneous* vaccination of the *entire* population, thereby eradicating the problem essentially by ensuring humans would no longer be carriers. While public health authorities have long thought this method superior, it requires mobilizing virtually the entire population. Nicaragua is one of the few countries that felt capable of this massive effort.

Mass participation in large part accounts for the success of the insurrection itself. By 1978, the year before victory, an overwhelming majority of the Nicaraguan people, from all walks of life, were directly or indirectly supporting the Sandinista-led struggle to topple Somoza and his National Guard. During the final insurrection against the dictatorship, Sandinista leaders admitted that spontaneous uprisings of the people took the initiative away from the leadership.

The motivation of so many of its leaders also distinguishes the Nicaraguan revolution. Motivations, of course, are difficult to assess, but what struck me as I talked with people throughout the country was the deeply religious purpose so many expressed. Many government and peasant leaders have described to me how their commitment was sparked in Catholic study groups where, as teenagers, they met with friends to discuss the Bible and reflect on the relevancy of Jesus' teachings in a society of gross injustice and misery. Moved by these reflections, some went to live and work among the poor.

These religious teachings stressed the innate value of each human being and, from this, the individual's right to control the resources he or she needs to live with dignity. The grounding influence of Christianity is reflected in many of the decisions made since victory. "Implacable in combat, generous in victory" has been a slogan of the Sandinista-led government from the start. The Sandinistas stand out for their lack of vengeance against their enemies. Immediately upon victory the government abolished the death penalty and went to great lengths to ensure legal trials for all of the captured National Guardsmen accused of crimes. (Much to the outrage of many Nicaraguans, whose loved ones had been murdered by the Guard, the government released half of the original 8,000 Guardsmen captured, for lack of sufficient individual evidence against them.)

Respect for the individual is also reflected in the Sandinistas' flexible economic policies, allowing people to choose what will work for them. Farm cooperatives, for example, are totally voluntary, although the government encourages them through credit and services where they appear to be economically appropriate. Indeed, in the countryside I've found dozens of varieties of cooperatives because the members in each place decided what would be best for them.

The Nicaraguan revolution also stands out for the extraordinary participation of women. During the fighting, women worked in supportive functions, as combatants, and even as military commanders; by the time of victory about 30 percent of the Sandinista forces were women. (In Margaret Randall's moving book *Sandino's Daughters*, Nicaraguan women tell what these new roles meant to them.) Today, women have important roles in government and in the mass organizations. The Nicaraguan revolution is also fostering the flowering of distinctly Nicaraguan culture in a country long considered a subsidiary of the United States. The first-ever Festival of Campesino Music brought national attention to previously obscure villages. And building on the national indignation against the U.S. government's wheat cut-off, the Nicaraguans organized corn festivals — including dances and imaginative cooking contests — to stimulate the pride of the people in their indigenous grain. Ninety new theatrical groups have sprung up as well as at least two dozen community centers offering workshops in painting, poetry, drama, music, and dance. Over a hundred poetry workshops supported by the Ministry of Culture are awakening creative expression in the slums, the factories, the army, the prisons, and even the police. For the first time, Nicaragua has a film institute — serving not just the city dwellers but bringing film by mule and backpack into even the remotest villages.

Finally, the Nicaraguan revolution does not use a cult of personality to glue the new society together. There is no Nicaraguan Mao or Fidel, and the leadership appears intent on making a common vision, not a personality, the binding force. Leadership is a collective undertaking: the three-person junta works closely with the nine-person National Directorate. The only personalities promoted as national symbols are the revolution's martyrs, especially Augusto César Sandino, who fought the U.S. Marines in Nicaragua in the 1920s and 1930s and was assassinated by the first Somoza in 1933. (The Sandinista Front for National Liberation, or FSLN, took is name for Sandino.)

A Common Legacy of Underdevelopment

While the Nicaraguan revolution is uniquely Nicaraguan, the country shares a common history with other under-developed countries whose economic and human develop-ment has been distorted by decades of external and internal exploitation.

That legacy involves not only the concentration of land and wealth in a few hands but also its fruits:

—Good land underused, and the best land used not for food for local people but for luxury export crops to further enrich the already wealthy elite.

—Extraordinary dependence on, and therefore susceptibility to, the international market. If any one of Nicaragua's four major export crops drops a few cents a pound on the London commodity markets, the country's entire econ-omy can be undermined.

—No experience in democratic process. Indeed, 45 years of ironclad dictatorship taught Nicaraguans that to speak out was to risk your life.

This legacy of underdevelopment results in innumerable sur-prises that can undermine even the best-intended policy, as the Nicaraguans have learned. So abysmal, for example, was the collection of national land tenure statistics under the Somoza dictatorship that the new leaders didn't even know how much land the government confiscated when Somoza and his allies fled the country. In the first months, they thought they had up to 60 percent of the land, which they could make available to Nicaragua's poor. But when the dust settled, they ended up with just over 20 percent—one-third of what they had expected.

Similarly, agricultural planners have been frustrated by the virtual absence of good roads in much of the country's food-growing regions. Thus, while peasants used the govern-ment's generous new farm credits to produce more rice and beans, much of the food never got to the markets. There was simply no way to transport it.

These are just two of the twists that have deepened our

understanding of the difficulties of building a more just society out of the ruins of an extremely unjust and inefficient one.

Not the least of the legacy of underdevelopment is the dearth of experienced leaders, technicians, and managers. Over and over again we have been struck by the youth of those who now must shoulder enormous responsibility. Nicaraguans in their 20s and early 30s, many with no administrative experience whatsoever, have taken charge of entire ministries of government.

Driving from the airport into Managua, Nicaragua's capital, the shells of bombed-out factories have continually reminded me that on top of the legacy of underdevelopment is the devastation of war. In Nicaragua this, too, is extreme because Somoza ordered the National Guard to bomb and pillage his own people to punish them for their impudence. About 50,000 Nicaraguans were killed and another 100,000 wounded, out of a total population of 2.5 million.

This costly war and Somoza's personal greed drained the country. The destruction of the war, capital flight, and the debt inherited from Somoza came to $4.1 billion, according to a U.N. study. The foreign debt alone, much of it incurred to fill the dictator's secret foreign bank accounts and to purchase arms, stood at a crushing $1.6 billion. In 1982, Nicaragua paid out 52 cents of every dollar earned from its exports just in interest and on repayment of its foreign debt.

As if all this were not enough, Nicaragua also confronts the economic crisis hitting all Central America. Prices for the country's basic exports have fallen while the prices of needed imports have risen. Of Nicaragua's export earnings, 40 percent goes for petroleum imports. In 1977, Nicaragua had to export 4.4 tons of coffee to import a tractor; only four years later, the same tractor cost the equivalent of 11.2 tons of coffee. By 1982, the price of sugar, another major export of the region, had fallen to the lowest level in ten years.

Not surprisingly, then, only two countries in Central America showed any overall economic progress in 1981. Nicaragua, in spite of these monumental obstacles, was one of them. Indeed, significant advances in Nicaragua's food production stand in sharp contrast to Costa Rica's food crisis.

By mid-1982, Costa Ricans were crossing into Nicaragua to buy beans and rice.

Lessons from Nicaragua

As a student of the causes and proposed remedies of world hunger for many years, the theme of my work at the Institute for Food and Development Policy can be summed up in one sentence: Hunger can be eliminated only through political and economic changes that redistribute power over food-producing resources. In 1977 Frances Moore Lappé and I completed the first edition of *Food First: Beyond the Myth of Scarcity* (Ballantine, revised 1979). Since *Food First* is more an analysis of the roots of hunger than a blueprint for change, we are often asked: How could any poor country, given the incredible legacy of underdevelopment, even begin to attack the roots of needless hunger? So naturally we sit up and take notice when a government claims—as does the Nicaraguan government—to be working to end hunger. Indeed, we take special note of Nicaragua because, before the overthrow of the dictatorship, most Nicaraguans had been made among the poorest people in Latin America, despite the agricultural wealth of their country.

But we have learned to be leery of governments' claims of concern for their poor. We've watched governments in India, Brazil, the Philippines, and other countries, claiming to be concerned about the hungry, launch costly aid-financed programs to increase food production. But despite production successes, hunger has deepened precisely because such governments repress movements for change that would redistribute power over basic resources, allowing people to feed themselves. We've watched other countries, some calling themselves "socialist," sacrifice the well-being of the rural poor for the sake of urban industrialization.

Of course no one can predict the future for Nicaragua. But I have been grateful for the opportunity to take this intimate look at a country attempting to put "food first." My perspective has always been critical, analyzing the high hopes and good intentions along with the mixed reality. But what has struck me over the last three years is the consistent and staggering discrepancy between my perspective, based on close contacts with Nicaraguans from all walks of life, and the one presented by the Reagan administration and the mass media in the United States.

Whatever happens in Nicaragua, Nicaragua *is* a school. Even if Nicaragua's leadership should become a new unaccountable elite, we would still have much to learn. We would have to learn *why* the country moved in this direction. We would have to ask what role the United States played in forcing Nicaragua to reduce political and economic pluralism.

Dismissing such an outcome as inevitable is too easy— and, I believe, profoundly wrong. First, it assumes that there is nothing we can do to stop our government's apparent attempt to make life in Nicaragua as difficult and repressive as possible. Second, it discounts the genuinely democratic spirit of participation we have witnessed in so many Nicaraguans. From my experience, I feel certain that Nicaraguans want to learn from the mistakes of previous revolutions, not repeat them.

TWO

IMAGINE YOU WERE A NICARAGUAN . . .

T HIS BOOK IS A STORY OF A SOCIETY STRUG-
gling to remake itself. It is a story of sacrifices, compromises, achievements, disappointments, fears, and hopes. It is
a story of people willing to risk their lives for change.

To understand why so many Nicaraguans have been willing to risk their lives for change, we must try to imagine ourselves as typical Nicaraguans before the overthrow of the
Somoza dictatorship.

Imagine it's 1977 and you are a 17-year-old Nicaraguan.
Your family, like two-thirds of all rural families, has either no
land at all or not enough to feed itself. If yours is "lucky"
enough to have a little plot of land, half or even more of
what you grow—or a steep cash rent—goes to the landowner in the city.

Last year you watched, helpless, as your little sister became
repeatedly ill with diarrhea. Your parents saw her losing her
strength but there was no one to help. In all of rural Nicaragua there are only five clinics with beds. The first few times
your sister pulled through. But by then she was so weak that
when measles hit, you watched her die after four painful
days. The year before, your brother died right after birth; your
mother and father have lost five of their children.

You cannot remember a day when your mother was not

13

worried about having enough food for your family—and, of course, you never really did have enough or your little sister wouldn't have died from measles. You heard once on a neighbor's radio that Nicaragua was importing more and more corn, beans, and sorghum. And you've heard about the incredible *supermercados* in Managua. But without money you can't buy food no matter how much there is.

The seven people in your family share a single-room shack, divided by a thin partition. The floor is dirt, there is no electric light, no toilet, no clean drinking water. You are outraged when you hear Somoza boast to some American reporters that "Nicaragua has no housing problem because of its wonderful climate."

You hardly know anyone who can read and write—except the priest, of course, but he's from Spain. You'd like to learn but there is no school. Anyway, you must work.

To buy a few simple tools, some cooking oil, sugar, salt, and kerosene, your father has to borrow money. But the only source of credit is the local moneylender who makes him pay back half again as much and sometimes much more. Not surprisingly, your family is forever is debt.

Locked in debt and without land to grow enough food, your family is forced to labor on the coffee, cotton, or sugar estates. But such work is available only three to four months a year at harvest time. Since the pay is miserable everyone in your family must work to try to bring in enough: your mother, your grandmother, your older sister—about 40 percent of the coffee and cotton cutters are women—and your father and brother. You had to start picking coffee when you were 6. For filling a 20-pound bucket you earn only 16 cents. Working sunup to sundown, you might earn a dollar.

Your "home" during the harvest is a long, windowless barrack built out of unpainted planks or plywood. With the other exhausted workers—men and women, old people and children, sick and well—you sleep on plywood slabs, called "drawers" because they are stacked four or five high with only a foot and a half of space between them. There is no privacy for there are no partitions. There is no flooring, no window, not a single light bulb. The only toilet is the bushes. Filth all the day long. For three to four months a year this is home for you and for over 400,000 other Nicaraguans.

Working on the coffee estates is bad, but picking cotton is even worse. You found that out one year when your family had to travel even farther, down to the Pacific coastal cotton estates, to find work. At least coffee grows in the cooler regions. But on the coastal lowlands the blinding tropical sun hangs in a cloudless sky, bringing temperatures to well over 100 degrees. You had nothing to protect you from the cotton branches, the pesticide-saturated fields, and the maddening swirl of gnats and jiggers.

Placing your baby sister on the edge of the hot, dusty field, your mother picked cotton as fast as she could, filling her sack and rushing to the weighing station so she could hurry back to nurse. She didn't know that tests would probably have shown that her breast milk had over 500 times the DDT considered safe for consumption by the World Health Organization, a frightening contamination due to 20 to 40 aerial DDT sprayings a year of the cotton fields.

In the harvests, too, hunger is a constant companion. All you get are small portions of beans and fried bananas and, rarely, some rice or corn tortillas or a bit of cheese in place of the bananas. Yet for this food, about three hours' wages are deducted from your pay. Even here, you're sure the owner makes profits. You only see meat on the final day of the harvest when the *patrón* and his family put on a "feast."

As you grow older, you realize that even though your family has no land, it is not because your country lacks land. You learn—quite likely through a Catholic priest—that there are more than five agricultural acres for every Nicaraguan, and potentially twice that. The problem is that most of the land is owned by the few big landowners. The richest 2 percent own over 50 percent of the land, while the poorest 70 percent of landowners—and that doesn't include your father, who only rents his miserable plot—own only 2 percent of the land.

Not only do the rich own most of the land, you discover, but clearly they've got the best land. Their soil is most fertile and flat. Yet they waste its potential, using it mostly to graze cattle. By the 1970s, in fact, 10 out of 11 million acres used for export production were being devoted to cattle grazing.

While you are constantly hungry, you discover that 22 times more land goes to produce for export than to grow food for Nicaraguans. And much of the food-growing land is so poor and hilly that it should be in pasture.

While you are growing up your grandmother tells you stories of how things got to be the way they are now, stories she heard from her parents back in the 1880s.

In those days, the powerful people had large cattle haciendas, but they were less concerned about producing beef and milk than they were in just holding on to the land. For many who traced their descent from the *conquistadores*, land was the primary source of their status.

Because they needed few workers, these land barons were content to let people like your great-grandparents work parcels of land, although, of course, they never got legal papers for it. So, while your great-grandparents were poor campesinos, at least they could feed themselves from their small farm, called a *tierra*. They grew corn, beans, and some vegetables, had some banana and other fruit trees, and kept a few pigs and chickens.

Then, somewhat before your grandmother was born—in the 1870s and 1880s—the Nicaraguan countryside began to change rapidly.

The demand for coffee in foreign countries was booming and Nicaragua's landowning elite, as well as new immigrant investors, were quick to respond. With visions of coffee trees as money trees, they broke up scores of cattle ranches, planting pastures with coffee trees.

To give a law-and-order veneer to pushing your great-grandparents and tens of thousands of campesino families like them off their *tierras*, the coffee entrepreneurs pushed through a "Law of Agrarian Reform" and other legislation. It put up for auction indigenous people's communal lands and much of public and church land. Although your great-grandfather and other campesinos had worked the land for years, they stood no chance of getting it. They were easily outbid by the coffee interests.

When the poor refused to get off the land they had worked for decades, the new owners drove cattle onto the *tierras* to trample and eat the crops. Your great-grandfather was almost killed in 1881 when thousands of dispossessed campesinos rebelled. Five thousand were massacred.

The new coffee barons needed not only land but labor, especially at harvest time. Robbing your great-grandparents of their self-sufficient farms insured that they would have to go to work on the big estates. How else could your great-grandparents' family survive? And as if necessity were not enough, laws were decreed requiring campesinos to show proof on demand that they were employed during the coffee harvest.

To survive between harvests, your great-grandparents migrated toward the central part of the country, the "agricultural frontier." There a cattle rancher allowed them to slash and burn some virgin land in order to plant corn and beans. But once they had their first crop or so, the owner put cattle on the land, telling your great-grandparents they'd have to clear more land if they wanted to eat. It was in one of those clearings, your grandmother tells you, that she was born.

You understand now that the history of your family, like tens of thousands of Nicaraguan campesino families, is tied to coffee. But you wonder where all the endless fields of cotton came from.

Your father explains that while he heard some talk of cotton when he was a boy, it was only in 1950, just ten years before you were born, that "white gold fever" hit Nicaragua. In only a few years the white puff balls took over the Pacific plain as far as you could see, north to south and right up to the base of the volcanos. The cotton plants wouldn't hold down the rich volcanic soil and soon the region became plagued with dust storms.

By the mid-1950s, cotton topped coffee as Nicaragua's biggest export. Somoza saw to it that the cotton investors got cheap bank credit, for he personally reaped millions of dollars on the cotton boom. It's completely unfair, your father tells you, that the rich export farmers don't even risk their money; he and the other campesinos grow what people really need most—basic foods—yet they can't get even the smallest bank loan.

In the cotton bonanza, campesinos, most of whom did not have any papers for their lands, were bought out for next to nothing; failing that, they were forced off the land. Absentee landowners returned to evict their campesino tenants and rent out their lands to cotton entrepreneurs.

When campesinos resisted, the National Guard burned

their homes and crops and pulled up the fences. Indeed, some of the cotton speculators themselves were high officers in Somoza's National Guard, Nicaragua's army and police set up by the U.S. Marines. You understand more than ever why your father and all his friends hate the Guard.

Cotton took over the land that had been growing corn and beans, rice and sorghum, all the basic food crops of the people. The tens of thousands of displaced peasant producers at best wound up as sharecroppers and cash renters on plots of earth too small and poor to support them.

Some of the campesinos run off the land by the cotton invasion pushed east and north into the "agricultural frontier." There, just like your great-grandparents had done, they cleared trees and brush on the huge cattle haciendas only to be forced onto new uncleared land by cattlemen seeking to cash in on the next export boom—the 1960s boom in beef exports to the United States.

Pushed even deeper into the mountainous interior, these tens of thousands of campesinos are even poorer than your family. Almost half the year they are entirely cut off from the rest of the country: even a burro can't get through the muddy trails and dirt roads. Few have ever seen a doctor, even though the area teems with disease, including malaria and adult measles.

You think about all of this—what the priest says, your sisters and brothers needlessly dying, the stories of your grandmother and of your father, and what Somoza claims—every time you look down from your family's little hillside cornfield at the cattle grazing on the fertile valley plains of Somoza's lawyer.

*

Okay. Now it's 1980. You are yourself again, not a Nicaraguan. Maybe you are an American and this morning you pick up the newspaper and find a big story on poor peasants "invading" some farmland in Nicaragua. Your knee-jerk reaction might be—oh, those poor peasants have been stirred up by the revolutionaries who just took over Nicaragua. The revolutionaries are fueling hatred against all the landlords just to make themselves more popular. Those landowners *own* the land. They have legal title. The law has to be respected or it will lead to chaos. Not only that, it will destroy production.

But pretending to be a poor Nicaraguan peasant for even a few minutes might, we hope, have tempered that reaction. By helping you see the world through the eyes of the majority of Nicaraguans, we hope to have made a few points very clear, points that you will need to consider as you read the rest of this book. First, there is nothing legal or fair about the landholding patterns that have been created in countries like Nicaragua. As you have seen, it is not the peasants but the wealthy elites who have consistently invaded land by force. Second, there is nothing especially efficient about landownership concentrated on a few big estates. The land-use patterns that developed in Nicaragua were exactly the opposite of rational, productive use. Third, it doesn't take a band of revolutionaries to show people the deep injustices in their society. The poor generally know the source of their misery. What they lack is the power to change it.

THREE

THE PEASANTS' VICTORY

To UNDERSTAND THE AGRARIAN REFORM UNder way in Nicaragua today we have to understand the impetus behind it—not just the injustice and misery described in the last chapter, but the decades of struggles by the peasants themselves. In the industrial countries we are taught such a bleak view of peasants—as ignorant, simple-minded, and stunted by chronic hunger—that it is hard for us to imagine them fighting back. So in Nicaragua we sought to find out to what extent the rural poor were an active force in giving birth to the revolution.

Fighting Back

As elsewhere in Central America, the Nicaraguan peasants have not remained passive before the theft of their lands and the misery of their lives.

No one who wants to understand the Sandinistas in victory can afford to overlook their dependence on the campesinos during the war. From its founding in the early 1960s, the Sandinista Front for National Liberation (FSLN) worked with campesinos. What would have happened to the guerrillas pursued by the National Guard without the help of campesinos who knew the lay of the land? Campesinos fore-warned Sandinistas of the Guard's attacks and provided the guerrillas with food, water, and other vital supplies.

Both campesinos (owners of small plots of land) and land-less agricultural workers joined the guerrillas. One of the ear-liest attacks on the National Guard was carried out by a Sandinista guerrilla column made up totally of small farmers and landless workers under the direction of Colonel Santos Lopez, a campesino who had fought the U.S. Marines with Sandino in the 1920s. Several leading Sandinistas grew up as poor campesinos.

The National Guard's "cleanups"—indiscriminate killings in areas thought to be sympathetic to the Sandinistas—swelled the guerrilla ranks with rural recruits. They sought vindication for years of forced misery as well as for the Guard's murders of relatives and friends.

Many thousands—perhaps more than 10,000—of those who died in the war against the dictatorship were campesi-nos, landless rural laborers, and their families.

Basta! Enough!

In addition to joining the Sandinista forces, peasants ex-pressed their demand for change by seizing plantation land to grow food crops for themselves, as we discuss in chapter 9. By the 1960s, more and more peasants were declaring, "*Basta!* We've had enough." Even official documents record 240 "land invasions" from 1964 to 1973 just in the provinces of Chinandega and León, where thousand of peasants had been evicted by large cotton planters.

These invasions were met by the armed force of the Na-tional Guard. Despite the violent repression, land seizures picked up after the 1972 earthquake. Using the increased U.S. economic and military aid after the earthquake, the National Guard set up makeshift concentration camps in areas with the most peasant resistance.

Domingo Gomez grew up in a poor campesino family on the east side of Lake Nicaragua, an area dominated by the large Santa Ana hacienda which belonged to a Señor Bon. Shortly after the triumph, at the age of 20, he recounted to me his childhood experiences in taking back land from the big landlords who had usurped it.

Over the years Sr. Bon expanded his hacienda by stealing, with the help of his lawyers and the National Guard, many small staple-food-producing farms to add to his ranch. Tensions ran high for years. Campesinos repeatedly tried to protest to the authorities but no one would even see them. Then in 1976, Domingo, his father, and some other campesinos began to meet at night in the house of the priest, who was active in CEPA. They listened to the Bible and discussed their problems—mainly their hunger and the theft of their land.

One night they made up their minds to act. "We divided up tasks," Domingo explained. "One person would steal wire for fences, another would make posts. The plan was that, working all night, we'd fence off the area we needed for a cooperative before the daylight, before the hacienda knew anything was happening. And we did it." But two days later the Guard came.

"We had only machetes and so we couldn't defend ourselves," Domingo recalled. "The Guard cut the fences and took our animals."

About that time Domingo and a few others made direct contact with the Sandinistas, who helped them plan and gave them some American-made rifles and handguns they had seized from a National Guard stockpile. "The priest was a big help," he explained. "He had a jeep and could hide the arms." Domingo, then 16, joined the Sandinista Front.

"In 1978, we invaded the hacienda, again by night. We put up fences and chopped lots of firewood. The next day we planted our corn. Thanks to the Sandinistas, we were able to defend ourselves. We stayed." (Today Domingo is a national-level leader of the farmworkers' association.)

Cristo, Campesino: The Liberation Message of Christ

But what accounts for the courageous self-assertion demonstrated by many Nicaraguan peasants? Part of the answer can be found in a "subversive" message that began to circulate throughout the countryside in the 1960s. The message: Each

human being is important before God and therefore has the
right to the resources necessary to live in dignity. This "subversive" message was being spread by none other than the
Catholic Church, which, next to Somoza, was perhaps the
most pervasive force in Nicaragua.

Pope John's Vatican Council (1961–65) helped open the
Catholic Church to the daily trials of the world's poor. Then
the 1968 Medellin Conference of Latin American Bishops
endorsed the reawakening of the liberation imperative within
the Christian tradition. Throughout Latin America many
bishops, priests, and sisters studying the documents from
these historic councils began to seek ways to make the gospel a living reality for rural people.

In Nicaragua some of the leadership came from the Jesuit
Fathers. In 1968, with the support of the Nicaraguan bishops, they created CEPA, the Educational Center for Agrarian Advancement. Initially, CEPA simply trained campesino
leaders in appropriate agricultural techniques; but CEPA did
this in the context of Biblical reflection. Soon CEPA's work
began to embrace the social and political implications of the
Christian gospel for those who worked the land. CEPA published *Cristo, Campesino*, a comic book whose recurring message was "You have a right to land." Thousands of copies cir-
culated throughout the countryside.

Another highly significant development during the same
period was the Catholic Church's decision to foster a lay
ministry. With so few priests, the Catholic Church in Nicaragua had never been able to place many priests in the rural
areas. However, with the Vatican Council's emphasis on the
priesthood of every Christian, the Nicaraguan Church began
to train lay persons to perform many sacramental and other
religious functions in rural areas where there were no priests.

These specially trained lay people were called "Delegates
of the Word." By 1975, in one remote interior province
alone, there were over 900 Delegates working closely with
Capuchin Fathers from the United States. The Delegates
formed Christian "base communities" in which campesinos and landless workers discussed their problems in light of
readings from the Bible. The Delegates were also trained to
teach literacy and basic health care. Some Delegates also
took part in CEPA training sessions.

CEPA itself, as we have seen, was started basically to teach farm skills so campesinos could better help themselves. No political impact had been intended. Nonetheless, more and more CEPA activists and Delegates came to understand that no matter how hard they worked at it, campesinos could not substantially better their conditions as long as the society was fundamentally structured against their interests. Gradually, the CEPA activists and the Delegates of the Word began to understand that campesinos would have to unite and organize political action. In serving the plantation workers, the Delegates soon concluded that "to hunger and thirst for justice" meant that workers had to organize to demand basic health services, drinking water, livable wages, and year-round employment.

Early on, the Somoza regime sensed the dangers of a socially interpreted gospel. The National Guard labeled Delegates of the Word "subversives" and began to harass them. Campesinos disappeared in areas with a strong Delegate presence. Eventually the National Guard repression claimed the lives of Delegates, too, provoking the official church into opposing Somoza.

After 1975, in some northern areas, the National Guard regularly banned all religious meetings. As the repression intensified, many Delegates and Christian base communities were forced to go underground. Instead of quelling the resistance, such repression actually fostered these Christians' collaboration with the Sandinistas.

Many Christians working in CEPA developed into active supporters of the Sandinista National Liberation Front. Several key CEPA activists became directors of the Association of Rural Workers (ATC), which, as we will see, the Sandinistas established in 1977. Some CEPA activists opted to become guerrilla freedom fighters. During 1977–78, at least four CEPA organizers were assassinated by the National Guard.

As the level of CEPA's commitment deepened, the Catholic hierarchy tried to restrict its activities and to discourage it from collaborating with the Sandinistas. Finally, when the bishops left it no other option, CEPA cut its ties with the Church hierarchy and became an independent Christian organization closely allied to the Sandinistas.

Agricultural Workers Organize

Building on the awareness in part created by CEPA and the Delegates of the Word, in 1976 the Sandinistas started to organize Committees of Agricultural Workers, first among the coffee workers in the Carazo and Masaya regions.

Formed on some 20 coffee estates during the harvest period when growers needed workers most, the Committees demanded better working and living conditions. The first confrontations over economic conditions quickly became political, especially because the landowners frequently called in the National Guard, who beat, tortured, murdered, and imprisoned Committee members. It became apparent to all that Somoza stood behind the landowners.

Again the repression backfired. The Committees of Agricultural Workers spread south into the department of Rivas and north to Chinandega, from the coffee estates to cotton and sugar plantations. By late 1977, the northern Pacific zone, completely dominated by cotton and sugar estates, was the most militant area in the country.

Within a year the Committees were strong enough to form a national organization, the Association of Rural Workers (ATC), which united the Committees in several departments.

During the export harvest period when seasonal workers were together on the estates and were most in demand, the ATC organized rallies to denounce National Guard repression and demand just wages and working conditions. The Guard responded with tear gas, clubs, and even machine guns. ATC members joined anti-Somoza protests in Managua. In the first nationwide work stoppage, in January 1978, they barricaded main roads and cut communication lines in rural areas to protest the assassination of Pedro Joaquín Chamorro, the *La Prensa* editor who opposed Somoza.

In some areas the ATC demanded that the control of large farms be handed over to the workers. In April 1978, the ATC published the first issue of its newspaper, *El Machete*.

On April 9, 1978—just a little more than a year before victory—the ATC organized its largest march and a hunger strike in the town of Diriamba. The strike was a response to Somoza's callous assertion that the problem in rural areas was not hunger but the lack of a balanced diet! In what has been called its "first baptism of blood," over 1,200 ATC members clashed with the National Guard.

Despite tremendous repression, the hunger strike strengthened the ATC and the resistance. Many of the town's residents threw open their doors to the marchers under tear gas attacks. News of their hunger strike and of the National Guard's violence set off other hunger strikes by student groups, the national women's organization, and ATC members throughout the country.

From this point the ATC clearly saw itself united with the Sandinistas in an all-out war against the dictatorship. Often armed only with old hunting rifles and machetes, hundreds of ATC campesinos and farmworkers organized themselves in popular militias. Their courage contributed greatly to the final victory on July 19, 1979.

Taking Back the Land—Even Before the Triumph

The Sandinista agrarian reform actually got under way well before the final victory over Somoza, as land takeovers took place throughout the countryside in collaboration with the Sandinistas. They were most common around the Pacific Coast city of León during what turned out to be the final months of the popular insurrection.

For example, La Maquina hacienda, controlled by Somoza's mother's family, lay about a mile outside the city of León. There campesinos accompanied by Sandinista commanders reclaimed the land after the National Guard had retreated, just one month before the final victory. Also in the León area, over 1,000 dispossessed campesino families occupied 22,600 acres of Somocista-owned farmland four days before the end of the war and started bringing it back into production.

These land seizures were not only a matter of just vindication (*revindicación*) of the wrongful actions of the bigger landlords. Just as important was the need to provide food in the liberated areas. Working with the Sandinistas, the people of León had liberated their city, Nicaragua's second largest, in June 1979. But no one knew that the war would be over the following month, so food self-sufficiency for the area was top priority. To prevent disruptions in production, the

Sandinistas worked to ensure that farms around León belonging to landowners aiding in the fight against Somoza were *not* taken over. And to ensure future productivity, the Sandinistas also tried to prevent any looting or parceling up of the large, modernized farms seized from the Somocistas.

Upon taking back the land, the campesinos and landless farmworkers immediately set to plowing and planting food crops instead of the cotton and pasture grass that had prevailed on most of the farms. With the help of the Sandinistas, the campesinos formed cooperatives to work the land as a team. Some of the largest haciendas were turned into Enterprises of the People (*Empresas del Pueblo*) run by the Sandinista National Liberation Front (FSLN) itself.

Gladys Baez, a 38-year-old woman from the rural areas around León, described to writer Margaret Randall how campesinos took over a Somocista farm during this period: "We knew that whenever there's a war, hunger follows. And if the campesinos can't plan, hunger spreads everywhere. So with the help of Julio Vazquez, an agronomist who volunteered to help us, and a group of campesinos, we made an inventory of everything there was on a ranch in the area. We guarded against the indiscriminate killing of cattle, got people to spare the cows and to eat only what was absolutely necessary. . . . We saw to it that the campesinos had their seed."

Many of us imagine revolution in the countryside to mean peasants' revenge against landlords who have brutalized them for so many years. Even given all our knowledge about the outrages committed against the majority of rural people, we will never fully grasp their rage—rage born of "land stolen, wells poisoned, and food crops sprayed with pesticides by the *latifundistas*," as an ATC leader, himself a farmworker since the age of 9, told me shortly after the triumph. Yet, to a truly remarkable extent, the Sandinista Front succeeded in using its moral authority with the campesinos and landless agricultural workers to restrain their wrath against landowners, including the Somocistas, and to await due process.

Clearly, then, the revolution in Nicaragua was not won by an isolated guerrilla band, acting merely in the name of the people. It was won by a widespread movement with strong bases among the poor majority in the countryside. The revolutionary impetus came from decades of gross injustice; the courage to act, often from the liberation message of the gospel; the decision to act, from the brutality of Somoza's National Guard.

Rural policies that would be developed during the first postliberation years were not simply dreamed up by Nicaragua's idealistic new leadership; rather they evolved in large part in response to demands of the peasants and farmworkers themselves. In this book we focus on the Nicaraguan revolution's response to those demands—agrarian reform and new food policies in the interests of the poor majority.

FOUR

NO OWNERSHIP WITHOUT OBLIGATION

"**L**AND TO WHOEVER WORKS IT!" WITH THIS slogan, Sandinista leaders undoubtedly assured the campesinos and rural workers that victory against Somoza would mean land for them. After all, Sandino—for whom the Sandinistas took their name and inspiration—had started to implement an agrarian reform program in 1932 by helping campesinos form cooperatives. In their proclamations during the liberation war, the Sandinistas promised agrarian reform. The San José Pact, which formally united business people and the Sandinistas in the war, proclaimed agrarian reform a major part of the new Nicaragua.

The Sandinistas kept their word. On the first day after the full triumph over Somoza and his National Guard, Decree No. 3 of the Sandinista-led National Government of Reconstruction authorized the confiscation of all the assets of the Somoza family and its close associates (the "Somocistas"). In one fell swoop, this 17-line decree set in motion the nationalization of almost 2 million acres on approximately 2,000 farms and ranches. Overnight about 20 percent of Nicaragua's agricultural land became part of the "People's Property."

This confiscation decree left a full two-thirds of the farmland in capitalist hands. Here we use "capitalist" to refer to

31

landowners large enough to hire labor or rent out their land, or both. These landowners are different from small farmers ("campesinos") who usually use only family labor. These small producers, unaffected by the confiscation decree, controlled less than 15 percent of the nation's farmland.

Farmworkers around Estelí—an area noted for its courage against Somoza's brutality—told me shortly after victory that they were disappointed that the new government had not expropriated more land. Ill-treated for years by this or that landowner, they were shocked if his land were not taken away.

In late September 1979, a top official of the agrarian reform, Salvador Mayorga, and I paid an unannounced visit to a cattle hacienda near Estelí that had been expropriated because it had belonged to Somoza's lawyer. The workers demanded to know why the adjacent ranch had not also been expropriated. "The owner's a pig (*cochino*)," they complained. "No one wants to work for him." Mayorga's answer—that the owner had not fled the country and was not considered a close ally of the dictator—did not seem all that satisfying to them.

Agrarian reform is a drama that unfolds in response to multiple, often conflicting, pressures on the government—and the Sandinistas seem to understand this well. The only citation from Karl Marx I've seen around the agrarian reform ministry seems to be a favorite of the Sandinistas: "People make their own history, but they do not make it just as they please; they do not make it in circumstances chosen by themselves, but under circumstances directly found, given, and transmitted from the past."

So while "Land to whoever works it!" might have been an effective rallying cry during the war of liberation, it got quietly buried once the victorious leadership had to confront the urgent need to get the capitalist farmers and ranchers controlling most of the country's exports back into production. These exports were needed more urgently than ever to import food, medicines, oil, and capital goods into the war-devastated country and to reduce the enormous foreign debt. Moreover, the Sandinistas' choices were limited by Nicaragua's proximity to the likely-to-be-hostile U.S. government. To resist any U.S. destabilization pressures, the Sandinistas knew they had to do everything within reason to build support among all social classes for the future of the revolution. "Building the material basis for national unity, not demagoguery, is the order of the day," a member of the Sandinista directorate told me three months after victory.

In this book, we will repeatedly see that the Nicaraguan agrarian reform is a balancing act. On the one hand are the pent-up demands from campesinos and landless farmworkers. On the other are political and economic constraints, not all of which are readily understood by the rural majority. In charge of this delicate process, the Sandinistas placed one of the most respected members of the National Directorate of the Sandinista Front, Jaime Wheelock. When the agricultural development and agrarian reform ministries were combined to form a single ministry (MIDINRA) in late 1979, Commander Wheelock rose to head the superministry.

Virtually all of the Sandinista leaders are young and inexperienced in government. Wheelock, at 34, was no exception. He readily admits his own inexperience. "We are militants in a revolutionary cause who knew little about the process of an agrarian reform, in theory or in practice," Wheelock told a group of us foreign advisors only a few months after victory. Nevertheless, Wheelock had a special familiarity with ·many of the agrarian problems of his country. The son of a well-to-do cotton grower, before the war Wheelock had written a carefully documented study of the social and economic impact of Nicaragua's cotton production.

"We are not guided by or tied to preconceived models. Our approach to each problem is very practical," he told Oxfam America's Larry Simon. "Some people call us Marxists, some call us Communists, and at the same time others are labeling us reactionaries, rightists, bourgeoisie—as happened during our recent trips to the United States and Colombia. But we must respond to problems in practical and concrete ways." In another interview Wheelock stressed, "Just as we made the revolution a Nicaraguan revolution without copying models, so we are not going to make an agrarian reform by imitating other countries. Of course, we do take into account the experiences [of other people]."

The first step in this balancing act, as we have seen, was the nationalization of all the properties that belonged to

Somoza, his family, his lawyers and other cronies—the So-mocistas. Since most of this land had been abandoned when Somoza and his friends fled the country, the new government's move was not politically difficult. The government did not have to evict landowners. In fact, most members of the landowning class even supported the government's take-over of Somoza's land, for they too had come to despise So-moza at least by the final months of the war. Thus the con-fiscation of Somoza properties did not ignite any brouhaha over private property rights. In addition, the agrarian re-form's birthright came without a price tag: "compensation" to Somocistas was out of the question. Everyone knew much of this land had been stolen in the first place. Indeed, this first step can most accurately be thought of not as agrarian reform but as the confiscation of the property of a handful of criminals.

Uneasy with the seemingly loosely defined label "Somo-cista," I wanted to learn how the Attorney General deter-mined who was a Somocista. Most identified themselves by fleeing, I was told. Some of these were business partners of the Somoza family or officials of the National Guard or both. Others had obtained juicy loans from the public domain. The sticky cases were those where the owners had not fled but where neighboring campesinos and workers denounced an owner as a Somocista. The local prosecutor then had to conduct an investigation and proceed through the judicial system inherited from Somoza. Expropriated owners had a right to appeal their cases in the courts. As one government official commented to the *Miami Herald* about these land-owners, "They win some and they lose some."

Although it is not widely known, Nicaraguan law did not allow the confiscation of Somocista properties registered in the names of wives and dependents (provided they had not fled the country, of course). Given the barbarisms of the Somoza family, such respect for formalities was hard for me to comprehend. "We are trying to bring about justice within an inherited unjust legal framework—it's not easy," Ruth Herrera, a high-ranking Sandinista and General Secretary of the Ministry of Agricultural Development, told me.

Once all these cases had been decided, the government controlled 20 percent of Nicaragua's agricultural land, or about one-quarter of the large estates. That amounted to 43 percent of the total acreage in the large estates, those over 850 acres. Somoza himself had controlled about a third of the land that was confiscated, according to one rough (and unverified) estimate. The estates taken over by the government were for the most part large, modernized, export-oriented farms on the best soils and modern export-oriented cattle ranches. Two-thirds of the land was made up of farms larger than 4,350 acres.

Obligation of Ownership

Although the large landowners supported the government takeover of Somocista lands, many watched anxiously for the government's *next* move. Wouldn't the new government— and all this talk of revolution—encourage peasant invasions of land on all capitalist farms and ranches? Wouldn't the new government set a ceiling on the amount of land any one person or family could own? Many landowners no doubt feared that private property was the real target of revolutionary change.

The Sandinistas, however, saw it differently. First, there were the practical considerations. The Sandinista leadership felt it couldn't take on any more land, even if it had wanted to. The ministry was swamped by an enormous administrative undertaking once the government decided to organize state farms on the newly publicly owned land (see chapter 7). Many of the farms had been run-down and abandoned by the Somocista owners who, in the final two years, had ceased to invest and sought only to liquidate their assets and get them to Miami. On some, land seizures and even military battles had taken their toll. On virtually all, production was at a standstill. Neighbors, relatives, and common thieves were smuggling abandoned machinery, irrigation equipment, and livestock off to Honduras and Costa Rica.

During my first visits I'd be bouncing along in a jeep with agricultural officials and every few minutes a message about some critical problem on one or the other of the 2,000 state farm units seemed to come across the CB system—"There's no truck"; "there's no seed"; "there's no payroll." Indeed, some agrarian reform officials feared they would become so tied up in day-to-day management problems of the state farms that it would be impossible to make further reforms. "Now we have to do the last thing any of us ever wanted to do—administer," Vice Minister and Director General of the Agrarian Reform Salvador Mayorga told me with a look of frustration at the end of a typical 16-hour day, two months into the revolution.

Second, the government resisted confiscating additional land because it was vitally concerned with reactivating production. It did not want to reduce production by taking land out of the hands of those using it efficiently. Nor did the government wish even to hint at land redistribution that might threaten landowners, giving them an excuse for not getting production going again.

Third, the Sandinistas' philosophy of agrarian reform is not anti-private property. Rather, the Sandinistas believe that the right to productive private property carries with it the obligation to use that property for the benefit of the society. Private property rights are guaranteed by the government but *only* if the owner is using the resource: owners letting their land lie idle, for example, will be subject to expropriation.

In actuality, however, the government did not take over additional land during the first two years, even if it were lying idle or being run-down; the ministry had all the land it could handle. The only exceptions were farms where campesinos or farmworkers put tremendous pressure on the ministry.

More generally speaking, then, the goal of the Sandinistas has not been public ownership of all the means of production. It has sought public ownership primarily where it represents the only practical way to keep production going—as in the case of the farms abandoned by Somoza, or the national banking system, bankrupt as it was at the end of the war.

Indeed, two years into the revolution private ownership still prevailed. "Very few people realize that 80 percent of agricultural production is in the hands of the private sector, as is 75 percent of industrial production," a key official in the Ministry of Planning, Xabier Gorostiaga, pointed out at that time. The 20 percent of agricultural production that does belong to the state is deliberately called "Area of the People's

Property." "The Sandinistas want to instill in people the idea that this area belongs to the people. The state is not the owner, it is only the administrator," Gorostiaga commented.

A Further Obligation of Ownership

To the Sandinista leadership, the right to private property, as we have said, carries with it a positive obligation: to use that property for the benefit of the society. Its philosophy of private property also appears to carry with it a negative obligation: *not* to use that ownership as a basis for exploiting others or, stated another way, as a base for amassing wealth to the unfair advantage of others.

Therefore, while the government guaranteed the right to private property, in the first months of the revolution it established rent ceilings for agricultural land. The Sandinistas considered the prevailing rents to reflect the monopolization of land by a few that left the majority competing against each other for land. Moreover, they considered high rents, as well as sharecropping, to be disincentives to greater food production. The new rents work out to be about 85 percent less than the previous going rates. For corn and bean production, the maximum rent is now only about 100 córdobas ($10) per manzana (1.7 acres); for cotton, about three times as much.

Combined with government credit for small food producers, these rent controls would make a difference even in the first year for countless tenants, sharecroppers, and small producers, the Sandinistas hoped. One survey indicated that 10 percent of the laborers in the coffee harvest were able to cultivate corn and beans for the first time in their lives. Still, all did not go well: it now seems many landowners refused to rent at the legal rates. One apparently common landlord ploy was to refuse to lend oxen for plowing if the campesino insisted on the new rate. Only in those areas where the peasant and farmworker association, the ATC, was strong were the rent ceilings widely respected.

While many agrarian reforms have started by giving land titles to tenants and sharecroppers, the Sandinista agrarian reform appears much more conservative. In regard to rent, it no more interferes with private property than do urban rent control laws in many "free enterprise" industrial countries.

By making rents low and outlawing evictions, the Sandinistas sought to provide secure tenure to poor campesinos while side-stepping the bugbear of private property.

Socialize the Surplus

The fact that the new government sought to tie these obligations to the right to private property does not mean that it hoped the capitalist sector would be hamstrung and eventually wither away. The goal, according to Minister of Agricultural Development Jaime Wheelock, is not to socialize (bring under public control) all the means of production but instead to socialize (use for the public good) the surplus that the private sector produces. The government sought to allow the private producer a decent rate of profit but tap the additional surplus. This surplus could be tapped by mechanisms common in most capitalist societies, such as control over credit, export sales, foreign exchange, land use, labor relations, prices and marketing, and, of course, taxation. One of the first acts of the new government, consistent with this philosophy, was to establish the Ministry of Foreign Trade to handle the marketing of almost all exports, thereby putting an end to private producers falsifying foreign sales and depositing the proceeds in Miami or Panama bank accounts.

As we'll see in chapter 5, the Sandinistas went to great lengths to try to foster the confidence of private producers and to keep them producing.

FIVE

THE FAILED PARTNERSHIP: BIG GROWERS AND THE STATE

WHEN MANY NORTH AMERICANS IMAGINE "revolutionary Nicaragua," they assume that all the land once belonging to the big plantation owners must now be in the hands of hungry peasants. Not so. Recall that only lands belonging to Somoza and his close associates were confiscated by the government after the fall of the dictatorship.

For the first three months after the victory, the new government thought it had control over 60 percent of Nicaragua's agricultural land. But at a planning session in late October 1979 in Jaime Wheelock's office, a young researcher presented us with startling new estimates, which caused an anxious stir in the room. The large- and medium-size farmers and ranchers, he reported, controlled over two-thirds of the agricultural land. They accounted for 72 percent of cotton production, 53 percent of coffee, 58 percent of cattle, and 51 percent of sugar cane.

Could private capitalist farmers and ranchers be counted on to maintain and expand urgently needed production? That became the big question for the rest of the afternoon session.

Without public control over the bulk of the export production, the new government realized that the recovery of the economy would hinge in large part on how effectively it

39

could motivate these private growers to revive and eventually step up production. This partnership in the countryside was the heart of the new Nicaragua's plans for a "mixed economy."

Aware of their importance to the economy, the large- and medium-size growers organized into producers' associations and drove some hard bargains. Not all the negotiations were formal. It was not unusual for government officials to spend Sunday afternoons in the countryside chatting with, say, some cotton growers to determine just what were their complaints and demands. Moreover, a number of leaders and other officials of the new government came from major land-owning families; they could readily test government proposals on close relatives and family friends.

While the government appealed to patriotic desires to rebuild a better Nicaragua, it was not overly idealistic or naive. In fact, the new government offered the private producers a package of incentives unprecedented even under the Somoza dictatorship:

—Enough credit, at an interest rate below the rate of inflation, to cover all working costs (seeds, fertilizers, fuel, equipment repair and replacement, all wages).

—Guaranteed prices for export crops, calculated to ensure a profit, and renegotiated yearly with the producers' associations in advance of annual planting. The government promised to absorb any drop in international commodity prices but to share with producers the benefits of any unexpected price rises.

—Low-cost government financing for replanting coffee trees infested by coffee blight.

—A seat for the association representing big growers and ranchers (UPANIC) on the Council of State and on various technical commissions.

—Rent decreases, primarily intended to help peasant producers, which also benefited many commercial growers, especially of cotton. In the mid-1970s, 40 percent of cotton growers rented their land from absentee owners, many residing in Miami and California.

—Low taxes on personal income and company profits.

Under this incentive package, the government put up the working capital, guaranteed minimum prices at which any reasonably efficient producer could make a profit, and absorbed any sudden drops in international market prices, while allowing the producers to own (as well as sell and bequeath) the land and equipment. It was tantamount to paying big producers a salary with bonuses tied to performance.

Why such a sweet deal? First, the government didn't want to drive the big producers out since it couldn't take on any more farms and ranches itself. Its hands were full dealing with the Somocista properties. Moreover, the government didn't want the big producers to leave the country because they constituted so much of the nation's scarce technical and administrative experience.

Behind the government overtures to the commercial producers were two other assumptions. The government believed that these incentives would stimulate production, especially of export crops. Through the foreign exchange earned, the government would gain funds it desperately needed for redistributive development as well as social programs. This would be especially true, the reasoning went, since the government had nationalized virtually all export trade and maintained a low rate of exchange, paying producers the official 10 córdobas per dollar, whereas the legal private ("parallel") market gave 25 to 40 córdobas to the dollar. In February 1982 this exchange rate was modified in favor of the producers as a further effort to stimulate production: producers could obtain part of the value of their exports effectively in dollars. Second, the Sandinistas believed that national unity was essential in the face of foreign hostility. By not nationalizing private producers and instead building their confidence in the new government, the Sandinistas hoped to avoid a confrontation that might give the U.S. government a rationalization for intervention in Nicaragua.

All this sounds reasonable. But did it work? In the judgment of many, it did not.

At a late night meeting on the eve of the second anniversary, a high official told me, "The private farmers, the big ones and the medium-size ones, have blown a historic opportunity. Once we might have thought we could rely on the private sector at least for a holding action. But now we see most of them are taking us backward economically." In his view, the majority of big producers not only failed to revive production but were systematically draining the rural economy.

Why Did They "Blow It"?

What looked to the Sandinistas like liberal offers may not have seemed so to the big growers, who believed they were losing a great deal. Under Somoza the big growers had unlimited access to cheap labor. Now with lowered land rents, increased employment on the state farms, and substantial government credit going to campesino producers, many poor peasants in the countryside saw themselves freed from the need to seek demeaning and arduous plantation work. "The *patrón* can't humiliate us any more" is the way I have heard many of them put it. With fewer workers competing for jobs, for the first time the big growers had to negotiate with workers. And under the new order, not only was there no National Guard to prevent agricultural workers from organizing, but the government actually encouraged unions. To the Sandinistas, such worker organizations are the motor force of agrarian change.

"It's unbelievable," an old field hand told me, radiating with satisfaction. The ATC association on a cotton plantation near León had gotten the plantation owner to pay for the workers' medical treatments. Previously, the only medical bills the owner paid were for the horses. On another plantation, when the owner refused to pay the minimum wage, workers organized an ATC local. When the landowner attempted to break up the organization, the workers first struck; then they took over the plantation.

The big growers saw their profits threatened as the government sought to enforce the minimum wage law, mandated improvements in living and working conditions, and directly competed with the owners' price-gouging "company stores" by offering the rural poor basic goods at fixed low prices. Even though all these changes were not effective everywhere overnight, the direction was clear.

Despite these changes, the big growers knew that they could continue to make good profits. After talking with many of them, I'm convinced that their fears for the future were what caused them to dig in their heels against the new government. Knowing that the countryside was alive with the demands of hundreds of thousands of people who had been ruthlessly exploited for generations, it was *la Revolución* that threatened them. And perhaps it was inevitable that at the beginning of a revolution the fears of the rich affect their behavior so that their fears are self-fulfilling. Certainly, as we will see, that seems to be the case in Nicaragua.

Throughout the first year or so, the majority of private agricultural producers appeared undecided about how much they would cooperate with the new government. For one thing, since the Carter administration seemed willing to live with the new order in Managua, many of Nicaragua's agrarian capitalists felt incapable of effectively mobilizing themselves politically and economically against the new government. Still there was a palpable uneasiness and suspicion on every side, each feeding on the other's fears.

After the election of President Reagan, whose party platform called for the overthrow of the Nicaraguan government, the mood in the countryside was expectant. Adding to the tension was a serious incident in late November 1981, which revealed that at least some big growers had moved into direct sabotage of the new government and its agrarian program. Jorge Salazar, president of the Union of Nicaraguan Agricultural Producers (UPANIC), was discovered by police to be carrying concealed arms in his car and was killed in a shoot-out with police. Investigations revealed that Salazar and others, including the president of the Rice Planters Association, planned to assassinate Sandinista leaders in co-ordination with an invasion by Somocista elements.

"Death by a Million Cuts"

Visiting Nicaragua at the end of 1980, I found Sandinistas and opponents alike predicting that 1981 would test the partnership between the big growers and the state. I returned to Nicaragua twice during the first half of 1981. I found the ATC, the newly created association of small- and medium-size farmers and ranchers (UNAG), the pro-Sandinista media, rural workers, and government officials themselves all accusing private producers of "decapitalization." Decapitalization referred to a range of economic sabotage by some large private farmers and ranchers:

—Cutting back on cultivated acres.

—Laying off needed workers and technicians.

—Selling off machinery and livestock, often to buyers in Honduras and Costa Rica.

—Using government production loans fraudulently—converting part of the loan to dollars on the street market, then sending the dollars to foreign bank accounts.

—Over-invoicing for imported machinery, spare parts, fertilizers, pesticides, and so on in cooperation with "friendly" corporations in Guatemala or Florida. (The grower or rancher, arguing that the imported item is essential for production, gets dollars from the national bank—at the 10 to 1 rate rather than the 25 to 1 rate on the street market—plus, perhaps, a loan. The extra dollars wind up in a Miami bank account.)

—Faking or inflating fees and commissions to foreign firms or individuals, again as a way to siphon dollars out of the country.

—Paying excessive salaries, often in advance, to themselves and their family members.

—Asking for a government loan on the grounds of "saving jobs" once any combination of the above had caused financial losses.

The whole process adds up to "death by a million cuts," a top government economic planning advisor told me in June 1981. "It's not as if there are just four or five of the big guys," he explained. "If there were, you could round up one or two and make an example of them." Knowing that I was a *norteamericano*, he added, "It's like moonshine in Kentucky." There's one big difference though: in Nicaragua the "moonshining" undermines the entire economy.

In his opinion, the Sandinistas had originally underestimated the danger of decapitalization because they had underestimated the number and importance of the medium-size producers. By mid-1981, some ranches and farms were so decapitalized that, counting in debts, their value was negative.

Specific examples of decapitalization have frequently been pointed out by campesinos and farmworkers and their organizations. Of the almost 900 acres of the San Pedro hacienda in southeastern Nicaragua, on approximately 100 grow coffee trees. In July 1981 the ATC charged that a large portion of the trees were ruined or on the verge of ruin because of lack of weeding and control of the coffee blight. The hacienda's 1980–81 coffee harvest dropped to one-quarter what it had been the year before. The ATC claimed that by mid-1981, 70 percent of the capitalist farms and ranches in the region had been similarly neglected.

On his 2,800-acre Namaslí hacienda, near the Honduran border, Alfonso Ramos had 800 acres in coffee trees. In 1980 he got credit from the National Development Bank to cover all projected production expenses. Yet it looked abandoned to a journalist visiting the hacienda in June 1981.

Before the revolution, Ramos employed 200 workers; in 1981, only 27. Left unattended, the coffee trees were hard hit by the coffee blight. When coffee trees are not cared for with weeding, fertilizer, pest control, yields are reduced for years to come. Ramos had also stripped the estate of almost all the machinery, including seven tractors, harvesters, and irrigation pumps—some taken into Honduras. An investigation revealed that he had sold the machinery, converted the money to dollars, and smuggled them out of the country.

Beef production also suffered from economic sabotage. By mid-1981, the government estimated that over 200,000 head of cattle had been rustled across the Honduran border since the start of the revolution. (Exports of beef from Honduras showed a sudden and inexplicable jump of 20 percent.)

In June 1981, the San Martín slaughterhouse laid off its 188 workers and announced it was closing for at least two months. The owners claimed a lack of animals, but the local ATC disputed this excuse. After borrowing money from the National Development Bank, the owners had sent checks totaling over $100,000 to Miami and had withdrawn 7 million córdobas from the company accounts to buy dollars in the street, the government charged. The owners, all vociferous critics of the government, included the head of COSEP, the powerful big business chamber of commerce.

Decapitalization hurt sugar production, too. The sugar mill on the San Pedro hacienda used to grind 5,000 bundles of cane daily; in 1981 it did not grind any at all. In 1981, the Ministry of Agricultural Development charged that a large number of landowners simply refused either to cultivate or to rent out their lands. Some 30 percent of the normally cultivated land was being left idle, the ministry estimated in July. Driving through the Pacific Coast and Matagalpa and Estelí regions in June and July, I saw fields covered with weeds and pasture grass where the land had obviously been plowed and planted in previous years.

A Bad "Climate"?

A vicious circle of self-fulfilling prophecies was at work. The more landowners decapitalized, the more they were denounced by workers and by the government, and the more insecure all landowners felt (and were). Thus the circle starts again, but this time with more people.

Hitchhiking in Managua in June 1981, I was picked up by a coffee planter in a tinted-windowed Mercedes. He insisted on speaking English and kept calling me "friend." Earlier in the year he had come back to the country from Coconut Grove to "get out what I could while I could," he told me. He was frightened by the worsening "climate," by the mood of more and more workers and campesinos pressuring the government for a harder line (*mano dura*) toward the landowners. The threat of the worsening "climate"—fear of eventual expropriation—is the reason landowners most frequently give for decapitalization.

Yet even Somoza and the National Guard had not provided a secure climate for the wealthy. For years before the Sandinista-led victory over Somoza, those who could often sent their money out of the country. They feared that one day Somoza would fall, despite all the U.S. backing, and they would lose their capital. With the war, of course, the process accelerated. A United Nations commission estimated that $800 million was taken out of the country between 1977 and July 1979. In the last six months of the Somoza dynasty, $315 million disappeared from the country, equivalent to three-quarters of the nation's total export earnings in a good year.

In the new Nicaragua, landowners have found themselves facing two options. One option is to make some córdobas by, say, growing cotton. This option means wading through government paperwork, hassling with increasingly demanding workers, locating spare parts, worrying about the weather, and wondering if enough laborers can be hired for the harvest and at what price. The other option is to decapitalize, to sell off assets to get some córdobas, which can be exchanged for dollars on the street market. With dollars one can either speculate on their value going up, deposit them outside the country, or go to Miami and buy clothing, appliances, and gadgets for resale in Nicaragua at a nice profit. Of course, an energetic landowner could do both: borrow, produce, and then use the profits to speculate in dollars, perhaps never paying back the government loan. Thus it's hardly an exaggeration when the government calls the big operators who are investing in long-term production "patriotic."

Decapitalization as a Political Weapon

Decapitalization could be understood as simply the big operators looking out for their individual interests. Their actions, however, take on political dimensions whether or not they are directly intended. Production failures that the big landowners themselves help to generate can later be cited as proof that the Sandinista-led government is a failure. Those who criticize the government most loudly for failure to meet production targets are often decapitalizing rather than producing, Sandinista Directorate member Bayardo Arce stated in March 1981.

At least some big landowners actually use decapitalization as deliberate provocation, many believe. If the big landowners can force the government to feel it must take over farms or businesses to keep the economy from collapse, these confiscations can then be cited as proof that the government is "repressive" and "communist." Such "proof" can weaken international support, making it harder for the government to get foreign financial aid. Moreover, some of the dollars drained out of the country by the big landowners probably finance the ex-National Guardsmen training in Florida and Honduras who are responsible for murderous raids on campesinos, teachers, and health workers in the northern border regions.

The Peasants React

Decapitalization of farms and ranches often outrages agricultural workers and campesinos. To them it is far from an abstract concept; they experience its consequences in "flesh and bones," as they say in Spanish. Poor workers, having responded to the government's pleas to restrain their own wage demands in the interests of the nation, then see the extreme selfishness of those infinitely better off than they. In visits to Nicaragua in the first half of 1981, I found widespread anger in the countryside against decapitalizers.

Angry workers on a cotton plantation near Chinandega told me that the *patrón* had taken out a $50,000 loan from the government to import a new tractor from the United States. They led me to a shed where they showed me a beat-up old Ford tractor that the *patrón* in fact bought locally for only a fraction of the loan, probably depositing the rest in a Miami bank account.

In late June 1981, a large group of campesinos from the interior of the country marched into Managua. "We have been forced to farm small plots of marginal land, trying to grow enough food," one of them told the press. "And now we see the gentlemen farmers letting hundreds and hundreds of acres of good land go idle."

The ATC made it clear that if owners were not disposed to plant, its members were. It was not an idle threat. In numerous cases the ATC moved in to complete the coffee harvest when private estate owners fired workers or left trees unpicked.

In the months leading up to the second anniversary, more and more campesinos and rural workers took it upon themselves to implement the government's dictum: no ownership without obligation. Land seizures increased. Often working with the ATC, the largest association of agricultural workers, and UNAG, the union of small producers, they took over the farms and ranches of those unwilling to fulfill the responsibility of ownership.

In June 1981 alone, the San Pedro hacienda, the Rio de Janeiro hacienda, the Namaslí farm, the San Martín slaughterhouse and numerous other properties were taken over by workers and campesinos. In Nueva Segovia, Jinotego, and Matagalpa, hundreds of campesinos and workers seized decapitalized farms. The ATC and UNAG leaderships pressured the government to legalize what they considered just seizures—and to do so quickly. "Children's stomachs cannot wait," they argued.

The direct action of campesinos and landless farmworkers made it impossible for the public or the government to ignore the issue. Especially in the two months building up to the second anniversary celebrations, union meetings, press conferences, official speeches, and articles and editorials in the two pro-revolution newspapers all denounced decapitalization. On July 8, I watched a demonstration of workers and campesinos from many parts of the country in front of the Government House. They demanded that the government take measures against decapitalization; they suggested confiscation. *"Contra la descapitalización—confiscación,"* the campesinos and workers chanted over and over.

The decapitalization law on the books since March 1980 was absurdly ineffective. The government had to prove in the courts that the owner had decapitalized before the state could intervene, and the courts were inadequate to move quickly. Moreover, the law required legal proof that assets or dollars had been taken out of the country—something rarely possible. The process took so long that by the time the courts decided against the owner, it was literally too late.

"Yes, against decapitalization, confiscation," declared Edgardo Garcia, head of the ATC, at a news conference. "But *timely* confiscation—not when there's nothing left but ruins, debts, and a bankrupt farm." As a final, absurd touch, the existing law also required the government to pay the owner the value of anything expropriated even if it got only an empty shell; this was tantamount to a financial incentive to decapitalize.

The campesinos and workers were demanding a law of

"preventive intervention." Under this law, the farmworkers' accusation that a landowner was selling off his machinery would be sufficient not only for an investigation but for an immediate confiscation of the farm by the Ministry of Agricultural Development. If the investigation proved the owner innocent of the charges, the property would be returned to him or her. Decapitalization should include taking money out of a production unit and not necessarily out of the country, the ATC demanded.

Implied in such a law would be a greater role for workers and campesinos. Already in May the ATC had organized 25 workshops to help farmworkers detect and deal with decapitalization. The Sandinista newspaper *Barricada* commented, "In the private sector the workers are pressuring more and more to penetrate the 'secrets' of production." Workers now wanted the right to access to the financial information of the *finca* or ranch. "The financial data really belong to the people because, after all, they had to be given to the people's bank to get the loans for building production," a coffee estate worker commented. The ATC's Edgardo Garcia insisted that the National Development Bank should immediately respond when the farm's union asked for information about the bank's financing of the farm.

In the government's view, it had given the private sector a "historic opportunity" to enter into a mutually beneficial partnership. While many "patriotic producers" continued to develop their property, the government concluded that, for the most part, the big operators "blew it."

By the eve of the second anniversary in July 1981, workers, peasants, and big owners alike waited tensely to see how the government would change "the rules of the game."

SIX

SPILLING CREDIT IN THE COUNTRYSIDE

IMAGINE YOURSELF A PEASANT WITH SIX ACRES of land on a Nicaraguan hillside, four days by mule from the nearest town. One afternoon in early 1980, you suddenly hear the thump-thump of a helicopter. A few minutes later the helicopter lands 50 yards away and a young fellow steps out saying he is from the agrarian reform ministry. He offers you a loan to produce more corn and beans. The interest rate? 11 percent—one-third the rate of inflation. Is this a dream? Is this the revolution?

Small farmers are among the poorest people in Nicaragua, isolated on the poorest soils and on plots often too small even to support their own families. Because their plots are so small and their soil poor, two-thirds of them cannot survive from their own direct production. They are forced to seek supplemental wage work during other people's harvests.

While they use only 14 percent of the farmland, these 200,000 small farmers produce about 60 percent of Nicaragua's corn and beans, the basis of the national diet. "Small farmers" refers to both owners and renters cultivating about 34 acres or less—much less in many cases. They represent 76 percent of the total number of farms.

Perhaps no segment of Nicaraguan society has experienced such a dramatic economic change in the new Nicaragua.

Most small producers had never before received government credit, the kind of credit that even American farmers expect from their government. In the first year after the triumph, almost half the small farmers got government credit—and at low interest rates. Small producers got seven times more credit in 1980 than in the year before victory, 1978.

The Sandinistas had several motives for this massive small farm credit program. First, under Somoza the country increasingly had turned to imports to ensure enough of the national diet—corn and beans, the foods the small producers grow. Food production was neglected in favor of export production; then came the war's disruption. Now, if small producers would use the credit to buy the fertilizer, seeds, and tools they need to significantly increase production, the country could save needed foreign exchange.

Second, "spilling credit on the countryside," as Jaime Wheelock called it, was, along with the literacy campaign, the best way the Sandinistas could think of to make the revolution real for the campesinos immediately. Having fought for years in the countryside, the Sandinistas had become intimately aware of the plight of small producers, whose only credit sources were landlords, moneylenders, and merchants who charged usurious rates of interest. Thousands of small farmers had actively supported the Sandinistas during the war. So the Sandinistas wanted to express their gratitude as well as to build support for the difficult times ahead.

Third, the government wanted to help make up for the earnings lost to poor campesinos due to a steep drop in the number of harvest jobs because of war-related cutbacks in cotton acreage.

Finally, the Sandinistas viewed the credit program as an organizing tool. With the enticement of lower interest rates for cooperatives than for individuals (8 percent compared to 11 percent), the government hoped to encourage small producers to form cooperatives or credit associations. From the administrative viewpoint, working with cooperatives was much easier than dealing with thousands of individuals. The Sandinistas also tended to see cooperatives, however rudimentary, as facilitating social advancement (literacy, modernization of production, culture, public health) compared to isolated, individual production.

"...the generosity of revolutionaries."

While the leaders' logic and good intentions in distributing credit massively in 1980 seemed impeccable, not everything turned out quite as hoped. Looking back on the experience a year and a half later, Jaime Wheelock commented, "These are mistakes made out of a romanticism, which, in a sense, is a negative result of the generosity of revolutionaries."

First was the sheer administrative challenge to a ministry that itself was less than a year old. Because of the logistical difficulties of getting credit to tens of thousands of farmers often in remote areas, some campesinos received credit so late that they were still harvesting their corn and beans as the season arrived when their labor was desperately needed on the export crop farms.

Second, crop yields in at least several regions were lower than ministry projections. The problem was compounded by the fact that the government had set a low guaranteed purchasing price for corn and beans, based on its somewhat optimistic calculations of producer costs. Thus some small producers simply didn't earn enough for their crop to repay the loans, although they were free to sell to private buyers at higher prices than the government guaranteed.

Third, in incredibly inaccessible areas (remember the helicopter!) farmers received credit, but then no one came to buy their harvests. According to the ministry, up to 50,000 acres of corn and beans (about 10 percent of the crops) may have been "lost" in this fashion. Realizing they had no one to buy what they had produced, some campesinos harvested only what they could use for themselves and their animals. (This did allow them to eat better than before.)

Finally, the credit that many received simply exceeded the economic potential of their land. So even if a campesino family could get all the seeds, fertilizers, tools, and work animals they could use, the money obtained from selling their crops was nowhere near enough to pay back the credit. Because campesino families probably consumed more than ever before, indebtedness was made even more likely. Thus, even with good crops, many did not sell enough (or get a high enough price) to avoid winding up in debt.

So despite all the good intentions, studies of the 1980

"spilling of credit" to campesinos showed that the increased credit had little impact on production, in part because much of the credit was used for consumption—a new pair of shoes, sugar, kerosene—rather than production.

Indebtedness Crisis

Compounding this disappointment, the repayment rates on the loans turned out to be less than hoped for. As in most countries, however, small producers performed better than larger producers (or state farms) in repaying their debts. Before long, a growing number of small producers were demanding that their debts be forgiven. Moreover, the minority of small producers who had received loans from the Somoza banks (now nationalized) wanted them wiped out. But many government policymakers feared that debt forgiveness would set a bad and difficult-to-reverse precedent. And bank officials worried over the government's growing fiscal crisis. Foreign loans to finance more credit would burden the economy for decades to come.

With the bad record of repayments the first year, national bank officials were reluctant to renew lending to small producers for 1981. But the ATC and the Ministry of Agricultural Development, through its influential director, Jaime Wheelock, pressed. With the government-wide decision in March 1981 to launch an all-out food production push, the balance of power settled in favor of renewing credit for small producers, although the total amount was significantly reduced.

The long debate, unfortunately, delayed the distribution of new credit. Delays in credit caused delays in planting in some areas. Around León, for example, only 25 of 68 small farmer cooperatives received timely credit, partially undermining the launching of the campaign to increase food production by small farmers.

The indebtedness problems of the first year reverberated in the second. Many campesinos who had been unable to repay the first loan refused loans the second and third time around. They feared that, as under the Somoza dictatorship, the credit was offered only to set them up for foreclosure and seizure of the little land, animals, and equipment they had.

"Today there are still poor campesinos who have the idea

that the government is going to trick them or rob them of their property," a campesino explained. "There are still campesinos who won't go to the bank because they are afraid they'll never see their money again."

For this reason, many campesinos applied for financing for only part of their land, keeping a "fallback area" in case of crop failure. In some regions where anti-government forces were particularly strong, this fear was exacerbated by anti-government commercial producers and others. They told the campesinos that the government's generous offering of loans was a "communist" trick to take their land—and even their children—away from them.

Unplanned Beneficiaries

The Sandinistas wanted the poorest campesinos to be the prime beneficiaries of the new credit. But their hopes were frustrated by the failure of credit policies to explicitly and effectively favor the poor and by the unanticipated impact of inflation.

The rush of credit to so many small producers without corresponding increases in the availability of farm inputs set off a sudden price spiral in the countryside for work animals, tools, seeds, fertilizers, pesticides, and transportation. Because many campesinos used the unprecedented cash the loans put in their pockets to satisfy pent-up desires for sugar, salt, shoes, clothing, and other consumer goods, their prices jumped too.

Inflation, as always, hit the poorer campesinos harder. The real beneficiaries turned out to be the rural middle class—truck owners, merchants, and the richer campesinos with animals and equipment to rent. They gained in profits and assets as the flood of credit intended primarily for poor campesino producers rebounded to them.

Moreover, even though the majority of the campesinos receiving bank credit for the first time were probably the poor, most of the total *amount* of small-producer credit did not go to them. There were no special lower interest rates for the most disadvantaged campesinos. Nor did they get more favorable prices when buying inputs or transporting their crops.

Thus the outcome of Nicaragua's rural credit program

turned out not very different from those in other countries around the world. In our investigations at the Institute for Food and Development Policy we have seen, again and again, how the better-off small producers corner the benefits of most small-producer credit programs. The better-off small producers—the minority who generally work their land mostly with hired labor—have all the advantages. They own their farms, have registered titles, and thus can offer the bank collateral. They are experienced in working with the government and have developed better entrepreneurial skills. Not surprisingly, therefore, most of the multiple-year credit went to them, credit they could use to buy young animals to fatten or to put in coffee or fruit trees.

Landholders too large to qualify for the subsidized small producer interest rate actually received considerable credit, subsequent ministry investigations discovered. In the *departmento* of Boaco, statistics on this type of lending were deliberately kept off the records, while bank officers in two other regions only considered for credit those with nine acres or more, even though the majority had less. (*Poder Sandinista*, a Sandinista Front supplement to *Barricada*, denounced the practice.)

In one region with unusually good data, the rich campesinos, who are small coffee producers, got six times more credit per family than the poor campesinos, who are tenants producing corn and beans. This provoked fears within the new government that small coffee farmers could become an elite among small farmers, dampening enthusiasm for the food production so urgently needed. Tenants with experience in planting got twice as much credit as farmworkers getting access to land for the first time.

For all these problems and injustices, however, we should not forget that even in the first year over 70,000 campesino families obtained bank credit for the first time in their lives. *Relatively speaking*, they experienced the most dramatic change of all producers.

Lessons

While many people might assume that policies aimed at justice should treat all farmers the same, Nicaragua's leaders have learned it's more complicated than that. To be effective in favoring the poorest, they have learned, it takes time, organization, and mobilization to identify the different social strata within the peasantry, much less design and implement unequal policies for unequal people. (This task is especially unlikely and difficult during a food production emergency.)

To many North Americans it might seem quite reasonable that the better-off campesinos get the lion's share of the credit; after all, they have the most land and animals to work with and the most experience. But what appears "reasonable" might not be if the goal is not only to produce more food but to ensure that more underfed people are able to eat from their own production. To achieve this goal it is necessary to take a course that might at first appear slower and therefore less efficient. Yet favoring the poorer, less secure, less experienced producers might turn out to be the best course to eradicate hunger.

Finally, even at its worst, the new government's track record in credit for small farmers is a far cry from the small farmer credit programs financed by the U.S. Agency for International Development under Somoza. In these programs an estimated 80 percent of the total credit went right off the top to the big export operators.

What has impressed us is that the new government recognized and publicly acknowledged the unintended consequences of its credit policies. This is in stark contrast to so many governments and international lending agencies, such as the World Bank, which often try to cover up the fact that the well-off benefit disproportionately from their rural assistance programs, often to the detriment of the true poor.

SEVEN

THE STATE FARM: DISCREDITED MODEL OR PRAGMATIC ADAPTATION?

"**U**P THE STEPS, THROUGH THE FRENCH doors and into what was once the living room. The Miami-chic 'still life' in gilded frame still hangs on the wall; a large fringed hammock with 'SOMOZA' woven on the side is slung across a corner. A set of shelves bear model ships, crystal ornaments, china horses, and six mugs with naked-lady handles, posing provocatively over the rims.

"Under this display sits a labourer on a sofa with muddy boots and work clothes, a booklet *The Role of Unions in the Revolution* in his cowboy hands. Another is looking at the cartoon version of the Economic Plan for 1980. Together with the four others in the room, all leaders of the local ATC, they have a study session, held every week. This is the first time that the meeting has been held in the former land-owner's house; old taboos die hard. Outside, other farm labourers and their children cavort in the swimming pool. The people have finally reappropriated their property."

This description of a ranch near Boaco, which had belonged to Somoza's uncle, comes from the diary of Hermione Harris, a British development worker who lived in Nicaragua for several years. The ranch was a state enterprise at the time she visited, a few months after victory.

To many North Americans, "state farms" evoke the worst

59

of socialist dogmatism and bureaucratic incompetence. Some might agree with the standard ideological justification that on state farms "the people" own the land (via the government) so that the whole society supposedly benefits. They might also agree that because the farms are controlled by the state, rational agricultural planning becomes possible for the first time. But, most North Americans would ask, Haven't state farms proven themselves production fiascos in the Soviet Union and Eastern Europe? Don't the workers come to feel as alienated as on any private estate? Doesn't state planning lead to inflexible directives out of touch with local realities? With such doubts in mind, most North Americans, upon hearing about state farms in Nicaragua, assume that revolutionary leaders are once more clinging to a discredited model.

Nonetheless, the Sandinista leadership is adamant in denying that its decision to convert confiscated Somocista estates into state farms was a "knee-jerk" socialist response. The leaders reject any suggestion that they were opting to follow a Soviet (or Cuban) blazed path. Rather they feel they had no option. "We were not choosing a model," commented Jaime Wheelock. "The model was chosen for us by the realities."

First, the Sandinistas feared that if the 2,000 or so confiscated properties were parceled up, productivity would drop. Two months after the final victory, Luis Franco, a Christian Brother appointed to coordinate government services to cooperatives in the province of León, explained to Oxfam America's Michael Scott:

"The production units formerly owned by the Somozas, the military, and their associates were large, highly mechanized plantations into which huge investments in the millions were channeled, often from the national treasury. Breaking them up into a myriad of parcels would decrease or eliminate the possibility of employing the technology and machinery that had been put into them and, consequently, would reduce their productivity. We realized that it was absolutely necessary to keep the production units intact. Had we not [acted] immediately, the campesinos would have occupied this land themselves and would have parceled it out in the traditional way." Indeed, I was told that the Sandinistas had

to act swiftly after triumph to minimize sacking of the Somocista farms by workers and campesinos in several areas of the
country.

A second rationale for state farms is that parceling out the
land would inevitably be unjust. How would it be decided
who should get a parcel? Only permanent workers on the
farm? What about seasonal workers who are often worse off?
Jaime Wheelock, like Solomon, shunned such a decision:
"Distributing the land is easier said than done. . . . What do
you do in the case of a sugar cane plantation where there's
only one processing plant? Who gets that? How do you decide who should get the choice parcels?"

Third, the Sandinistas thought it would be easier to create
more jobs—so desperately needed by landless farmworkers—
on large farms than on small parcels worked by family labor.

One way to keep the confiscated farms intact would have
been to continue and extend the pre-victory *comunas*. *Comunas* were cooperatively worked farms that campesinos and
farmworkers in some liberated areas hurriedly set up after
they seized Somocista lands. Yet soon after triumph the Sandinistas concluded that for the sake of production they had
to ask the peasants to hand this land over to the state. It was
a difficult decision: "Is there any precedent for undoing after
victory the agrarian reform model that was carried out during
the insurrection?" agrarian reform director Salvador Mayorga asked me during my first visit. That the Sandinistas succeeded in changing the war-time *comunas* into state farms
without much conflict testifies to the moral authority of
the Sandinistas in the eyes of the campesinos and landless
workers.

But why did the Sandinistas opt for state farms over
comunas?

Painfully aware of the financial and production crisis in
which the war left the country, the leadership of the agrarian
reform felt it had to do what would most quickly revive production. The *comunas* were actually functioning on only a
few farms. It thought that organizing genuine cooperatives
on the 2,000 or so confiscated farms all over the country
would take too much time.

But the leadership perceived an even more basic problem

with encouraging more *comunas* on the confiscated land. With victory, restoring the nation's capacity to earn foreign exchange for a whole range of imports became just as much an emergency as producing food. And it was feared that if campesinos and farmworkers were granted direct control of the farms, almost all set up to produce for export, they would plant food crops instead. As state farms, the Sandinistas figured, the Somocista properties could continue to use their infrastructure to produce mostly for export, with profits going for the public's well-being. The Sandinistas were equally concerned about increasing food production, but they saw government support, especially credit, for the small campesino producers as the best way to achieve this goal. Land scarcity, they believed, was not the root of Nicaragua's food problem.

While Wheelock and other leaders stressed how circumstances dictated developing state farms on the confiscated land, the Sandinistas nonetheless expected some positive consequences. They hoped, for example, that state farms would foster worker participation in management and that, more than with individual farms or cooperatives, the profits could be used to benefit the poor majority in Nicaragua. Also, the Sandinistas believed they could avoid some of the problems state farms have encountered elsewhere. Whereas state farms in the Soviet Union, for example, entailed the collectivization of small, privately owned farms, in Nicaragua the process simply involved the transfer to public ownership of already existing large, centrally managed farms.

For the first year and a half, just bringing some coherent organization into the over 2,000 confiscated farms was a major part of the work. Two or three neighboring farms were consolidated into State Production Units (UPEs), each with an administrator. These 800-odd UPEs in turn were grouped according to proximity and type of production into 170 *complejos* (complexes). Each *complejo* is under an administrator who appoints the UPE administrators. Several *complejos* are organized into *empresas* (enterprises) that have a roughly similar production. Whereas in Nicaragua everyone refers to "UPE," we will use the term "state farm." Bear in mind, however, that most "state farms" (UPEs) are a grouping of what once were several farms or ranches.

The Sandinistas' goal "is not to repeat the mistakes of the type of bureaucratic socialism that people have known up to now," according to Peter Marchetti, an American Jesuit priest who is a resident advisor on the agrarian reform. "Their principal goal is to continually, as much as they can, reduce the responsibility of bureaucratic units." He notes that in regard to state farms "the government has taken a very creative step and put each enterprise on its own with respect to the national bank. . . . Each unit [is] independent and has to work out its own efficiency."

Are State Farms Profitable?

Are the state farms generating an economic surplus? Or are they a net drain on the economy? Two years into the revolution, these questions were being debated at the highest levels of the government.

Most Americans, thinking of the U.S. Postal Service or Amtrak, probably expect the worst of state farms. They expect "lemon socialism," in which the public takes ownership of the inevitable money-losers in the economy while private corporations hang on to the lucrative operations. In June 1981, Augusto Zeledón, administrator of the ex-Somoza coffee farm La Fundadora, told me that every group of visiting foreigners asked him about the profits of the farm. "You can count on the question," he said. In fact, only an hour before, a U.S. visitor had asked him, "How are the profits divided?" He told her, "Well, we haven't had any yet to divide."

In examining the profitability of state farms it is easy to forget the past—how Somocista operations made their sizeable profits. They made such profits largely by exploiting workers—by paying less than even the minimum wage, by providing miserable working conditions, by laying off most workers for several months each year, and by corruption. They helped drain the national treasury by fraudulent borrowing, making profits by building up debt. The state farms are also facing the same fiscal crisis devastating other export-oriented farms in Central America: higher prices for imported inputs such as fertilizer and pesticides and lower prices for the commodities produced.

Improved Services

During the first year or so, part of the farms' earnings were returned to the workers not only in the form of wages, but also in social services. Most of these services—clinics, schools, etc.—were built right on the farm. To avoid growing inequalities in standards of living between state farms, the government decided to organize these services, especially in health and education, on a *regional* level and through the Ministries of Health, Education, etc. A cattle ranch might invariably have a greater profit margin than, say, even an efficiently operated coffee plantation, given the relative value of beef to coffee—but should the ranch workers automatically benefit from better clinics or schools? In addition, the government wants to avoid concentrating social services on the minority of the rural population permanently employed on the state farms. Regionally organized services can also benefit seasonal laborers and campesinos and their families living in the region. "This is most important," note two scholars of Latin American agrarian history, "since other Latin American agrarian reforms, such as the Peruvian, have tended to exacerbate rural inequality by concentrating the provisions of social services in only the reformed sector, thus excluding the majority of the rural population."

Rather than each farm or grouping of farms using part of its earnings for social services, each will have to calculate its profits and, like a private firm, pay various taxes to the state. Each grouping of state farms also allocates money for investments on these farms. Some may be for better cultivation practices, such as mulch fertilization of coffee trees. In the short run these may mean higher costs and, therefore, lower profits, but they should provide greater productivity in the long run. Other investments, such as irrigation, intensify production and provide more year-round employment.

Profitability

It is hardly surprising that the state farm sector, for the most part, has been a drain on the government given these longer term investments, the problem of building new worker incentives, and the run-down condition in which many of the farms were taken over. In 1980, the state farms got over 25 percent of the total agricultural credit, yet produced only 14 percent of the value of agricultural production. In terms of loan repayment, an officer in the national finance corporation told me that the state is "our worst client."

At the same time, there has been considerable debate within the ministry about the notion of "profitability." Some have pointed out that the performance of the state farms cannot be measured in the same terms as private farms. For instance, the state farm policy of providing more year-round jobs may, at least in the short term, work against profitability. Some argue that the *volume* of production should be considered more important than profits (defined as revenue minus expenses). For it is the cotton, sugar, or coffee (or locally grown food substituted for imported food) that earns the *dollars* or other "hard" currency that the economy needs. In this view of profitability, the only cost that truly makes a difference is the foreign exchange cost of *imported* inputs such as tractors and fertilizers. Proponents point out that córdoba costs are not the same for the state enterprise as for the private enterprise since the government can print córdobas, while private farms get them only in exchange for the the exports they sell through the government. They do caution that too many córdobas in circulation can be inflationary. Yet boosting the volume of exports, no matter what the córdoba cost, is the goal for them.

In its simplistic form, this approach could cover up gross inefficiency and lead to a flagrant disregard for cost accountability. Underlying this view on profitability, however, is the intriguing idea that, despite the increased expenditures for cash and social wages, the state agroexport enterprises would easily show a profit if the dollar-córdoba rate were revised from 10 to 1 to, say, 17 to 1 (bearing in mind that on the legal "parallel" or "tourist" market, the dollar easily fetches 25 to 1).

In 1981 the ministry decided to clear the state farms' books of pre-victory debts, at least those in dollars. Being saddled with enormous past debts, it was thought, would lead farm administrators and workers to despair of ever turning a profit, a despair that would become a self-fulfilling prophecy. Clearing the books has been difficult since Somoza and his associates often kept false records and had many bank records destroyed when the end seemed near.

Generally, costs in the state farm sector are running higher than expected—due, no doubt, to reduced labor productivity and administrative problems. If the trend is not reversed, it could easily jeopardize the state's ability to deliver on social services. (The early 1981 cutbacks in previously budgeted expenditures for "nonproductive" social services are an ominous warning.)

Measures are being taken to reverse the trend. First, as we have already stressed, a major effort is under way to develop accounting systems on the farm and *empresa* level. While some sort of bookkeeping was to be in place by mid-1981 on every farm, the target date for the full system is 1983.

The goal is to get a grip on whether a particular state farm is losing money. If it is, government thinking is that either changes must be made or a *deliberate* subsidy set. It is crucial to calculate and budget a precise and appropriate subsidy rather than say, "Oh, we don't run the dairy farm to make a profit anyway," an attitude that could easily cloak a multitude of needless inefficiencies.

Questions of profitability have helped lead to some key decisions regarding state farms, which show how free the Sandinistas are from any Marxian dogmatism that state farms are inherently the "superior form of production." As we will see in a later chapter, after initial resistance, the government gave in to the demands of landless seasonal workers and campesinos for land to plant food crops by lending them idle lands on the state farms. Even more significant was a decision that state farms that cannot be operated profitably because they are too small or too remote, or for any other reasons, would be turned over to independent cooperatives of landless campesinos. The government is also open to turning unprofitable state farms over to individual peasant families when the families are clearly not interested in cooperatives. By the end of July 1982, over 300 state farms had been titled over to peasants and landless laborers, comprising 40 percent of the land titled over in the first year of the Agrarian Reform Law.

Handing over lands in the state farm sector to land-hungry rural people reduces the pressure to expropriate idle or underutilized land on the private estates. For a government still trying to work out a productive *modus vivendi* with private commercial farmers, this has no doubt been an important consideration.

The leadership's state farm policy has responded to Nicaragua's historical circumstances and has resisted any idealized concept of either urban-based planners or ideologues. In chapter 11 we'll see that it has a similar policy on agricultural cooperatives. But first let's look into the difficult problems the state farms are tackling in trying to increase production while meeting the just demands of the workers.

EIGHT

WAGE AND PRODUCTIVITY DILEMMAS

"LET'S SUPPOSE THAT EACH OF YOU EARNS 1,000 córdobas a month, and we decide to double that to 2,000. What would happen? There would be more money on the street. Isn't that so? So the goods we have would be bought up very quickly, with more money around, and we would start to have shortages. And when shortages start, things begin to get more expensive. So that within a short time your 2,000 córdobas would buy the same that 1,000 córdobas bought you before."

Comandante Tomás Borge, the only surviving founder of the Sandinista Front, was talking to workers at the Pedro Rivas Recalde state farm. They were demanding higher wages to help offset the inflation, which had already eaten up most of the increase in the minimum wage established soon after victory. Without more goods, Borge told them, more money is no help.

It was a message few workers wanted to hear. After the seemingly impossible victory over Somoza, anything seemed possible. Low wages had been one of the starkest signs of their oppression. So it was hard to understand why, with the dictatorship overthrown, they the workers couldn't immediately enjoy the profits once hoarded by the rich.

Under Somoza, labor legislation included a $2.10-a-*day* minimum wage for agricultural workers. But few workers ever got it. In practice, wages typically ranged from 80¢ to $1.70 a day, except for skilled workers such as tractor operators. Mandatory fringe benefits, such as meals or transportation, were seldom delivered. Some workers have told me that they didn't even know such laws had ever been on the books. At the very best, it seems, Somoza sometimes enforced the rules when he wanted to teach particular growers a lesson.

A few months following victory the new government boosted the minimum wage by 30 percent. But because the government paid the minimum wage on state farms and attempted to enforce it elsewhere, the *average* rural wage may have gone up over 60 percent. Fringe benefits or equivalent cash payments amounted to further increases. (Well into the first year, however, administrators of some state farms paid less than the minimum wage, according to the Sandinista Front's newspaper *Barricada*. The explanation I was given in the ministry was that some farms were *de facto* self-financing for many months, and the administrators did not have the money.)

Yet two years' inflation seemed to have canceled out real gains in cash income for most permanent and seasonal workers on the state farms. During the insurrection, inflation was 80 percent annually. Since victory, it's been 25 to 35 percent a year with every indication that it will be rising over the foreseeable future. On the first anniversary the government raised the minimum agricultural wage 18 percent to help offset inflation. While some ministry people can calculate a few points' gain here or there (largely by costing in the fringe benefits), everyone admits that workers universally feel they are earning "*lo mismo*"—the same.

On many farms, state and private alike, workers have persisted in demanding higher wages. On some state farms workers have gone on strike. At the Altamira rice farm (formerly Somoza's, therefore now a state farm), workers struck for five days during March 1980. Strikes in early 1980 over wages at the sugar mills, the state-owned Ingenio Monterrosa and the huge, privately owned San Antonio, were particularly costly. Cut cane quickly rots and work stoppages at San Antonio were estimated to cost over one-half million córdobas ($50,000) a day.

The workers' ignorance of the cost accounting on each state enterprise exacerbated the conflict over cash wages. On a state-owned dairy farm in Managua, for instance, the unit production costs in 1980 were over 35 percent higher than the selling price. But the workers weren't told this. So, knowing that total production was up, they couldn't understand why their wages weren't also hiked. They were bewildered when told that the dairy farm was losing money.

In resisting wage demands, the Sandinista leadership has had to fend off opponents on both the left and right. Groups such as the Frente Obrero ("Workers Front," an ultraleft communist labor group) tell the workers that the Sandinistas, in their unwillingness to increase wages, are defending the country's monied interests. At the same time, the rightwing newspaper, *La Prensa*, tries to discredit the government by harping on the fact that workers' wages buy no more than before.

Government and Sandinista Front spokespeople invariably respond to wage demands by admitting that they are just, but saying they cannot be satisfied given the economic crisis of the nation. Leaders such as Jaime Wheelock have often gone personally to talk with disgruntled workers to explain the government's dilemma. When the Frente Obrero organized strikes at sugar mills calling for a 100 percent wage increase, the Sandinista Front's Organizing Secretary responded: "This minuscule organization [the Frente Obrero] is quite ignorant of the situation of the country and real problems that we face. They are making a series of proposals that are totally pie in the sky. These proposals are very nice, very interesting, but quite unrealizable."

The ATC has generally been successful in countering such groups. This success is the fruit of a long relationship of trust with the workers built by ATC leaders over years of organizing—under great risk—in many of the country's sugar mills and other agroindustrial centers. At the same time, the ATC has pushed for more health and housing improvements and for government stores selling basic foods at low fixed prices in the countryside.

Social Wage

In a similar vein, the government's primary response to the dilemma has been to try to shift the focus of rural workers' demands away from the cash wage to the "social wage," meaning improvements in health services, meals, housing, etc. Not only are they less inflationary than cash wage increases but they respond to the dire need (especially following the war) for improved living and working conditions. Many Sandinistas also favor increases in the "social wage" because they do not foster the individualism they feel would thwart the future development of the country.

The government has also responded to wage demands by trying to keep food prices down (so low wages could buy more) by importing an unprecedented quantity of staple foods during the first two years after the war. By 1981, the government set low fixed prices for the basic necessities (corn, beans, cooking oil, sugar, kerosene, soap, salt, etc.) and subsidized farmers.

In addition, the ministry set up ENABAS stores on 149 state farms serving over 16,000 families, or 8 percent of the rural population. The stores are managed by workers selected by the farms' labor unions. Unfortunately, these stores are not always as well stocked as hoped.

In retrospect one might judge that the *first* move of the new government in 1979 should have been to announce an economic emergency—austerity for all. Yet I know from conversations with Jaime Wheelock and other Sandinista leaders how repugnant it was to them to call for belt-tightening by the poor just after a war in which the poor paid the heaviest price. How difficult indeed when the poor can see all around them an elite loath to sacrifice even imported luxuries, yet making political hay out of shortages and price increases.

Year-Round Work

The Sandinistas based their initial rural policies on the assumption that what many rural poor want, above all, is year-round work. Under Somoza, over a third of those working in agriculture were not only deprived of land but were employed only three or four months each year. So within one year after victory, the Sandinistas had doubled—even tripled—permanent employment on many state-run farms compared to when the same farms belonged to Somoza and his associates.

With the rush of expectations after the overthrow of the dictatorship, every worker on a confiscated farm seemed to be badgering the administrators for a permanent job for a brother-in-law or a cousin or a friend who previously could get only seasonal work. Benjamín Linarte, administrator of the large Altamira rice complex, told me that if he took down the "no job openings" sign at the entrance, at least 150 people would show up looking for work on the first day alone. Many administrators obviously gave in. After all, the farm was the people's property, wasn't it? And surely these were "the people."

Many thus gained permanent work during the chaotic early period in which often there were no payrolls and the new books, for what they were worth, were kept at ministry headquarters in Managua. (It was two years after victory before the ministry knew the exact total of permanent workers on the state farms.)

The problem is, of course, that unless production increases at least as fast as the payroll grows, labor productivity (output per person-hour worked) plummets. That means it costs more to produce a pound of rice, sugar, or coffee. The Sandinistas have no short-term answer to the problem. In the short run, the ministry has attempted to use the additional workers for socially useful ends. On some farms, for instance, they build new on-farm services such as clinics and stores. On the Germán Pomares sugar complex, where all 1,015 workers are now permanently employed, many repair houses, buildings, and roads during the "dead season." (About 400 of these workers had only seasonal work on the plantation "before.")

One obvious alternative would be to replace machines with handwork. Concerned about the many unemployed in his region, the administrator of the highly mechanized Altamira rice farm considered just such a move. He had many reservations, including the workers' fear that standing in irrigated fields would give them arthritis. But on my last visit to Altamira in March 1981 I saw so many giant John Deere tractors paralyzed for lack of spare parts that I wondered if he would be forced to overcome his reservations.

In the longer term, the government hopes to be able to invest in irrigation so that food crops can be grown and harvested during the months before planting the export crop. Then there would be no "dead season." But given the falling and very low prices for Nicaragua's major exports, that day could be a long way off. The increasing difficulty of securing long-term loans from World Bank-type sources, largely because of opposition from the Reagan administration, would also make this more difficult. A more immediate measure to deal with the dead season is lending or renting unused land on state farms to workers who form production cooperatives, as we discuss in chapter 11.

Falling Productivity

During the 1980 agricultural cycle, the state farms employed more persons per unit of land yet produced less value than the private capitalist farms. This falling productivity could not all be attributed to the additional number of workers given year-round employment. Perhaps even more significant was the fact that on many publicly owned farms, the average workday in practice has dropped from seven to about five hours or even less. When workers were paid to do a set piece of work, they finished as soon as possible, with quality often suffering.

Even the official workday, at least on some farms, has been reduced from eight to seven hours. On the state farm La Sorpresa in the province of Jinotega, a mid-1980 report stated that the workday had been reduced from eight to seven hours but that many workers put in only three. Farm workers were completing only half as much work in a given day as compared to before the revolution. At the same time, the state-owned Germán Pomares sugar mill estimated that labor productivity had dropped by at least 25 percent.

On the Altamira rice farm, the pilots of the small planes that sow the rice could optimally cover 182 acres an hour but were sowing scarcely 106 acres. When the pilots had been paid by the number of acres sown, they earned an average of 30,000 córdobas a month. Under the new order, they have a fixed monthly salary of 9,500 córdobas, only 500 córdobas less than the Minister of Agricultural Development earns.

Why the falling productivity? From the outside one might be baffled. After all, wouldn't workers want to work *harder* now, hoping their production would benefit the whole country's development? In a December 1979 address to the national assembly of the ATC, Jaime Wheelock asked if workers on state farms were wage laborers? No, he answered, "they are producers of social wealth, and the consciousness of the producer is quite different from that of the wage laborer. . . . He knows that each stroke of the machete is no longer to create profits for a boss, but perhaps to create a new pair of shoes for a barefoot child who may be his own."

But agricultural laborers saw it differently, at least initially. They had labored at hard, tedious, and even dangerous work for years to make others rich. The new order gave them an immediate chance for only one tangible good—less work. Many office-bound people in the ministry caricatured this notion as *"Revolución es piñata,"* referring to the candy-filled paper animal batted about at parties. But many workers saw themselves taking what they called their "historic vacations." The fact that they can do so speaks to perhaps the most fundamental change in the new Nicaragua—the loss of fear. Workers don't feel in danger of being brutalized or fired by their employers.

Ruptured is the old system in which export crops were produced through repression (the National Guard, dismissal without just cause, unions effectively prohibited), and through depriving people of enough land (and credit and good prices) to provide any alternative means of survival. For decades the shortage of workers during peak harvest periods should have given workers bargaining power to win higher pay and better working conditions. But actual repression or very substantial threat of repression by the National Guard thwarted that natural development.

Many permanent agricultural laborers with a little parcel of land in food crops expanded it or rented land for the first time. Moreover, lowered rents and abundant credit led small farmers to reduce the time they put in on the *"gran producción"* in order to tend to their own crops. Workers staying home to work their own plots was the main cause of absenteeism on the Germán Pomares sugar complex, for example.

Wage Policy

The departure of technically trained managers for jobs on the private farms also probably contributed to the drop-off in labor productivity. A primary reason has been the difference in paychecks. As a matter of general policy, the new government has collapsed the differential between the highest- and lowest-paid public sector employees. The Minister of Agricultural Development, for instance, was paid only eight times as much as the lowest-paid permanent farm worker; the ratio had been 78 to 1 under Somoza. By reducing the higher salaries and raising the lower ones, salaries for state farm managers have averaged slightly over twice that of permanent workers or 2,611 córdobas ($261) a month, making it easier for private farms to lure away state farm managers with higher salaries.

My visits to state farms indicate that women generally receive lower wages than men. The administrator on the ex-Somoza coffee farm La Fundadora, near Matagalpa, at first tried to give equal pay for equal work in fertilizing the coffee trees and other tasks, he told me in June 1981. But the men insisted on being paid at a higher rate, threatening otherwise to work less.

Moreover, women do not get the higher-paying jobs, such as tractor drivers. Women typically have jobs such as cooking meals for the workers and cleaning out the administration buildings. When this fact is pointed out to (male) administrators and ATC leaders, they see it as "natural" because "the women don't know how to drive tractors." Conversations with women workers on a dairy farm near León made clear that they would like to milk cows and drive tractors, but they also said that they didn't know how. Yet asked if they would like to learn, they unhesitatingly responded, "Of course!"

New Incentives

The Sandinista leadership has repeatedly stated—and shown—that it is determined to work out a mix of noncoercive means of motivating workers. "We are seeking to replace negative incentives with positive incentives," one Sandinista explained to me. A good part of the search is simply trying to get the workers to understand the importance of their work given the economic crisis in which Somoza left Nicaragua. On a state tobacco farm, the workers are reminded that their tobacco's quality is world renowned and they must work so that it doesn't lose its reputation. By contrast, the Somocista owners of that farm forced workers who performed poorly to stay for extra hours of unpaid work.

Recognizing that the drop in productivity can be related to the failure of workers to connect increased production and profits with improvements in the cash and social wage, the ministry is trying to open every farm's balance sheet to its workers. But to do this the ministry itself has had to develop farm-level accounting methods. In practice, if not in theory, the entire state sector was run out of one big purse during the inevitably chaotic first couple of years.

During the initial period of any true social transformation a drop in productivity is to be expected because workers will celebrate their freedom by rebelling against a history of exploitation in their workplaces. As the Sandinistas see it, eventually the workers will have new reasons to work, encouraged by a new form of authority—one coming from the workers themselves. By the end of the second year, this was beginning to happen. Augusto Zeledón, administrator of La Fundadora coffee plantation, told me in June 1981, "At first there was a lot of disorientation. Workers were coming two, three hours late and going off early to work their own plots. But now they are working practically a full day. What has made a difference is that I spend a lot of time talking to the workers in the fields. And the workers have gotten more organized and learned what they can do, especially through setting up and managing the store here."

Unlike their counterparts at similar periods of the Cuban and Chinese revolutions, the Sandinistas do not seem to be ideologically opposed to some linkage of wages (both cash and social) to increased productivity. In fact, a system of incentives perceptibly tied to advances in production and efficiency seems imperative. Workers themselves need to set norms of work—easier for some jobs than others—so that a schedule of incentives can be agreed upon, not imposed. An accounting system that everyone understands is also necessary to encourage increased efficiency as well as increased production. Questions about the types of incentives compatible with the goal of decreasing sharp inequalities among rural people—lest state farmworkers become a labor aristocracy in the countryside—and the best balance between individual and group incentives are still being debated within the ATC and several ministries.

The challenge is to make the state farms profitable without resorting to coercion or exploitation of the people who work on them.

NINE

IS SEIZING THE LAND REVOLUTIONARY?

A BOVE ALL ELSE, THE POOR MAJORITY IN NIC-aragua yearned for land—land for food, land for security, land to free themselves from the humiliation of having to sell their labor and even that of their children to a *patrón*.

By the last years of the Somoza dictatorship, well over two-thirds of those working in agriculture had been either totally deprived of land or deprived of enough land to support themselves. Since there was work on the plantations for only three to four months of the year, 80 percent of the land-poor Nicaraguans had to subsist catch-as-catch-can. They hunted small wild animals and harvested fruits with seasons different from the export crops. They had their children beg or peddle loaves of bread, flowers, or coconuts in the cities. And they sold their labor power for an hour or a day at a time to anyone who would buy it—anything to scrape together enough money to survive until the next harvest season.

Their hopes for land were reinforced by the Sandinista slogan in some of the war zones: "Land to whoever works it!" Land takeovers organized by outraged peasants were part of the Sandinistas' strategy against Somocistas during the war. But once they were in charge of the country's economy, the Sandinistas had to confront the implications of a sweeping "land to the tiller" reform. Immediately the Sandinistas called for a halt to land takeovers. Their primary concern: if most of Nicaragua's rural people became landowners, would there be enough workers for the export plantations, which generated 80 percent of the foreign exchange—foreign exchange needed more than ever by a country devastated by war and debt? Moreover, if the Sandinistas did not discourage land takeovers, the big landowners controlling most of the export crop land would feel threatened and seek to liquidate their operations. The Sandinistas also feared that spontaneous land takeovers would result in thousands of tiny plots, too small ever to produce efficiently.

Reinforcing all this pragmatic reasoning was the belief of many Sandinistas at the start of the revolution that a wage-earning ("proletarianized") labor force represented historic progress. They felt it laid the foundation for eventual worker self-management. Thus, increasing the number of peasants, especially individual small owners, would be a step backward. "There have been many agrarian reforms that in one stroke have handed over the land," Jaime Wheelock stated in 1979. "But this type of land reform destroys the process of proletarianization in the countryside and constitutes a historical regression."

Not surprisingly, the landless were confused. A Chinandega campesino summed up the bewilderment of many a few days after the July 19 triumph: "I don't understand it at all. One minute seizing the land is revolutionary and then they tell you it is counterrevolutionary."

In seeking to discourage land takeovers in the months following the triumph, the new government tried to improve wages and working conditions on private and state farms rather than redistribute land ownership. With hindsight, a privilege rarely granted to revolutionaries, it appears that the Sandinistas probably underestimated the depth and strength of the demand for land. For as the months went on, there were innumerable land takeovers, spontaneous as well as ATC-organized, especially of lands that had not been planted and where landlords refused to rent land at the new legal rates. The situation was especially tense in areas like the northern provinces, where the campesinos lived far away from most wage-labor plantation jobs and could barely survive on marginal lands rented from the big growers.

The fact that the Sandinista-allied association itself, the ATC, was involved in land seizures in some areas reveals a fundamental tension within the Sandinista Front in the early period: Is seizing the land revolutionary or counterrevolutionary?

The ATC, whose members were experiencing cases of gross injustice in the countryside every day, argued that land seizures represent the just response of the rural majority. The Sandinista directorate, feeling responsible for the long-term survival of the revolution as a whole—lest all the gains of the rural majority be ultimately reversed as in Chile after Allende—tended to oppose post-victory land seizures. Of course, there were also ATC leaders who saw the "bigger picture," as well as top Sandinistas moved by the authentic popular demands. Once again, it was evident that agrarian reform was never a fully successful balancing act.

By early 1980 the conflicts over land seizures were moving inexorably toward a center-stage showdown. In late 1979 the courts moved to return to owners those farms and ranches spontaneously taken over by peasants and farmworkers, if it could not be proven that the owners had close ties to Somoza. For the ATC, however, *any* return of properties to private owners signaled a halt in the process of agrarian reform just when so many workers and peasants believed it should move forward.

On February 17, 1980, the ATC organized an unprecedented demonstration through the streets of Managua to the Plaza of the Revolution. Brandishing placards, banners, and machetes, over 30,000 campesinos and landless rural workers from every part of the country demanded that "not one single inch of land be returned." They also demanded measures against landowners who refused to resume production, pay the minimum wage, or carry out recently decreed improvements in working conditions and fringe benefits. It was clear that the Sandinista Front had made up its mind to side with these demands: a Sandinista Air Force plane was even called in to bring campesinos from some remote areas to the rally.

The Sandinista Front obviously supported the demonstration because it proved to any who still doubted that there was popular support for a further decree. Jaime Wheelock, Minister of Agricultural Development and a member of the directorate of the Sandinista Front, addressed the demonstrators: "We know that your demands are just, and this march gives us the confidence to advance and make further transformations." While Wheelock reiterated the need for the agrarian reform to proceed in an orderly fashion, avoiding "anarchic and spontaneous actions," he insisted that "there are elements among the landowners who must be hit hard if their lands are left idle. . . ."

On March 2, taking its legitimacy from such a groundswell of demand in the countryside, the government decreed that all lands taken over up to that time would remain in the public domain, the Area of the People's Property. Still, it was a balancing act: in recognition of the rights of private property, the former owners who could not be proven to be Somocistas would be compensated. Thus, in effect, the decree was an exercise in eminent domain. Farms belonging to small producers were exempted from the decree. And the government assured private landowners that further land takeovers would be strongly discouraged.

Workers and neighboring land-hungry campesinos wanting part of the land to plant food crops put pressure on state farms as well as large private farms. At first, many state farm administrators refused these demands. They had two fears: loss of labor for the harvest and loss of land that might eventually be needed to expand production.

But as the pressure built, the ministry tended to give in, at least allowing the landless to "borrow" unused acreage on state farms, theoretically on a season-to-season basis. The workers had to pledge to work the land cooperatively and promise to work for wages on the state farm when they were needed. In fact, the peak seasons for work on the export crops and work on the staple food crops generally do not conflict. Many state farms did have more land they could effectively use; lending it to the landless helped deal with the unemployment problem in the countryside without increasing the total payrolls of the state farms. With the strong pressure for land in spring 1981 and the all-out push to boost food production, lending idle state farm acreage became official policy.

The land-lending policy enabled the government to make a stronger case against the big growers, for if the state farms were not using all their land, it was difficult to criticize private owners for keeping lands idle. The government also figured that its lending of idle land in exchange for an agreement to work when needed would automatically put pressure on many private landowners to do the same, since the large private farms and the state farms compete with each other for harvest workers. This pressure on the big private growers would also help meet the hunger for land.

Under pressure from the newly organized union of small and medium producers (UNAG), the government decreed at the same time that lands traditionally rented out, and idle lands, must be rented to the landless. Many landowners refused to obey the law, charging much higher rents than allowed in zones where there was a great demand for land, or planting pasture or sorghum rather than renting the land.

"We Won't Be Hungry Any More"

Just when many in the government hoped that there would be no more land takeovers, they picked up again as the time for the spring 1981 planting of corn and beans approached. As campesinos told me, "with the smell of moist earth after the first rains, people yearn to have some land."

But this food crop planting season came at no ordinary historical moment. The new Reagan administration, sharply hostile toward the Nicaraguan government, abruptly cut off $9.8 million in credits for importing U.S. wheat, reinforcing the idea that Nicaragua must become self-sufficient in food production. At the same time, many commercial farm owners were leaving their lands idle and illegally liquidating their assets. From the ATC and UNAG in the field, as well as from the ministry itself, came repeated reports that many campesinos and farmworkers could no longer be talked out of seizing idle farmland. Peasants and workers were particularly outraged by the landowners who refused even to rent idle lands.

One such landlord was Adolfo Pastora, who planted only 85 acres of his 24,000-acre farm. Pastora often resided outside the country and repeatedly refused to rent land to any of the hundreds of nearby poor campesinos.

A group of these campesinos went to the local agrarian reform official to demand the land legally. The official told them, "You know that's against our policy of national unity. That is going to send a cold chill through every private producer in the country. Maybe we can find a way to give you a piece of land, but to expropriate all this—we don't want to do it." But the peasants were not persuaded, as they told me later. They told the official he was mistaken and that he should consult with his *jefe*.

Working with the ATC, they organized demonstrations in front of government offices in the nearby towns. In May 1981, 600 went straight to the head office of the agrarian reform in Managua. There they found Salvador Mayorga, the director of the agrarian reform who had worked with some of the campesinos during the liberation war. He heard them out, then agreed to order confiscation of the farm. The triumphant campesinos returned to the Pastora farm and started planting.

When I visited them several weeks after the takeover, their enthusiasm was evident. The sun shone down on their newly planted crops, their guarantee of plenty to eat in just a few months. Along with the new crops, there was an obvious new sense of self-respect. An old campesino, with deep wrinkles in his face, told me that since learning to read and write in the literacy campaign, "I don't bow down and conform any more. I used to hide, but now I stand up."

"We won't be hungry any more," said a woman with a child in her arms, pointing to some vegetables she'd planted nearby. Standing in a rough-hewn, smoky, communal kitchen, she told me about her life. At the age of twelve she had gone to Managua to work as a maid so that she could send money back to her family. "When my employer sensed the coming popular victory, he fled to Miami," she explained. "I returned to my family here in the country."

The next morning back in Managua, I picked up *La Prensa* and read the big three-inch headline: "Courts Rule the Pastora Farm Should Be Given Back." Adolfo Pastora had returned from abroad and hired some top lawyers. *Barricada*, the Sandinista afternoon paper, interviewed some of the same campesinos I had spoken with. One had told me of losing his thumb in an accident on the Pastora farm when he was 14 years old. Pastora refused to help him. "We will die before we give back one inch of this land," he told *Barricada*.

Less than three months later, the peasants were vindicated by the new agrarian reform law, which made them legal owners.

TEN

A CONSERVATIVE AGRARIAN REFORM?

E VERY DAY FOR TWO YEARS THE PRESSURE
mounted on the government to come up with a comprehensive agrarian reform. Not only did many of the big
growers fail to use their land productively, but some were also
draining money and productive assets from the country,
often with the help of generous government loans. From the
campesinos and seasonal farmworkers came an additional
pressure on the government to act: illegal seizures of idle
land by those outraged that good land lay unused while they
went hungry. By mid-1981, everyone in the country, rich
and poor alike, wondered when the revolution would enact a
land reform and what it would be like.

A year earlier Minister of Agrarian Development Jaime
Wheelock had assigned some key people in the ministry to
work day and night to draft a comprehensive agrarian reform
law. And on July 19, 1980, the first anniversary of the victory over Somoza, the government announced that the agrarian reform law was ready and would shortly be presented for
deliberation to the Council of State. But the law, though
drafted, was never presented.

A few months later, I asked ministry officials why the new
law had never been presented. The ministry was reluctant to
take on the administrative burden of expropriating a myriad

of idle properties, scattered here and there, I was told. There was, after all, enough idle land in the state sector, the vice minister for agricultural planning explained to me. "We need time to get our own act together first," he observed wryly.

I was also told that the ATC, the farmworkers' association, felt it hadn't had a large enough role in formulating the draft. It wanted a more flexible law.

More fundamentally, the big growers, lobbying through their producer associations, had objected to a land reform, *period*. And, as it became increasingly apparent that Ronald Reagan would be the new U.S. president, the Sandinista leadership put top priority on the broadest possible unity, anticipating heightened U.S. hostility.

There also seemed less urgency for the new law. The mere announcement of an impending law that would require owners to use their land productively, at penalty of losing it, had the effect of "motivating" many cotton growers to get on with the overdue planting of their fields, Vice Minister Salvador Mayorga told me. At the same time, the rural poor were seizing fewer farms and ranches because the main season for planting corn, beans, and other staples had passed. As the pressure waned, the draft law wound up on the revolution's back burner.

But just for the time being. During my visits to Nicaragua in the first six months of 1981, I found a clear acceleration of "decapitalization" and other forms of economic sabotage by many of the larger private producers. As a consequence, the rural poor grew increasingly impatient. They couldn't understand why the government didn't act to stop it.

The Sandinista leadership was responding, however. It was at work in the ministry, in the farmworkers' association, and in the newly created small producers' union (UNAG). Carefully and deliberately, they sounded out campesinos and large producer associations, farmworkers, administrators, and ministry workers around the country—all now enriched by two years of on-the-ground experience.

Then, on July 19, 1981, government and Sandinista leader Daniel Ortega read out the proposed Agrarian Reform Law to the applause of half a million Nicaraguans gathered to celebrate the second anniversary of the victory. The proposed law went to the Council of State where certain changes were recommended and then back to the junta, which made it official in late August.

The law is pragmatic; some have even called it conservative. I've been told that many larger landowners had expected something "much worse." Virtually unique among land reforms, it places no ceiling on land ownership and emphatically reiterates the state's guarantee to protect the right to private property. But the law does set out once and for all the criteria and legal process for judging whether a landowner is meeting the obligation of ownership, making the land produce efficiently.

At the time the Agrarian Reform Law was announced, ministry officials estimated that perhaps as much as 4 million acres, roughly 30 percent of the country's agricultural land, was abandoned, idle, or inadequately used and therefore could eventually be redistributed.

In its provisions for redistribution, the law reaffirms the Sandinistas' commitment to a mixed economy in the countryside. Internal government projections are that in due course, as a consequence of the application of the law, 40 percent of the agricultural land will wind up belonging to independent campesino credit associations and production cooperatives, 25 percent to the state, 5 percent to small individual owners, and 30 percent to medium and large individual owners.

Large and even very large owners, however, are not excluded from the government's vision of the new Nicaragua. The obvious case in point is Sr. Pellas, the largest private landowner in the country, whose San Antonio complex produces almost half of the country's sugar and all the Flor de Caña export rum. He has no reason to fear expropriation for he has continued to invest his own capital, increasing both the area planted and total production. Pellas has been singled out for praise by the government on several occasions.

Since the law does not affect lands put to proper use, it will not shift any productive farms and ranches into new hands, a transfer that has disrupted production, at least in the short term, under other land reforms. Furthermore, production of food crops should be boosted by moving thousands of farmworkers, traditionally unemployed much of the year, onto fertile but idle lands.

At the same time, the government hopes the law will increase the production of export crops by the nation's commercial producers; the law sought to remove any uncertainties they had, thus hopefully encouraging them to invest. Many—some in blatant bad faith—had complained during the first two years that they could not commit themselves to producing or investing given their uncertain future. They complained that the government had not legally defined the role of private farming and was looking the other way when the poor took over idle or underused lands. Hanging over them was the knowledge that virtually all other Latin American revolutions had placed ceilings on land ownership— some even confiscating an *entire* property, not just the part exceeding the limit. The new law explicitly forbids land seizures by peasants and workers. But it also makes more precise the obligation of landowners to produce, and sets forth the legal consequences of failure to do so.

Land Redistribution Under the New Law

Under the law, any abandoned land can be redistributed by the government. In such cases, there will be no compensation. Idle or underused land on very large holdings (over 850 acres in the prime Pacific Coast region; over 1,700 acres in the rest of the country) are also subject to expropriation. The total amount of land owned by one individual or partnership, regardless of how many separate farms, is used to determine the size of the holdings. Lands with titles transferred to other members of the same family are considered part of the same holding, thus short-circuiting a classic land reform evasion tactic. ("Idle" is defined as not cultivated for at least two years; "underused" refers to farms where less than 75 percent of the land suitable for farming is in use; cattle lands are underused if there is less than one head of cattle for each 3-1/2 acres on the Pacific Coast and for each 5 acres in the rest of the country.)

Making the acreage provision so generous indicates that the law does not target the medium-size producer. The main targets of the reform are not so much big farms but large cattle haciendas that pasture relatively few cattle, often on prime cultivable land.

If only part of an estate is left idle or underused, the entire estate will not be expropriated, the law states. Only the neglected land will be seized. In one case, an owner was cultivating only 300 of 1,200 acres. The 900 idle acres were expropriated and given to a cooperative made up of nearly landless workers. The government then gave the owner a loan to irrigate the remaining 300 acres so he could increase production on that land.

Over the protests of farmworker and peasant organizations, the law prescribes compensation to owners for all idle or unused land taken over. However, owners caught decapitalizing (selling off machinery or cattle) will not be compensated.

The law also seeks to end the exploitation of poor farmers by absentee landowners. On farms larger than 85 acres in the Pacific Coast area and 170 acres elsewhere, any lands being rented for cash or labor, or being sharecropped, can be expropriated. The applicable farm size for rented land is set lower than for idle land because the poor tenant/absentee owner relationship is considered so unjust and economically backward.

But small farms are exempt. In some areas, truly small, poor farmers who work the land themselves also rent out part of it. While they will not be affected by this part of the law, it is hoped that in due course the agrarian reform will provide their tenants with their own land. The earlier decree placing a low ceiling on rent remains in force.

Of course, the government can expropriate very large farms that are entirely rented out to commercial producers, often the case with cotton plantations. In this case the government can opt to rent to the same producers, but with the rent going for the public good rather than to an absentee landlord. The logic behind this decision is that unlike the actual operators of the rented cotton plantations, the absentee owners contribute nothing to production.

"The government is not dividing the people according to an abstract logic that often creates a tremendous amount of social conflict," Father Peter Marchetti, an American Jesuit rural sociologist employed by the Ministry of Agricultural Development, told us. "We are not going to expropriate the land of those who own, say, 200 acres, as was the case in Chile and in most other reforms that have set a limit on size. In this sense, the Nicaraguan land reform is much more just because it punishes only those who are parasites on the peasantry and on the society."

Even in compensating for expropriated land, the law recognizes differences among landowners. Landowners whose land is taken over will be compensated according to tribunal judgments of how drastically they underused or destroyed the productivity of their estates and whether they did so out of neglect or to drain money out of the country. Those judged to have done the least harm will receive bonds at 4 percent interest that can be claimed in 15 years. The worst offenders will get bonds at 2 percent interest that mature in 35 years. An owner without other sources of income and unable to work will receive a pension of at least 1,000 córdobas a month.

Who Gets the Land?

Just as those who fail to produce are to be expropriated under the law, so the most industrious of the poor peasants are to be the first to receive land. Campesinos who banded together during the first two years of the revolution and have proven themselves responsible by obtaining good yields, working together in some form of cooperative, and paying back their loans from the bank, are to be the first to receive land titles.

Preference is also given to families of heroes and martyrs of the liberation war and to those who risked their lives. The next priority is impoverished small farmers who need more or better land just to meet their basic needs.

Preference is also given to those willing to organize themselves in some form of cooperative. The government's encouragement of credit associations and production cooperatives rather than scattered family farms can better take advantage of economies of scale. This not only includes crop processing centers and other production facilities but social advances such as clinics and schools. But cooperatives remain voluntary. In fact, the first titles under the new law were awarded on World Food Day 1981 to individual families in the Wiwilí area, where Sandino had worked with the peasants over 50 years earlier.

Next in line to receive land are landless farmworkers. They are given lower preference because the government fears that once they have land of their own to cultivate food crops, they will be reluctant to work in the export crop harvests, which are so critical for the nation's foreign exchange earnings. The ATC is organizing landless-worker families into "Seasonal Worker Committees." These committees will report idle lands and organize themselves to receive and work them cooperatively. But they are also committed to making their members available for work in the export harvests when needed.

State farms have the next priority to receive newly expropriated lands. Putting state farms so far down the list reflects the view that the primary task is to get the already established state farms to function well as modern, efficient poles of development before even thinking of expanding them. In some areas, especially those lightly populated, newly expropriated land might be combined with existing state farms to create more rational production units.

Minister Jaime Wheelock has stressed that state farms, like private farms, must live up to the production responsibilities that come with ownership. State farms that cannot prove themselves to be producing efficiently will, like private estates, be turned over to the landless and the land-poor. In the first year of the Agrarian Reform Law, over 300 state farms were turned over to campesino cooperatives and individual family farmers. In many areas, during the first year of the new law, most of the land titled over to peasants has been state land.

The lowest priority in land redistribution goes to the urban unemployed who want to return to the countryside to produce basic food staples.

The exact amount of land that agrarian reform beneficiaries will receive will vary according to the quality of land and local circumstances; the guideline is that the minimum acreage be sufficient to yield an income equivalent to the legal minimum wage.

Land titles granted under the law come free and unencumbered. By contrast, in many other land reforms the beneficiaries have had to pay for the land. The Nicaraguan agrarian reform titles cannot be sold; for this reason, opponents of the revolution, both inside and outside Nicaragua, have argued that the government is defrauding campesinos. But the government's intention is to forestall any new process of land concentration. And the land titles can be used as collateral for loans from the state banking system.

The agrarian reform is also designed to work against the land fragmentation so characteristic of rural misery in much of the third world: while the land titles can be inherited, the land cannot be divided among heirs. Land received under the law can be transferred to a cooperative and, if none is adjacent, it is possible to exchange it for equivalent land suitably located to become part of a cooperative.

Rational Land Use

The new Agrarian Reform Law aims for more than greater justice in the use of Nicaragua's agricultural land; it also provides for more rational use of the country's agricultural resources. Under the Somoza system, rich soils, well-suited to growing crops, were usurped by powerful ranchers for grazing cattle, while peasant producers were forced to grow food crops on low-fertility, easily eroded hillsides suitable for grazing. An "agricultural development zone" provision of the law authorizes the agricultural ministry to identify the best agricultural uses of each productive area and to guide the appropriate commercial, peasant, and state production to those uses. Such land use planning could not only increase production but also make easier government technical assistance to producers. Moreover, concentrating certain crops in certain areas will facilitate the efficient use of crop processing industries such as rice-drying plants.

A good example of the use of this provision of the law is a mammoth sugar cane development scheme in Tipitapa, not far from Managua (although investment in sugar cane is in itself controversial). Over five years, cane will be planted on 50,000 acres, half belonging to private owners. The projected state-owned mill will be the largest and most efficient in Central America, using only cane waste products for fuel and indeed generating a surplus of electricity. The project is slated to cost $250 million, with $103 million of that financed by Cuban government aid.

Implementation: The Hard Part Starts

A land reform that sets an arbitrary ceiling on landownership can be implemented virtually overnight; one that uses effi-cient production as its criterion instead of size takes longer. The Nicaraguan land reform, if it is to be effective, requires careful case-by-case study; even then there will no doubt be differences in judgment. The Sandinista leadership has stressed that its agrarian reform will take years to implement. Since the law cannot be properly implemented quickly, it hopes there will be time for many "wait and see" producers to realize they can live—indeed, can prosper—with it.

If Nicaragua were land-scarce, the government might be tempted to apply the new law harshly—redistributing land whenever there was a shred of doubt about its productive use. But the Nicaraguan revolution's great luxury is its over-all abundance of land, so tremendous that even in the most optimistic scenario about the performance of the larger land-owners, it is hard to imagine there would not be enough land to distribute to the landless and the land-poor. (In some areas, however, they might have to be relocated to land else-where in the country).

"We plan to do it right, however long that takes us," the Director General of the Agrarian Reform, Salvador May-orga, told me shortly after the promulgation of the law. Im-plementation procedures reflect considerable concern for due process. Yet at the same time they recognize the danger that landowners might use the legal process to obstruct progress indefinitely—a tactic that has stymied land reforms in other countries. Such delays would undoubtedly provoke land sei-zures, thus placing the government in the ironic and politi-cally untenable position of arresting the rural poor in the name of the revolution's agrarian reform. Thus special courts have been established to streamline adjudications. While landowners have the right of appeal, final judgments are to be handed down within 30 days.

For its implementation, the law established two new struc-tures. First is the National Agrarian Reform Council, with parallel regional councils to carry out the functions of the national council on a regional level. The council sees that studies to assess properties that might be affected are carried out in collaboration with the farmworkers' and farmowners' unions. Landowners are required to show evidence of their productivity. The council also identifies individuals and cooperatives capable of properly using confiscated lands. The national council is made up of top officials as well as technicians of the Ministry of Agricultural Development and Agrarian Reform, the director of the National Finance Corporation, and representatives of both the farmworkers' association (ATC) and the small and medium producers' union (UNAG). Interestingly, final authority in deciding whether an expropriation procedure should be set into motion rests with the national council; otherwise, it was feared, local tensions might make the land reform process either overly radical or overly restrained.

The second new institution for implementing the agrarian reform is a system of agrarian reform tribunals to resolve any claims of injustice or irregularity as well as other disputes. A national tribunal supervises a network of regional tribunals. Members of the tribunals are appointed by the national government and, from what I have seen, generally include a small farmowner or farmworker.

In the first year of the Agrarian Reform Law, 242 properties totaling approximately 400,000 acres and belonging to 94 families were affected. Somewhat over 60 percent of the land was expropriated because it was judged to be idle or underutilized. One-quarter had been abandoned by the owners; the remainder was rented or sharecropped.

Of the 94 owners, 18 filed legal appeals. Six appeals were upheld and the council's decision overturned; the land was returned to the six owners. Of the land expropriated so far, titles have been distributed for only 40 percent of it, to 6,503 campesino families, nearly all in credit associations or production cooperatives. Salvador Mayorga's explanation of this gap was that it takes more time to identify good beneficiaries, especially if the emphasis is on cooperatives, than to identify bad hacienda owners. "We're working on it, but we don't want a single beneficiary to fail," he told me. "So we won't be rushed—even by President Reagan."

ELEVEN

COOPERATIVE WORK: WILL IT WORK IN NICARAGUA?

A LONGSIDE THE STATE FARMS AND THE PRI-
vate commercial growers, the Sandinistas are encouraging the development of cooperatives—gradually and
voluntarily. For the Sandinistas, setting up cooperatives represents a vindication of the rural-based leader who fought to
free Nicaragua from the U.S. Marines. Half a century ago in
the mountains of Nicaragua, Augusto César Sandino started
cooperatives among campesinos, cooperatives that Anastasio
Somoza obliterated in 1932, the day after he had Sandino
assassinated. The Sandinistas took their name—and considerable inspiration—from this hero.

Sandinista leaders offer a variety of reasons for the new
government's promotion of cooperatives. Some are philo-
sophical: working together is morally superior to working
alone, which can foster selfish attitudes and the exploitation
of others, including family members; cooperative ownership
works against the emergence of conflicts based on growing
differences in wealth. But for the most part, leaders I've
talked to stressed practical reasons.

During the years of fighting against the dictatorship from
guerrilla bases in the countryside, many Sandinistas witnessed
the isolation and extreme deprivation of the Nicaraguan

campesinos. Campesino families often live miles from other families. With few and very poor roads, many have no access to schools, clinics, churches, or even the simple pleasures of social life among friends. Thus cooperatives are seen as one way of drawing people together to make possible at least a better, more social, life.

The new government also knew that developing Nicaragua's food potential required getting credit and technical help to the country's numerous campesino producers. The government wanted to set up stores selling basic goods throughout the countryside to give campesinos an incentive to produce. These monumental tasks would be possible only if the government could work with organized groups of small producers rather than with over 200,000 individuals.

Finally, the new government hoped that as Nicaragua developed it would be able to use agricultural machines, machines economically justifiable only if used on large holdings. If the countryside remained carved up into tiny plots, even small tractors would not make sense. Such an argument for cooperatives is not lost on the peasants: in conversations with countless campesinos, I have found tractors high on their list of desires. And they readily appreciate the need to share a tractor with other small farmers. The Nicaraguan government has solicited donations of tractors; the Soviet Union has been the principal donor.

To many North Americans, cooperatives no doubt connote the kind of idealism that leads both to coercion and to the undermining of production. And these fears are hardly surprising: if one believes that people will not cooperate willingly and that individuals working solely in their own self-interest are always the most productive, then surely cooperatives are suspect. In addition, in such countries as Tanzania, coercion has been used in forming cooperatives.

Keeping these doubts in mind, I've asked many questions in studying the new Nicaraguan cooperatives. What forms will these cooperatives take? Is the model rigid or flexible? To what extent will it be imposed rather than simply encouraged? And does the concrete evidence from the first three years' experience indicate that cooperative production might work in Nicaragua?

The First Step: Credit Associations

One type of Nicaraguan cooperative, the Credit and Services Association (CCS), resembles farm cooperatives here in the United States in certain ways. In it, small farmers keep their land individually, but join together to purchase fertilizer, seeds, etc., in bulk and at a better price. Each member receives credit for production expenses individually, but elected representatives pull together the information and negotiate with the government bank on behalf of the entire group. In fact, it's more of an association than a cooperative. The Sandinistas hope these credit associations will be "schools of democracy" where campesinos accustomed to living in isolation will learn to build communities and gain confidence in working together. These associations, they hope, will serve as stepping stones to cooperatives in which land is worked together and work animals and equipment pooled.

To encourage peasants to form these associations, the new government offered them credit on a priority basis and at a substantially lower rate than for individual small producers. Peasants responded: over 1,200 credit associations were registered in the first year.

In most, however, the cooperation revolved around obtaining bank credit and perhaps technical assistance. Other activities were as individualized as before. Thus when credit was restricted during the second year (with some first-year debts not paid back and less credit available), many of these associations virtually disappeared. During this period, I talked with a member of a credit association near Estelí from which many members had recently withdrawn: "I don't have the words to explain why we don't work well together," he told me. "It's a disease that goes way back, a lack of experience."

But not all of these associations fall apart. Not surprisingly, more are thriving in regions where peasants were more actively involved with the Sandinistas during the war against Somoza. They already have some experience in building organizations, and many of these credit groups see themselves as precursors of "real" production cooperatives. At a cooperative I visited in June 1981, the members had decided to pull down their fences so that they would gradually grow accustomed to the idea of working their lands together. This practice of "invisible fences" has since been encouraged with other associations in such "advanced" regions.

The farmworkers' association, the ATC, was charged with organizing these credit and services associations until the creation of UNAG, the union of small farmers and ranchers, in April 1981; the government agency PROCAMPO provided technical assistance. Those associations receiving fairly regular visits by ATC and PROCAMPO people have tended to become more solidified; the visits themselves bring about meetings and give legitimacy to the leaders. But the capacity of the ATC and the government to make such visits has been limited.

On the other hand, many campesinos have mistrusted ATC organizers with urban student backgrounds. Organizers were rushing things—trying to accomplish everything at once, one campesino told me.

The credit associations vary from place to place because campesino members adapted the general model to the way they wanted to do things. Some were formed by small landowners together with people renting land. One that I visited in Apantillo del Sabalar was started by 20 landless laborers who originally came together through their involvement in a Catholic Action group. They pressured the medium-size producers in whose harvests they worked to rent them cheap parcels of land here and there. After the members of this group formed an association and received credit, reaped an ample harvest, and repaid the loan, the small landowners in the area got interested, too. "They made many other people, especially small owners like us, interested in the cooperative and getting a loan from the National Development Bank," a small landowner told me. "So we joined the cooperative, too."

For over a year the landless and the small landowners worked in the same cooperative. Then a technician from the government PROCAMPO divided the group in two—one for the landless, the other for the small landowners. His move reflected the Sandinistas' belief that cooperatives can function best in the interest of their members when members have similar assets. If small landowners are mixed into the same cooperative with landless seasonal workers, Sandinista leaders fear, the small farmowners will tend to take control of the administration of the cooperative and skew credit and other services to their personal advantage. This often occurs because better-off campesinos are more experienced in dealing with outside agencies and in record keeping. The better-off landowners even tend to hire other members of the association. In time, the Sandinistas fear, the cooperative would become something of a corporation in which some of the members would stop working in the fields at all and non-member laborers would be contracted.

At another credit association on a 3,500-acre cattle ranch in Boaco, the members are essentially *colonos*, workers living on or near the hacienda. The hacienda owner lent the members 226 acres at no charge; in exchange, the workers promise to work (for wages) on the hacienda when they have free time. Launched with only 26 members, the cooperative now has 38. To expand, it had to overcome some people's fear that joining the cooperative means indebtedness and the prospect of jail if one cannot repay a loan. This fear of debt also prevented some from taking their full share of available loans. Campesinos will undoubtedly be more inclined to take such risks if their confidence in the new government grows.

The leadership of this cooperative is optimistic; the growth in membership is proof it is making life better, the general secretary told me. Optimism was also evident in a member who declared: "Last year we didn't harvest any crops. Now we see some really good crops coming in. We're not going to perish." And the owner, who bought the cattle hacienda only a few years before the overthrow of Somoza, told me it was functioning better than ever. He supports the revolution and has not joined the big cattlemen's association in Boaco.

To the Sandinistas, the credit and services cooperative is both an end in itself—a way to facilitate production by getting farm credit to the small producers—and a stepping stone to cooperative ownership and work. We'll see over the coming years whether this evolution actually takes place.

Production Cooperatives

The Sandinistas are not merely waiting, however, for this evolution; they are actively encouraging peasants to begin working the land cooperatively in what they call Sandinista

Agricultural Cooperatives (CAS). Even before final victory the Sandinistas had seen to it that lands taken by campesinos and workers (under 250 acres) were not parceled up but worked collectively by 10 to 30 families.

In a CAS, the type of cooperative most favored by the Sandinistas, small farmers pool their land, equipment, and animals. There are no government rules determining how a CAS is to be run: it has been up to the members themselves to set the norms for work and decide how to divide up what is produced. Generally the profits are divided three ways: first, to the individuals according to the amount of work performed; second, to community projects such as clinics, schools, or meeting halls; and third, to capital improvements such as plows or a tractor.

Sandinista leaders hope that such genuine cooperatives will serve to reduce rural inequalities. Members generally share in earnings according to the work they perform without regard to the land or other assets they contributed in forming the cooperative, although some CASs have made exceptions. Moreover, workers hired to help out during peak periods share in earnings on the same basis as members.

But at this stage, few small farmers have opted to collectively work their lands. As one ATC organizer told me, even the word *colectivo* is enough to scare off most small owners. It's no surprise then that after the first three years of the revolution the entire country had no more than two dozen CASs formed by peasants who had been small landowners before the revolution. Very early the ATC and the ministry began to see that CASs were a long-term goal, not an immediate prospect. The leadership made it very clear that nothing should be forced.

Given the peasants' fears about pooling their land, it's understandable that most of the cooperatives now in operation were either formed before triumph, where the Sandinistas were especially active in working with the small producers, or made up of close relatives where a basis of trust already existed.

Tres Esquinas ("Three Corners") near Estelí falls into both categories. Its 11 members cultivate 49 acres in common. Six "pulled up their fences," as they like to say, to put their lands together. They also decided to collectivize a 5,000-córdoba ($500) debt belonging to the member who had contributed the most land. But the members did not give up all their assets to the CAS. One kept 17 acres of pastureland, since only cropped land was included in the CAS; two others contributed oxen but kept cows for their private use. Five previously owned no land at all; three of these were sons of the most well-off member, the owner of the 17-acre pasture. Two others had been agricultural laborers, sometimes working for the landed members before the formation of the CAS.

Tres Esquinas is almost an extended family operation. Except for the two who previously had been laborers, all are related; the two ex-laborers were likely to marry into the family, I was told.

The elected general secretary of the CAS is the member who had had the most land. He had worked closely with the Sandinistas since 1973 (which is considered very early): his house sometimes served as a command post. The two laborers joined the Sandinista combatants at the time of the September 1978 insurrection. "We experienced the collectivization of the war itself," one of them commented.

This CAS has received a great deal of government backing in the form of technical advice, credit (a year after the triumph the cooperative was over 20,000 córdobas in debt), and access to purchase of inputs. The other CASs have probably received similar help.

The government has been flexible in encouraging cooperative farming. Finding small landowners resistant to pooling land, the government, through the ATC, has organized cooperatives of the formerly landless and land-poor farmworkers—primarily on rented land but, increasingly, on land belonging to state farms. State-farm land is lent rent-free on a seasonal basis to those agreeing to work the land together. These cooperatives were also called CASs, but many in the ministry referred to them as "nongenuine CASs" to distinguish them from those composed of small landowners. For that reason, they were increasingly called "work collectives."

About 1,300 such work collectives were formed in the first year, despite the government's initial ambivalence. It feared that members with land to cultivate would no longer seek work in the export harvests so crucial to the country's balance of payments. But once the workers were on the verge of seizing land, the ATC decided to get involved to provide the best "orientation"—to encourage the workers to work the land together and share its fruits. However, the ATC has not been able to do in-depth work with many of the more than 1,300 such cooperatives, Edgardo Garcia, the head of the ATC, told me.

Of these 1,300, about two-thirds are on land rented from private owners under the new low rates; the rest are on land lent by state farms. Traveling around the countryside, I realized that probably no two are structured exactly alike because the members feel free to shape them as they see fit. In some, the land is truly worked cooperatively. In others—usually where the members had had their own plots as tenants and sharecroppers—the members worked as if they individually owned plots. But even in these cases there was a fair amount of shared work.

Each cooperative elects a president, a bookkeeper, and a supply person. For the work in the fields, a leader is elected each year. Once elected, the leader discusses the work with everyone and group decisions are made; in the case of disagreements, the leader has the final say.

El Sol is a good example of how the government works to promote cooperative work on idle lands on state farms. El Sol is a cooperative made up of former agricultural laborers on a cattle hacienda that had been taken over from a Somoza associate and turned into a state enterprise. As soon as the hacienda was taken over by the ministry, the workers began demanding land to grow food for themselves. At first the ministry resisted; but then it realized that if it did not relent, the workers would simply seize the land and divide it up among themselves. To prevent this, the ministry offered to lend the land on the condition that it be farmed cooperatively.

While some were not initially in favor of working the land cooperatively, now they are generally pleased. Work is done collectively, with a government loan paying daily wages to the members, technically an "advance" on profits. Once the loan is repaid, the members plan to divide the harvest based on the number of days worked by each member, also figuring in work done by members' children. They are growing rice, beans and corn and expect not to have to migrate for seasonal wage work as in previous years. However, the members promised the ministry that when they were free they would work for the going wage during peak periods on the hacienda.

Throughout 1980 the biggest complaint of the cooperative members was the uncertain, season-to-season arrangement with the ministry. The administrator of the hacienda was concerned that more pasture land would be needed as the cattle herd was rebuilt after the massive slaughtering by the Somocista owner. The CAS members were asking the ministry for barbed wire to fence off their land from the cattle. But the ministry fears a fence would de facto make the land concession permanent. (Many CASs on state farms, even without cattle, have sought to fence off their fields as a symbol of a permanent arrangement.) The harvest-to-harvest uncertainty also tends to inhibit the cooperative members from making long-term improvements on the lands. Eventually the government's decision to redouble its commitment to national food self-sufficiency convinced the ministry to more permanently cede idle lands to cooperatives formed by seasonal workers.

By the end of the first two years, there were officially 3,820 credit associations and CAS production cooperatives with a total of 62,359 members, comprising 53 percent of all small producers. Indeed, the Sandinistas were concerned that both types of cooperatives were formed faster than the government's capacity to provide them with basic productive services. In fact, all too many cooperatives failed economically for this reason.

Analyzing this experience, the ministry and the leadership of UNAG decided to select 150 cooperatives—half CAS and half credit associations—and strengthen them by making sure they were properly supported, especially with technical assistance and machinery. These cooperatives would also get priority in long-term improvements of their productive capacity, such as irrigation installations. In early 1982, cooperatives were selected in each region of the country on the basis of the past two years' experience. Criteria included stability, profitability or reasonable potential for profitability, commitment to cooperative work, and, for the credit associations, evidence of a tendency to collectivize not only credit but also services. The leadership emphasizes, of course, that it will not abandon the other cooperatives; but, as one official told me in May 1982, "we want less hit-and-miss." They hope that these successful cooperatives will give a good name to cooperatives in general and thereby encourage other peasants, including small landowners, to form cooperatives, especially on the lands being granted through the new Agrarian Reform Law.

In sum, the Sandinistas are promoting cooperative work by making credit available on more favorable terms to small producers organized in some form of cooperative. And, wherever they can, they are making cooperative work a condition for the landless seasonal workers getting land. Campesinos and rural workers are generally responding, for they can see the benefits to themselves. But the government has been much less successful in getting small landowners to pool their land, because unless cooperatives are lent machinery by the ministry or a private farm, it is very difficult to explain the advantages of collective work. The capacity of a cooperative to accumulate the surplus needed for capital investments and community projects (schools, roads, clinics, etc.) probably seems too ambitious and thus too distant to be an effective incentive. The moral or social benefits of "learning to work together" are likely too vague to attract many poor peasants who have coped with a hostile environment for so long by minimizing their risks.

The Sandinistas' forms of persuasion have been positive, not punitive. They adhere strictly to their view that cooperative work must come about voluntarily. They seem willing to take the time for a gradual transition, experimenting with varying forms of organization. The Sandinistas see cooperatives as only one part of the rural economy, operating alongside individually owned private farms as well as state farms. The Sandinistas thus set themselves apart from revolutionary leaders in several other agrarian societies, who, with the same high ideals, have sought a more uniform and rapid transformation by using force when deemed necessary.

TWELVE

CORN AND BEANS FIRST

O UR BOOK *FOOD FIRST* EXPOSES HOW, IN SO many countries, more and more land and financial resources go to produce luxury crops for export while the production of local food crops is severely neglected, even in the face of widening hunger and growing national dependence on imported food.

By 1979 Nicaragua had become an extreme case in point. From the early 1950s to the mid-1970s, the agricultural land used to produce luxury export crops expanded almost 40 percent. By the 1970s, 90 percent of all agricultural credit was earmarked for export crops with virtually none for local food production. In 1955, Nicaragua imported 21,000 tons of grains; by 1978 this country of rich farmlands was importing over ten times that amount. What forces were behind these developments?

As dramatized in chapter 2, the history of the Nicaraguan countryside has been the story of more and more people forcibly deprived of land. It is the history of more and more people denied decent-paying jobs or even year-round work. As elites took ever greater control over Nicaragua's productive resources, fewer and fewer people were able to grow food for themselves or earn enough income to buy the food they needed. In economic terms, they could not make "effective" their demand for food. With such great poverty, the local market for corn, beans, and rice was so weak that growing them never looked like a promising business. The well-off, moreover, craved American-style foods, some of which (notably wheat-based foods) could not be produced economically in tropical Nicaragua.

Thus the land-controlling elites naturally saw their road to profits in producing luxury crops for foreign consumers and importing the status goods they desired. In the few instances when they did put prime lands into basic food crops, such as when world cotton prices were down, it was to produce corn and sorghum to feed cattle destined for the U.S. hamburger market. In sum, the logic of the elite-controlled economy was to ignore the basic needs of Nicaraguans in favor of producing for foreign markets. In the mid-1970s, almost 70 percent of the country's entire gross national product was in export production, in contrast to 10 percent for Mexico and 18 percent for Chile. Maintaining such an *economic* system required force, the *political* system of a military dictatorship.

Then the disenfranchised overthrew the dictatorship. No one could seriously expect the food situation of the majority of Nicaraguans to improve overnight. Indeed, at least in the short run, the prospects were alarming.

The liberation war itself compounded a "normal" food situation, which was already desperate for many Nicaraguans. The final offensive happened to coincide with the period when the fields should have been prepared for planting corn, beans, and the other staple foods. In some areas I visited, campesinos told me that during the war they had eaten the seed saved for planting for fear of starvation. Food production was forecast to plummet 40 percent in the first harvests following the victory. Moreover, food stores in the war-ravaged cities had been stripped bare by looting, and food prices in the markets jumped 50 to 100 percent in the final months.

With victory, the revolution brought new jobs, higher wages, new money throughout the countryside through campesino credit, and cuts in rents for land and for urban housing. These programs directly and indirectly released some of the pent-up demand for more food. In fact, during the first

18 months following victory, the demand for food leapt a phenomenal 45 percent.

How was the new government to cope? It was determined to abolish hunger from Nicaragua and aware that for many Nicaraguans "the revolution is measured through the plate of beans." In this chapter we examine its efforts to improve the distribution of food, the supply side of the problem.

In the short run, the only solution was to import—massively and quickly—before speculation could drive prices even higher. While some countries, principally in Western Europe, donated food, a tremendous amount had to be purchased on credit. In the first few months, more food was imported than in the whole year preceding the war. In 1980, the beans and corn imported from the United States equalled almost a third of what was produced locally. The cost in precious dollars was staggering.

At the same time, the government sought to increase peasant production of corn and beans by an unprecedented offering of credit and by decreeing sharply lower rents for tenant farmers, most of who produced corn and beans.

Yet there was a strong tension within the new government, which I noticed during my first visit after victory. Since I was known as the coauthor of *Food First*, everyone assumed I would advocate priority to local food production. But many in the government worried that policies encouraging peasant food production—making it easier to get land to farm, cheap credit, technical assistance, and good reliable prices—would undercut export production as the poor majority in the countryside found it no longer needed to work in the export harvests. "Food First" policies, they feared, would reduce the country's ability to earn dollars just when dollars were needed more than ever to pay off the Somoza debt, to pay for imports vital to reconstruction, and to pacify the potentially counterrevolutionary well-off classes accustomed to imported consumer goods.

Others stressed the sad shape of local food production and wanted to focus attention there. In the agricultural year 1980–81, bean production had fallen to two-thirds of what it had been in 1977–78, while corn production showed virtually no increase.

Throughout 1980 and into 1981 the food debate roared on. Sometimes it seemed that there were as many viewpoints as there were participants; yet none were simplistic. To reach a resolution, research was carried out; developments internally and internationally were continually evaluated. In March 1981, shortly after a major consultation with about two dozen of us foreign advisors (no Cubans, no Soviets!), a rough consensus emerged within the Nicaraguan leadership. Ironically, it was the Reagan administration that brought deliberations to a dramatic conclusion. For at the beginning of April the Reagan administration abruptly canceled a $9.8 million loan to import wheat from the United States. Only days later the Nicaraguan government unveiled a major comprehensive program for achieving food self-sufficiency; all the ministries involved were instructed to give the program top priority.

Indeed, a prime motive behind the program is national independence. For as long as Nicaragua is dependent on food imports, its national sovereignty stands in jeopardy. This was especially true since in the first two years most food imports came from the United States, the country that has repeatedly intervened directly in Nicaragua's affairs, and from other Central American countries whose elite-controlled governments were increasingly belligerent toward the Nicaraguan revolution.

And there were other considerations. Nicaragua found that beans, the daily food of all Nicaraguans, were hard to find on the international market. Countries with far greater financial power than Nicaragua—Mexico, Venezuela, Brazil—corner much of the world market in beans. Beans purchased from California and Texas were expensive and, worse yet, were simply not to the liking of Nicaraguans, who insisted on their locally grown *frijolitos rojos*. A similar situation prevailed with corn. Nicaraguans are accustomed to *white* corn, which commands a premium on the world market. Oil-rich Venezuela is the major buyer of white corn and the major supplier is South Africa, a country whose government is hardly likely to be a dependable ally.

Moreover, the government found study after study projecting that international prices for grains and other staples were likely to rise significantly faster than those for Nicaragua's traditional exports: coffee, sugar, and cotton. Thus ever more cotton would be needed to buy a ton of corn or beans. In addition, if decent wages were to be paid while exports of cotton, sugar, and coffee remain competitive in world markets, expensive technology to increase labor productivity would have to be imported. Pesticides, fertilizers, and other imported materials already represented almost 40 percent of cotton production costs (while corn and beans were produced with virtually no foreign exchange costs). Finally, cyclical overproduction problems for cotton, coffee, and sugar result in periodic sharp drops in international prices and in marketing quotas.

Calculations indicated that on only 60 percent of the amount of prime land being used to grow the cotton that earned the dollars to import beans from the United States, it would be possible to raise the same quantity of beans—and they would be Nicaraguan beans grown in Nicaragua. Indeed, once domestic needs are secured and every Nicaraguan can afford an adequate diet, Nicaragua might well be able to export beans, white corn, and grain-fed poultry and hogs on better terms than its "traditional" agricultural exports. This capacity to generate foreign exchange for the nation could, in turn, give new prestige to campesinos, traditionally the most disparaged group in Nicaragua.

The Sandinistas also understood that making food production a priority would entail greater government support for campesinos. That in turn would help to build greater support for the overall revolutionary program among the biggest producer class in the nation.

Nicaraguan policymakers began to realize that "food versus export crops" was partly a false dilemma. Nicaragua could *both* produce more food for local consumption and more for export. It could increase its exports of coffee, sugar, beef, and cotton primarily by using the lands already devoted to their production more efficiently and fully. In addition, Nicaragua could increase food production by providing more support and better prices for peasant producers as well as by allowing peasants and seasonal laborers to plant on idle lands (as provided under the new agrarian reform law).

Fears about whether there would still be a sufficient labor force for the export crop harvests began to wane as policymakers realized that since peak work periods for corn and bean cultivation generally do not coincide with those for export crops it should be possible to work out agreements by which, in exchange for access to land, landless workers and campesinos would agree to work when needed in the export harvests (for decent wages and under ever improved conditions).

Thus in April 1981, a national food plan to achieve food self-sufficiency as soon as possible was unveiled. The initials of the Programa Alimentario Nacional, PAN, conveniently spell the word for bread in Spanish. (Some might say it is ironic that PAN also means bread since Nicaragua, for climatic reasons, cannot be self-sufficient in wheat.) From the beginning the government stressed that this was a very special emergency program requiring a national mobilization. Media, posters, and speeches proclaimed: "Food is a priority."

But how would PAN achieve its goal? From the start, the program stressed that food self-sufficiency means more than eliminating most food imports through improved local production; it also means assuring every Nicaraguan an adequate diet. As we stress in *Food First*, many governments in the world have claimed to be self-sufficient in food while the majority of children went hungry. Thus the program encompasses both increased production and more efficient and just distribution. The distribution side we will discuss in the next chapter; here we focus on the production side of PAN.

First of all, PAN is to motivate and support small farmers, traditionally the principal suppliers of the nation's staple foods (except rice, which is mainly produced on large, mechanized farms). But how? Studies of the first two years showed that better credit was not the best way to increase production. Raising guaranteed prices to producers was tried instead. The Somoza regime had favored low prices to campesinos, encouraging their exploitation by middlemen, so that campesinos would be forced to seek work in the export harvests. Keeping food prices low also allowed plantation owners to pay lower wages, giving them fatter profits.

Under PAN, the price paid to farmers for corn was hiked 25 percent; the price for beans, Nicaragua's most critical food, was boosted 50 percent. (These prices are still lower than those in other Central American countries.) The bean price represents a considerable savings over spending dollars to import U.S. beans.

At the same time it raised the guaranteed producer prices, the government committed itself to improving the rural distribution of consumer items such as kerosene, sugar, cooking oil, clothing, and radios at reasonable prices. Good crop prices are somewhat meaningless to Nicaragua's remote small farmers unless there are things they can buy with the money they earn, PAN planners had learned. Indeed, better prices would be canceled out by inflation if there were not a simultaneous improvement in the supply of consumer goods for purchase. Government credit to individual small producers and peasant cooperatives would continue at favorable interest rates, but it would be distributed with more care. For instance, credit would be distributed less as cash and more as production inputs, such as fertilizers, seeds, and tools. Clearly this will be easier with small farmers organized into cooperatives than with individuals on scattered, isolated plots.

The new Agrarian Reform Law, passed only four months after the launching of PAN, also promoted PAN's production goals. Under the new law, idle lands on both state and privately owned commercial farms and ranches can be turned over to peasants and landless seasonal workers, who invariably plant food crops. These lands are generally more fertile than those onto which most of Nicaragua's food producers had been pushed by the expansion of elite-controlled plantations. Thus the ministry hopes that average yields for food crops, pitifully low for so long, will be boosted even without costly imported chemical fertilizers (which are difficult to distribute in remote areas). At the same time, ministry agronomists have concluded that cotton is ruining some of the poor soils the cotton entrepreneurs cultivated. And since a considerable number of larger cotton growers have been showing themselves unwilling to plant their estates fully, it seems sensible to restrict the total cotton acreage to soils that can best withstand cotton cultivation. The government thus could hand over to peasant cooperatives land better suited to food crops, land more fertile and more accessible to urban markets than the interior, hilly land onto which the expansion of cotton pushed so many campesinos.

PAN also recognizes that producing more is not the only way to increase food availability. Of the country's corn crop, all too much is typically lost after harvest because of poor storage. So a government program is now teaching small producers how to build rat-proof, air-cooled corn cribs made from local materials, principally bamboo and thatch. They can be built in two to five days with little or no cash outlay. First 500 campesinos learned the new technique. Then each was to teach ten more campesinos so that by the end of 1981 the knowledge had theoretically spread to 5,000.

General observation in the countryside, even in the more remote areas, suggests that these pro-small producer policies mean that food producers themselves are eating better. Many campesinos have told me they are now raising more chickens and pigs so that they can eat better and boost their cash incomes. Under Somoza, ironically, they were among Nicaragua's worst fed.

Shifting Tastes

Achieving food self-sufficiency also involves reorienting eating habits toward foods that can be locally produced. The clearest example of this is the campaign to consume corn as opposed to wheat, which flourishes only in temperate climates and therefore must be imported. (Experiments are going forward, however, to cultivate wheat in one highland region. Apparently the campesinos there used to grow some wheat but the tradition was lost with the steady stream of wheat imports from the United States.)

Building on widespread public indignation with the Reagan administration's sudden cutoff of wheat credits, the government organized a series of corn festivals throughout the country. The theme was "Corn, our roots." (As with many slogans, this one translates poorly. The rhyming Spanish version is *"El maiz, nuestra raiz."*) The festivals did catch the imagination and national pride of the people. The symbol of the festivals was the indigenous corn god, Xilem. Cooking contests were held throughout the country for a whole range of corn-based foods, including tortillas and tamales as well as corn-based beverages, both alcoholic and nonalcoholic. Local winners were sent to a national corn cookoff in Masaya, where winners were awarded a trip to Corn Island, a Nicaraguan possession in the Caribbean complete with white sandy beaches. Even Sandy's, the local rival of McDonald's, got into the act, producing a *tortiburgesa*, or corn tortilla burger.

If corn is "in," the government would like to see beef "out"—or at least "down." Beef exports, the third most important source of foreign exchange, fell dramatically in 1980 in part because Nicaraguans ate more beef. The government would like to see more people eating fish instead. Nicaraguans have traditionally eaten fish, but a low catch and inadequate distribution has limited consumption. The government's plan is to make loans to fisherpeople to buy boats, tackle, and outboard motors. As with small farmers, these loans are being used to encourage cooperatives. By 1980, 26 new cooperatives were already producing 25,000 pounds of fish a month. A transport system is being organized to get fresh fish efficiently to market in Managua. In the Somoza days, fishing families would send one of their members to the capital by bus to sell the previous day's catch. Given notoriously fickle fish prices, sometimes these sellers would not even recoup their costs.

Even in its efforts to feed Nicaraguans better the government is meeting U.S. hostility. In early 1982, the United States blocked a $30 million loan from the Inter-American Development Bank to improve Nicaragua's fishing capacity and marketing.

Poultry and eggs are also seen as good beef substitutes. The war left the country practically stripped of small livestock, so in 1980 chickens were imported in an effort to boost animal protein consumption without reducing beef exports. But so many chickens were imported that the scheme was almost self-defeating. The cost turned out to be only $1 million less than the total earned from beef exports. Great effort has gone into rebuilding local poultry production, which can be significantly increased in months, compared to years for cattle. And in comparison to cattle, chickens are efficient converters of corn.

Efforts to introduce cultivation of soybeans and consumption of soy foods have also been one of the focuses of PAN's plan to improve the nutritional well-being of the Nicaraguan people.

The PAN program in the countryside got off to a late start for the 1981 major planting season because coordinating all the ministries took longer than anticipated. Still, when the 1981 harvests started coming into the market in early 1982, it looked like PAN was working. Bean production—perhaps the principal focus of PAN—more than doubled, to a level considered self-sufficient *despite* a 40 percent increase in national consumption. Corn production, however, went up less than 9 percent, probably somewhat less than the nation's need; corn consumption has increased 35 percent since the victory. Unfortunately, the unprecedented floods in late May 1982 wiped out a considerable amount of the stored corn harvest, leading the government to import corn in the second half of the year.

For many, these results confirmed the thesis that boosting producer prices was key: bean prices had been increased much more than those of corn. Reports from some areas indicated that campesinos got credit for corn but then, except for producing their household corn needs, switched over to bean production; or, instead of marketing their corn, they fed more of it to their pigs and chickens. In response to the first year's results, before the 1982 planting season the government announced a greater increase in the corn price than the bean price.

Rice production increased 45 percent—almost double the production of the last year before the liberation war. This means that Nicaragua has achieved self-sufficiency in this third basic food. Only the shortage of warehouses prevents the country from becoming a net exporter of rice, a deficiency an $11 million project with Mexico is designed to correct. Sorghum production reached a level more than double the last year before the war, more than sufficient for the nation's needs.

Poultry production was estimated by mid-1982 not only to have recuperated from the war but to have risen some 20 percent above the historical record. Egg production also showed sharp increases and by mid-1982 stood 30 percent above the prewar record. It was, therefore, possible to cut egg imports by two-thirds in the first six months of 1982 compared to the previous year, with every prospect of soon eliminating egg imports altogether despite greatly increased consumption.

Self-sufficiency has thus been achieved in several key food staples and near-term prospects are very encouraging for most others. By 1982, the third anniversary of the triumph, many Nicaraguans could take satisfaction from their country's dramatic advance toward the national goal of self-sufficiency in basic foods—no small achievement, especially during a time of significant increase in national food consumption. But what about the other goal of PAN, that every Nicaraguan have an adequate diet? This is the question for the next chapter.

THIRTEEN

CAN THE FREE MARKET FEED THE POOR?

NICARAGUA COULD IMPORT VAST QUANTI-
ties of food. And it could increase its food production,
even achieving self-sufficiency. But it could still fail to eliminate hunger. Because for poor people who don't grow their
own food, getting enough to eat depends on whether the
price of food is within their reach.

Confronting what looked like a potential famine at the
end of the war, the new government dramatically stepped up
food imports. World prices were steep and, still worse, had to
be paid in dollars. If these real costs were passed on to the
local food market, the poor majority would suffer. Many
might actually starve. No doubt that is what Somoza would
have done, but for the Sandinistas it was unthinkable. So
the government chose to subsidize massively the cost of food
imports and to forestall speculation by importing enough to
fill the markets for everyone.

Under this strategy, the government was footing the food
bill not only for the poor but for the middle classes and even
the rich. In fact, since the better-off could afford greater
quantities of food, they were disproportionately subsidized.
Any visitor to Managua in those days would have been struck
by the Intercontinental Hotel's world class, all-you-can-eat
buffet of largely imported foods for $1.75. Subsidized imports

were obviously a very indirect and thus costly way to help the poor majority.

But could the new government have helped the poor majority more directly? Limiting the amount of cost-subsidized foods a person could buy or making it available only to the poor would have been much less expensive for the government. But any such system would instantly have been labeled "rationing." And the word "rationing" strikes fear in Nicaraguans, including the poor. For years Somoza's U.S.-aided propaganda drummed in the message that rationing is the first foothold of "godless communism." Photographs of Nicaragua's well-stocked supermarkets were repeatedly contrasted with Cuba's drab ration books. No one from the Somoza regime, needless to say, pointed out that the majority of Nicaraguans couldn't afford to buy from Managua's supermarkets, while every Cuban was ensured at least a minimum basic diet.

During my visits to Nicaragua I often ran up against this fear of "rationing"—even though Nicaragua, unlike the United States during World War II, has never had rationing. I'll never forget a meeting with about 20 women from Ciudad Sandino, Nicaragua's largest working class barrio. In discussing their food problems, several poor women complained bitterly that the better-off in the barrio bought more food than they needed, hoarded it, and thus created shortages for others. There should be a fairer way of doing things—maybe cards or books where what each family buys could be recorded, they told me. "But," they emphasized, shaking their fingers, "we wouldn't want rationing."

Aware that poor Nicaraguans identify rationing with a lack of freedom, the Sandinista leadership from the start ruled out rationing, even of a single scarce item. After all, just what the U.S. government wanted Nicaraguans to believe was that Nicaragua was going to become "another Cuba." One day the Minister of Domestic Commerce was discussing with some of us foreign advisors the problem of the run on sugar supplies—supplies that theoretically were sufficient for all. "I was told I could do whatever I wanted to deal with the shortages, just as long as I didn't even mention the word 'rationing,'" he confided.

But the new government also ruled out rationing for practical reasons. The country's food is distributed by an unbelievable number of small vendors. (Managua's principal market alone had almost 10,000 small retailers!) Administering a rationing system with so many outlets would have been a nightmare for even the most experienced government.

With rationing ruled out, the government set its sights on several other measures to improve the poor's access to food.

First, more jobs. During its first year, the government succeeded in cutting the unemployment rate in half—down to 17 percent. (Unfortunately, the new jobs were mainly in government and other service occupations, which did not increase the supply of goods. The new jobs therefore worked against efforts to cut inflation.)

Second, higher wages for the working poor. The new government decreed a 125-córdobas-per-month raise for all those earning less than 1,300 córdobas. A household income survey at the time indicated almost 40 percent of the urban population should benefit. (To give you an idea of the potential impact on a poor family's diet, the "suggested" retail price at the time for corn (kernels) was 1.15 córdobas a pound; beans and rice 2.85 córdobas a pound each; and one egg for 1 córdoba.)

Third, lower prices for other necessities. Housing rents were sliced in half, and transportation, education, and medical costs were strongly subsidized, all to release more of a family's income for food. Finally, taxes on food were removed, while taxes on alcoholic beverages were raised.

Entering the Marketplace—On the Side of the Poor

The Sandinistas shunned the idea of policing the prices charged in the marketplace, a high official of the Ministry of Planning, himself not a Sandinista, told me in October 1979. After all, he pointed out, they had risked their lives to free a country terrorized by police. Besides, many of Nicaragua's food vendors were poor people and thus among the very people the Sandinistas most wanted to help. Moreover, he added, they had been warned against replacing market mechanisms with "bureaucratic socialism" by no less an authority than Fidel Castro.

What should they do? Could they maintain the private

marketing of food and yet be sure that the market would at least respect the needs of Nicaragua's poor majority? The Sandinistas decided to try. At the heart of that experiment would be the National Basic Foods Corporation, ENABAS, set up just two months after the fall of the dictatorship.

ENABAS was to work with both small food producers and with poor consumers, and to do so without excluding private merchants.

To help food producers, ENABAS offered guaranteed prices for their crops, calculated to ensure them a decent profit. Historically, the smaller farmers, backbone of the nation's food production, were at the mercy of local money-lenders and itinerant middlemen who offered them low prices at harvest—taking advantage of the fact that most had no storage facilities and no way to get their crops to market. These middlemen then resold at a high mark-up to large whole-salers who sometimes hoarded the food to make even higher profits as supplies tightened on the retail market. With ENABAS in the picture, it was thought, middlemen would have to offer better prices, prices at least equal to those offered by ENABAS.

To help consumers, ENABAS would store up enough of the supply of basic foods so that whenever private merchants speculated on rumored shortages or hoarded, it could release enough onto the market at a low and stable price to undercut speculators, without resorting to policing. By "capturing" 40 percent of the total supply of basic foods, ENABAS could "keep the market honest," or so planners thought. If for some reason ENABAS was unable to purchase locally enough foods to protect consumers in this way, it had the authority and the dollars to import.

And, to prevent exports of locally needed foodstuffs, ENABAS was also granted sole authority to export them. Exporting in spite of local needs is a temptation to private producers and merchants since corn and beans fetch higher prices in Honduras and Costa Rica than in Nicaragua.

All of these plans for a government role in new Nicaragua's food system appeared to be a sensible way to begin to right centuries-old injustices. But how has ENABAS done in practice?

Helping Producers

Largely due to the government's overall inexperience, ENABAS' efforts to boost food production showed little success during its startup year. In chapter 6, we describe the disappointing results in boosting food production through "spilling credit" in the countryside. But what turned out to be an even bigger disappointment for ENABAS was the difficulty in *purchasing* enough of what was produced, despite the fairly large corn crop in 1980.

While shooting for 40 percent, ENABAS was able to acquire only about 12 percent of the 1980 corn and bean crops. One reason was that ENABAS suffered a tremendous handicap compared to private traders: in payment, it offered only checks—something never before seen by most peasants. Private buyers offered not only cash but the goods campesinos needed but could not produce themselves: salt, sugar, kerosene, machetes, boots, cooking oil, and so on. ENABAS learned the hard way that an essential part of buying from small producers is selling to them, since many goods are hard to find in the countryside.

Even when campesinos were willing to sell, ENABAS often did not have the staff to handle the purchase, sorting, and transport of millions of pounds of grain. Transportation was a major bottleneck, especially with corn. Over three-quarters of the corn harvest comes from the interior of the country, where roads are at best passable only during the dry season in some areas. Corn, harvested in October, could not be brought to market in many areas until the dry season started in February. And with so much credit available and so much grain to transport, the price of mules and trucks quickly shot up. Even where there were roads suitable for trucks, ENABAS often lacked the trucks. It had only 38, when it estimated it needed 218. To try to bridge this gap, ENABAS rented trucks from private owners at high prices or borrowed trucks from other government agencies.

ENABAS' prices to producers posed still greater problems. Figuring out a fair nationwide producer price—one that would cover all the producer's costs plus allow for a decent profit—is a very tricky business. How do you anticipate the inflation in costs, in part due to the flood of credit hitting the countryside, and the varying yields in different areas and for different size producers? While the government wanted the price to be high enough to help the peasants improve their standard of living in relation to urban dwellers, it feared setting prices so high that consumer prices would have to be massively subsidized lest the poor be cut out. On top of all this, ENABAS found itself limited as a bureaucracy trying to compete with much more flexible private buyers.

Take the case of beans. Beans are the number one food crop of Nicaragua since *all* Nicaraguans want their daily *frijolitos*. Thus they are a food for which the better-off and the poor compete directly. In 1980, rains at the wrong time and a pest outbreak destroyed 20 to 30 percent of the crop in one key bean-producing region. Rumors of a bean scarcity set off a consumer scramble. And private traders appeared in full force in the countryside offering up to 500 córdobas per hundredweight; ENABAS could hardly compete, with its price set at only 220 córdobas. (In some areas the Sandinista-led ATC expended precious political capital with the campesinos trying to persuade them that the "correct" thing to do—"for the sake of the revolution"—was to sell to ENABAS at prices well below what they could be getting. Much to its dismay, the government felt compelled to forcibly stop some campesinos from trying to take their beans across the border into Honduras, where bean prices were much higher.)

ENABAS also failed that year to get the corn it wanted, but for different reasons. With so much credit and exhortations to increase food production, many campesinos planted lots of corn. But with the inflated costs—due to the rush for scarce inputs—and yields below government projections, many campesinos found the ENABAS price of 80 córdobas per hundredweight would not even cover the rent for mules to take it to ENABAS. So they declined to sell to the ENABAS buyers when they came around, hoping for better prices later from private buyers. In the end, the corn harvest was abundant, and ENABAS imported so much corn, that prices offered by private merchants plummeted to 50 córdobas. At that price, many decided that it wasn't worth harvesting more of their crop than they could eat or feed to their pigs and chickens.

To fight the speculation set off by the scarcity scare in the marketplace, ENABAS repeatedly imported great quantities of corn, beans, and other foods, especially during its first year. Administratively, importing was immensely easier than purchasing locally. But, as pointed out in the previous chapter, the costs were exorbitant and national security was jeopardized. In addition, especially with the beans, people complained that they did not like the imported varieties.

Looking ahead for the 1981–82 season, ENABAS thought it had learned some useful lessons. For one thing, to compete better with private buyers it would have to substantially raise the price it offered to producers. In addition, as part of PAN, the National Food Program, ENABAS would try to stimulate sales by seeing that campesinos could buy the basic goods they wanted (from farm tools to sugar to transistor radios) at nonexploitative prices.

To avoid expanding its fledgling bureaucracy, ENABAS would work through established merchants with good reputations instead of opening a network of government stores. These private outlets would get government credit as well as help in securing farm and consumer goods at the official wholesale prices. The "honest" merchants would be identified by UNAG, the union of small and medium farmers and ranchers. Thus the Sandinista-led government has been working to shift the responsibility for coordinating rural credit, farm input delivery, the purchase of crops, and sales of manufactured goods to rural producers into the hands of experienced local merchants with good reputations. The idea is to work *with* the market, not against it, and thus avoid creating a large, inexperienced government bureaucracy, however well-intentioned.

Nevertheless, *frijoles* has persisted as problem *número uno* for ENABAS—and therefore for Nicaragua's urban poor. Bean production doubled in 1981–82, apparently mainly in response to the much higher ENABAS-guaranteed price. But ENABAS has painfully learned that there are beans and there are beans.

For starters, Nicaraguans crave only the local (*criollo*) variety of red beans, even though some others are grown in Nicaragua and are generally easier to cultivate. (Black beans, much in demand by Brazil and some Caribbean countries, could be more easily produced in Nicaragua than the prized red beans, but Nicaraguans generally do not like black beans.) On top of this, beans of whatever variety vary in size, moisture content, firmness, and the amount of extraneous matter, like pebbles, mixed in. Considering all this, many campesinos sell their red beans and other good quality beans to private merchants for higher prices and then unload their "rejects" onto ENABAS. As if that's not bad enough, ENABAS has had difficulty properly drying and storing the beans (no doubt compounded by the lower quality of the beans), thus making its beans still less desirable.

In the marketplace and even at lunch counters, you will find people distinguishing "beans" and "ENABAS beans," and commonly paying more than twice as much for the non-government beans. So the poor majority winds up either paying through the nose for the beans they really want (and thus sacrificing something else they need) or they eat second-class beans. It's all politically costly for the government since every trip to the marketplace and every meal makes the government's logical constituency—the poor majority—more willing to listen to those who are out to discredit the revolution. For its part, the Sandinista government has been quick to publicize the real bean shortage in Costa Rica and the numbers of Costa Ricans coming into Nicaragua to buy beans.

Helping Consumers

While ENABAS fell far short of its goal of purchasing 40 percent of the basic foods produced in the country in 1980, it did succeed in becoming the wholesale supplier of 40 percent of most of the basic foods sold. It did so, of course, by importing. While this clearly was not ideal, at least ENABAS was in a position to be able to help poor consumers by deterring consumer price speculation, or so planners thought.

From the start the new government had hesitated to set consumer price ceilings for food items, fearing this might act as a disincentive for the country's food producers. But as more and more wholesalers and retailers took advantage of consumers by speculating on food prices, the government decided it had to act. Otherwise, all the measures designed to help the poor majority would come to naught. So in 1980 it set wholesale and retail price ceilings on 23 basic items, including beans, corn, rice, cooking oil, sugar, milk, soap, salt, and toilet paper. The prices of 50 other items were to be monitored in an effort to detect speculation and hoarding. From time to time over the next two years other items were added to the controlled list.

To allow retailers to make a sufficient profit, the plan was that ENABAS would supply them (as well as private wholesalers) at wholesale prices allowing for a retail profit margin. Priority attention was to go to retailers in poor neighborhoods.

While ENABAS was planned to help stabilize and keep down consumer prices primarily by operating as a wholesaler, it also developed its own retail network. That network's most important component consists of 11 supermarkets in Managua (where almost a quarter of Nicaraguans live). To some extent the government fell into operating supermarkets. In the Somoza days these American-style supermarkets—one chain was appropriately named "Colonial"—catered to urban elites infatuated with U.S. lifestyles; they emphasize luxury and processed items. In the final days of the war the supermarkets were looted, leaving them bankrupt. ENABAS decided to finance their reopening, entering into a joint venture partnership with the original owners and often retaining the old managers. But these "Supermarkets of the People" are the same only at first glance: although located in the higher income neighborhoods, they now have poor customers from the barrios. The poor come to buy not the frozen vegetables (still available) but the basics at official prices: rice, corn, beans, sugar, salt, cooking oil, cheese.

To supply the same basic foods in the barrios at the official low prices, ENABAS created a new type of store, the *tienda popular* or people's store. By July 1982, 71 of these state-owned stores were in operation, theoretically selling 37 basic items in simple wood-plank buildings. Among the common complaints I've heard in the barrios are that the people's stores are only open during working hours (mom-and-pop stores stay open until late in the evening); that they don't give credit; and that they don't carry some of the things people want such as milk, chicken, vegetables, cheese, and fruits.

Supplementing these stores is a fleet of government-owned trucks ("mobile stores"), which makes the rounds every two weeks in many poor barrios and villages in Managua province. Each truck has the capacity to supply a thousand or so families with the basics.

The purpose of the stores and the mobile units is to cut out the middlemen and provide the basics at stable prices, especially for poor families. But a major shortcoming has been that they are still fundamentally middle-class in their design—they sell many items in larger packages than the truly poor can afford and they do not offer credit. On some of my first visits to barrios, I was surprised to find that poor people were paying higher than official prices even when a local ENABAS store or mobile unit was selling the same item at the official price. Then a Catholic nun living in a barrio explained to me that the *pulperías* (mom-and-pop stores) allow their customers to buy on credit, crucial for families with irregular employment. That's why government calls to denounce those who charge high prices often meet with little response, she said.

In addition, ENABAS supplies basic foodstuffs directly to commissaries set up in workplaces with over 30 workers. The administration of the workplace is required to supply space, and the trade union elects a committee to supervise the store. Since most such large workplaces are in Managua, so are most commissaries. By 1982, 500 were in operation in the capital. One apparently negative side effect concerns women. Since most of the shoppers are men—because the workers in these kinds of workplaces are mostly men—the women in their families sometimes feel marginalized since they "don't get to handle the money," according to comments I've heard.

ENABAS has also sought to develop a special "franchise" relationship with private retail stores with good reputations in their neighborhoods. The idea has been to take advantage of the honest storekeepers' managerial ability and wealth of knowledge about neighborhood needs and not to tax unnecessarily the limited capacities of ENABAS. The stores are called *expendios populares* or people's outlets. Over 1,000 of them were in operation by the end of 1981. In exchange for a pledge to sell controlled items at the official retail prices, a store owner is guaranteed an adequate supply of the items at official wholesale prices, thus ensuring a reasonable profit margin. The store owners must supply their own financing (although some government credit is available) and pick up their inventory from ENABAS warehouses. Storekeepers should gain extra benefit from their relationship with ENABAS because people patronizing the stores to buy basic items at the low official prices would undoubtedly buy other things too. In Managua, the largest volume of sales for ENABAS is through the *expendios populares*.

ENABAS is also making use of a traditional private distribution system—the large markets filled with stalls for private vendors. By building new markets in neighborhoods all over Managua, the government hopes to close down or at least reduce the sprawling Mercado Oriental (Eastern Market). This market, on the edge of the area leveled by the 1972 earthquake, has mushroomed to almost 10,000 vendors, mostly poor women. Because of its location, the Oriental requires long and costly trips for vendors and consumers alike. And it is known for hard-to-control price speculation (especially by a few large wholesalers), unsanitary conditions, and prostitution.

Thirty-six new neighborhood markets with stalls for private vendors have been built in Managua alone. For over a year they were highly promoted by newspaper ads featuring large maps of Managua and the caption, "Find your new market." Other ads, in photo-cartoon format, emphasized that new markets have high quality produce, are cleaner, better stocked, and provide lessons on hygiene and food preparation. And they also offer such amenities as barbershops.

The new market in the Ciudad Sandino barrio is an example of those the government would like to see flourish. Ciudad Sandino began as a settlement camp for families fleeing the 1970 flooding of Lake Managua; today it has 72,000 residents. In October 1981, Ciudad Sandino opened its own open air market, the pride of the barrio. The new market should save considerable time and bus money. In addition, it should promote the economy of the barrio, providing sources of employment that have been almost nonexistent in the past. One vendor in the new market, Fernando José Silva, explained to me why he was so enthusiastic. For five years he worked in the Oriental, paying 12 córdobas each day in bus fare; the new market is only two blocks from his home. Another vendor, Eva María Ulloa, told me how she used to have to board the bus at 5:00 in the morning to get to the Oriental by 7:00. Now she walks to work in a few minutes.

But the government has been largely frustrated in its desire to close down the Oriental. On my visit in June 1982 it seemed to be almost as large as ever, although perhaps better organized. People claim they continue to go there because they know they can find everything there, even though the prices for scarce products might be much higher than the official ones. They also claim that the beans are better there, the fish fresher, and the vegetables cheaper. In June I found vendors illegally but openly selling beans at 5.70 córdobas a pound, while "government" beans were going for the official 2.85 a pound. And because more people want to shop at the Oriental than at some of the comparatively immaculate new markets, vendors want to stay on at the Oriental. In the new markets some vendors claim they must charge higher prices because there are fewer customers. By mid-1982, government policymakers seemed to be backing away from their goal of closing down the Oriental, even though they still believed it would be in the people's best interests.

In rural areas, ENABAS has established over 200 rural supply centers, which sell both basic foodstuffs and a few industrial goods at the official prices.

The Spoilers

As we have seen, shortages—often induced by rumors of scarcities and by hoarding by speculators—prompted the Sandinista-led government to fix price ceilings for basic necessities. Thus less than a year after victory its hopes for an unregulated domestic food market had been abandoned. These same factors have made it far more difficult to enforce price ceilings than to set them. Sometimes, as we will see, the government has quite literally been left holding the bag.

Price gouging, even on items with official price ceilings, has been widespread in private outlets. Many retailers say they can't always sell at the official price because when an item is scarce, and ENABAS supplies are tied up in its own stores and the *expendios*, the wholesalers won't sell to them at the official wholesale prices.

Many vendors dodge the rules by selling a scarce product, such as cooking oil, at the official price—but only if the customer agrees to buy something else (that she or he might not even want) at a higher price. Another tactic is to sell at the official prices when a nearby people's store or *expendio* is well supplied. But as soon as the rice or cooking oil or beans or soap runs out in the government-supplied outlet, then the private seller jacks up the price. A secret government survey in August 1981 showed that 93 out of 100 stalls in the Oriental were selling scarce basic food items above the official prices.

The government has been reluctant to use police methods to keep down prices. In addition, paying inspectors is expensive, and in mid-1981 there were only 40 for the entire country. Nonetheless, in the first six months of 1981, 625 wholesale and retail vendors were fined a total of 230,000 córdobas.

The Sugar Blues

Sugar is one product that illustrates the government's headaches in enforcing price ceilings. (While you might think people would be better off with less sugar, most Nicaraguans don't see it that way.) The trouble started in 1980 when the government underestimated the portion of the sugar harvest needed for the domestic market and thus "oversold" it—mainly to the Coca-Cola Company. Demand was growing for sugar, as for other food items, precisely because of the improved purchasing power of the rural and urban poor. One of the most successfully reactivated industries has been the bottled soft drink industry—the revolution tripled Coke and Pepsi sales in 1980, compared to 1978.

By April 1980, rumors of a coming scarcity of sugar set off an explosion in purchases. One rumor had it that Nicaragua's sugar had been sent off to communist Cuba—a Caribbean version of coals to Newcastle. Some who had the means began storing sugar for the future. Others began hoarding in order to speculate. Monthly sales of sugar soared to the equivalent of 12 pounds per person. Such increased sales, of course, guaranteed that there actually would be a shortage. Government supermarkets became easy targets; whole families would swoop down and buy up ten five-pound sacks. Speculators paid poor families to go into supermarkets several times, buying over 100 pounds of sugar a day to be sold at much higher prices in the Eastern Market.

The government first responded by using every communication medium to tell people that there would be enough sugar for everyone if no one hoarded, and that the country desperately needed the foreign exchange it could earn from sugar exports. Posters went up everywhere: "A good revolutionary consumes less sugar daily." I found the slogan convenient when explaining to startled juice vendors that, no, I really would rather not have a few tablespoons of sugar added to my glass of fresh orange juice, a common Nicaraguan practice.

A blitz of television and radio spots told how sugar can be bad for you. Dr. So-and-so, head of the school of dentistry of the national university, looked up from a patient's mouth into the camera: "We know that people who consume sugar are more likely to develop cavities." Fade to announcer: "Reduce your sugar consumption and help rebuild the economy of the nation. Each spoonful of sugar that we save permits Nicaragua to export more and thus obtain foreign currency to satisfy our needs and develop the country. When we consume sugar rationally, we are saving. Each teaspoon that we save is converted into foreign currency."

These sugar-is-bad-for-you spots probably did not have the desired effect. In my experience, most people were skeptical about such messages; they suspected the real reason they were being told something wasn't good for them was that the government couldn't deliver the item in question. Perhaps more effective was an incentive program. If a municipality reduced its per capita sugar intake, thereby allowing the country to export more, part of the dollar value earned was returned to the municipality in córdobas for financing local public works. The government calculated that this incentive program saved over $500,000 worth of sugar in only eight months.

Yet another installment in the government's sugar blues

came in late 1981. First were several production problems: heavy rains in May reduced the expected crop yields by 12 percent. Then work stoppages, organized by antigovernment communist unions in the sugar mills, cost 700 tons a day. Finally, the Mexican government ran into its own big sugar shortage and pressured the Nicaraguan government to sell it 17,000 tons of refined sugar. Since Mexico was helping the new government diplomatically and financially (including supplies of oil on long-term credit), the Nicaraguan government felt that it could not turn Mexico down. (However, I imagine there were many officials who were highly annoyed by the Mexican "request.")

Nicaragua was left with short supplies. What refined sugar was available the government decided to sell to small candymakers and bakers since raw sugar would be "unacceptable" to them. Left for sale on the retail market was only raw sugar, which normally would be exported. Raw sugar became the *cause célèbre* of the day. Antigovernment forces spread rumors that the beloved white sugar had disappeared from Nicaragua forever. Once again, rumors set off an all-out scramble—corruption, pilfering, black markets, etc.—to corner the scarce refined sugar. Progovernment papers churned out numerous articles explaining why white sugar wasn't available and that brown sugar is really better for you anyway. (A favorite headline of mine in *El Nuevo Diario* heralded the "Great Vitamin Properties of Raw Sugar." The article went on for paragraphs in a highly scientific tenor, citing experiments with monkeys who ate only raw sugar and didn't develop tooth decay. It made raw sugar sound like the greatest health food of all time.)

Several other basic foodstuffs illustrate the same story: government programs to make food available at stable, affordable prices undercut by profiteering as well as by those holding food in "reserve," for fear of shortages. Thus part of the national economic emergency declared on September 9, 1981 made it a crime to hoard, speculate, or disseminate false information that might provoke hoarding and speculation. In addition, in a major break with private marketing, the emergency decree placed exclusive authority for domestic sugar sales into the government's hands.

"Guaranty Cards"—*Not* Rationing

In early 1982, ENABAS introduced a system of "guaranty cards," thus sidestepping the dreaded word "rationing." The system had first been tried in a Managua barrio, apparently after the CDS neighborhood organizations pushed for it. When the government first introduced the cards in March, those against the revolution thought they had been handed a golden opportunity to discredit the government—"See, it's just going to be another Cuba!" But the cards, combined with putting sugar sales exclusively in government-supplied outlets, did stabilize the price at the official ceiling by making it possible for all families to buy about five pounds of sugar per person per month. (In the Eastern Market, some illegal sales of sugar—at much higher prices—persisted, but there was no crackdown, apparently in order to allow an escape valve for those who simply "had" to have more than five pounds of sugar a month.)

The CDSs, the Sandinista neighborhood organizations, were actively involved in organizing the sugar distribution system. They carried out a household census and issued the guaranty cards. (Several Nicaraguans tell about their experiences with sugar distribution in our companion book, *Now We Can Speak.*) By June, only three months later, the whole card system was so widely accepted that the maligners of the government were quiet, and I found government officials taking satisfaction in a small but politically important triumph. While the government had found it necessary to eliminate sugar sales through the private market, at least the government's sugar blues were over.

The Question of Subsidies

Government subsidies on food staples have been fundamental to whatever gains have been made in the food security of the poor majority. To counteract the effects of persistent unemployment and overall inflation, ENABAS has been wholesaling and retailing food for a lot less than it pays to buy it from farmers or import it. In 1982–83, for example, ENABAS is buying beans from campesinos at 3.50 córdobas a pound and retailing them at 2.85 a pound, plus absorbing all the costs of transport, drying, storing, packaging, administration, etc. With many millions of pounds, it adds up to a staggering cost.

Paying higher prices to help motivate producers further increases the subsidies. In fact, the government projected total ENABAS subsidies to come to a staggering 1 billion córdobas in 1982. Not only is this subsidy enormous, but it is not targeted to the poor. If anything, the poorest are discriminated against by programs that market low-priced foods through workplaces, since the really poor don't have permanent workplaces—that's their basic problem! By 1981, however, ENABAS started to eliminate people's stores and *expendios* from better-off neighborhoods in order to concentrate more in poorer neighborhoods.

A major threat to the well-being of those who need the food subsidies is that increasingly severe foreign exchange shortages will pressure the government to severely cut back or do away with the subsidy program. In spring 1982 the government placed large display advertisements in the newspapers to promote public awareness of the magnitude of the food subsidies, emphasizing that such outlays require sacrificing other programs.

Comparing the prices of staple foods in Nicaragua with prices elsewhere in Central America shows the results of applying the "logic of the majority" to food policies in Nicaragua. Beans sold for 2.87 córdobas a pound in Nicaragua, 4.60 in Guatemala, 4.80 in El Salvador and Honduras, and 7.50 in Costa Rica, according to an August 1982 *Barricada* survey. Rice sold for 2.94 córdobas a pound in Nicaragua, 3.30 in Guatemala, 4.00 in El Salvador, 4.80 in Honduras, and 7.00 in Costa Rica. (Prices were converted into córdobas at the official exchange rate.)

While their subsidized prices are already generally higher than Nicaragua's, Nicaragua's neighbors are being pressured by the International Monetary Fund to abolish consumer food subsidies. Following suit would be politically very damaging to the popular base of the revolution, and it is highly unlikely the Sandinistas would do so. But indiscriminate subsidies are incompatible with urgent fiscal austerity and, as the government itself points out, severely limit other programs of benefit to the poor majority. Thus the real challenge facing the

Sandinistas on the third anniversary of victory was to develop discriminatory subsidies—subsidies that discriminate in favor of the poor majority, placing the burden on those who can afford it. *That* would be revolutionary.

Are People Eating Better Now?

It's hard to document whether people are eating better now. We know that overall food consumption is up about 40 percent since before the war. Undoubtedly it is not the rich and the upper middle-class minority that are eating more, for they have never gone without. But the other Nicaraguans—the majority—cannot be lumped together when we try to assess their food well-being.

In the countryside, those with access to land—households making up perhaps 40 percent of Nicaragua's population—are now using more of what they produce, both directly and through consumption of small livestock, most observers agree. As the revolution lowers rents, abolishes sharecropping, and gives land or better quality land to the land-poor and landless, these campesino families will likely be eating better and have real food security for the first time in their lives. Asked how they're eating now, compared to before, many campesinos tell me, "We're getting by okay." And they proudly point out the many chickens and pigs running loose around their peasant homes.

Life is tougher for the majority in the city as well as for rural laborers without land. And prospects are threatening. A survey of Managua in early 1982 yielded no evidence of overall improvement in the diet of the poor majority. Managuans, without land to grow food and hardest hit by inflation, were eating more of less expensive foods. Rice, bean, and sugar consumption had gone up while milk and red meat consumption had dropped.

Such a survey, however, must be taken at best as an approximation of trends rather than as hard data. Also useful are the firsthand observations of those who have lived for years in the poorer barrios. In June 1981 I asked several Catholic sisters if the people were eating better now. "The children now look healthier, even chubby," one sister responded, with others agreeing. This sister is a nurse, versed in the signs of even first-degree malnutrition, which, according to a 1975 U.S. AID study, afflicted 42 pecent of Nicaraguan children under 4. She and other medical workers agree that infant deaths are many fewer than before, even though births are undoubtedly on the rise (apparently the usual postwar phenomenon). While improved family nutrition is a likely factor in this important advance for the poor majority, other causes could be even more important, including newly created neighborhood infant rehydration stations for babies suffering from diarrhea, a campaign to encourage breast-feeding and neighborhood sanitation efforts.

Steady employment is crucial in determining how well people eat. Families with at least one or two members regularly employed, no matter the wages, obviously fare better than those whose members live catch-as-catch-can. In the first two years, the government did greatly increase the number of jobs, mainly in the government sector. With a deepening fiscal crisis in mid-1981, the government started to make across-the-board hiring cutbacks. The overall economic picture for 1982 is bleaker still—and what is most frustrating for the Sandinistas is that so many crucial factors are outside Nicaragua's control, notably the steep slide in international prices for Nicaragua's chief exports. As in the rest of Central America, foreign exchange is growing very scarce. That spells disaster for the country's manufacturing sector, which is dependent on imported inputs as well as sales of its manufactures to the other countries in the region, facing their own financial crises. Large-scale factory shutdowns are likely, increasing unemployment. Growing inflation, still less than half that in neighboring Costa Rica in 1981, will chop away at the purchasing power even of those with jobs. While the real purchasing power of urban workers has dropped since 1978, government measures to control basic food prices have undoubtedly helped at least maintain the majority's food consumption. Government price controls were more likely to have been effective in neighborhoods with a greater degree of self-organization, where there is willingness to stand up to price gougers. Thus an important part of the majority's food security depends on large numbers of people organizing themselves on their own behalf. Overall food prices since mid-1981 have risen more slowly than prices of other goods, especially those imported or made from imported·materials. This is due to the general impact of the price ceilings on basic foods, controls (and built-in government subsidies), and the fact that food is mostly not imported. This is particularly the case since late 1981, when the growing scarcity of foreign exchange led the government to significantly hike taxes on imported consumer goods. As a result, lower income people are more likely to find items like shoes and radios out of reach, but food a relatively good buy.

The Last Straw

Ten days of better-build-an-ark rains (21 inches in one day alone!) struck Nicaragua's Pacific coast in late May 1982. According to a United Nations survey, rain and flooding swept away at least 20,000 acres of just-planted food crops, $3.6 million in stored grains, and innumerable rural roads, and did $350 million additional damage to the nation's economic infrastructure. This was a tremendous loss in a country where all goods and services produced in an entire year (GDP) are worth only $2.2 billion.

Arriving the day after the rains, I found a country outraged at the opportunistic hoarding and speculation by private merchants, especially wholesalers. Public sentiment was so strong that it was easy for the government to move quickly and decisively. The day after I arrived the national police were authorized to inspect food prices and arrest speculators. Fines were increased and jail sentences of up to six months were imposed. In the first two days alone, the media were filled with stories of the arrest of two big wholesalers and 111 retailers. One retailer showed receipts proving that he had paid so much to the wholesaler that he had to raise his price; his fine was dropped and his goods returned to him, while a stiff fine was slapped on the wholesaler.

Labor unions, the CDS neighborhood organizations, the national women's organization, and a lot of ordinary people were calling for a guaranty card system for beans, rice, and corn "since it has worked so well with sugar." At this writing (September 1982) a new law to do so is being intensely debated while ENABAS is rapidly expanding the number of franchised private retail stores (*expendios*) and, where necessary, opening people's stores.

Three years' experience has raised deep doubts whether the free market can serve the poor majority, at least in times of scarcity. It has also shown how difficult it is for a new government to set up an efficient, low cost alternative system.

PART TWO

FOURTEEN

TARGET: THE AGRARIAN REFORM

THE SAN JERONIMO COOPERATIVE LIES nestled in northern Nicaragua's Condega hills. Before the revolution, the estate belonged to a Somoza crony who fled with the dictator to Miami. For four years it was operated as a profitable state farm. In August 1983, the farm, complete with its coffee mill, was converted into a worker-owned cooperative.

Many of the cooperative's members formerly worked on the coffee estate during the harvests, and had secretly helped "*los muchachos*" during the long struggle against Somoza's *Guardia*. Proudly they will tell you they knew Omar Cabezas and several other *comandantes* when they were guerrillas in the hills. Pedro Pravia, the cooperative's elected treasurer, has worked for 36 years on the San Jeronimo estate and likes to speak of his "three experiences." "First we were hired hands for the *patrón*," he says. "Then with state ownership, we got a health clinic, our very first school, and higher wages." But the "biggest difference," he thinks, has come with the cooperative. "Now we are masters of our own farm. All the benefits we produce are for us. Now we have the means to improve our lives."

The 1983–84 harvest, the first since the San Jeronimo coffee estate became a cooperative, was a very good one. Profits were enough to buy irrigation hoses and make other improvements. In addition the cooperative's 69 members received bonuses based on the number of days each had worked. The bank loan for the year's working capital was fully repaid. Over 400 head of cattle grazed on the cooperative's pastureland. Following the coffee harvest, 50 acres were plowed and waiting for the first rain to be planted with corn and beans.

The San Jeronimo cooperative clearly demonstrated the advances Nicaragua's poor campesinos could make through the revolution. Too clearly—for some. Three times in early 1984 a band of contra terrorists slipped by night across the Honduran border and attacked the cooperative. Each time, the cooperative's own volunteer militia repelled the invaders. Then on May 23, 1984, several hundred contras attacked at dawn. This time the *compañeros* were too greatly outnumbered. "Fortunately," said Julio Calderón, a poor tenant farmer who had joined the cooperative and been elected its president, "our sentries spotted them in time to evacuate both our cooperative and the neighboring one and all the nearby small farmers." The cooperative's militia guarded the retreat. "The contras killed only one of us and failed to kidnap anyone," Calderón boasted.

But the contras inflicted heavy damage on the cooperative's facilities. We visited San Jeronimo within days of the attack— soon enough to stumble on such gruesome reminders of it as a blood-soaked tuft of hair from a wounded contra. The contras' mortar fire had burned the coffee mill to the ground. A large storehouse was also reduced to charred rubble. It had contained machinery and 100-pound sacks of fertilizer, the cooperative's offices and account books, the kitchen and dining hall used during the harvest, recently purchased building materials, school supplies for adult evening classes, and medicines and clothing left by Austrian volunteers who had helped with the harvest. Several members' homes and those of some neighboring small farmers were also torched. The total loss had just been assessed at 10 million córdobas, 20 times the cooperative's profits that year. As we sifted through the ashes of his office, Pedro Pravia said sadly, "We were so satisfied with what we had achieved. We were just beginning. And now comes this attack."

On our visit to San Jeronimo we were accompanied by

Orlando Picado, an official from the regional agrarian-reform headquarters. Boarding our jeep as we passed through Estelí, he looked preoccupied. We asked him what was wrong. He spoke gravely of a major contra attack that morning at Ocotal, less than 50 miles away, and of the ambush and cold-blooded murder of two of his co-workers. Painfully aware that such attacks would not be possible without the support of my government—and that most people knew it—I felt at once outrage, embarrassment, and helplessness. Then Orlando's T-shirt caught my eye. Iowa State University. Noting the surprised expression on my face, Orlando grinned, "We're anti-imperialist, anti-Yankee, but we're not anti-American."

San Jeronimo is only one of 11 cooperatives in Nicaragua attacked by the contras in the first six months of 1984. It is no coincidence that cooperatives are a prime target. The contras attack whoever and whatever symbolizes the new Nicaragua: cooperatives, a peasant family that has received land through the agrarian reform, rural health workers, agricultural technicians working with peasants, a Managua high school student volunteer for the coffee harvest, fields planted in corn and beans where only a handful of cattle grazed before the revolution, rural adult education centers and literacy *brigadistas* (mostly young volunteers); and at least 27 agricultural technicians.

The contras (and the CIA) reason that the Sandinistas' unprecedented developments in health services, schooling, farming assistance, and food distribution form the basis for support of the revolution in the countryside. These services, then, must be destroyed. The contras practice cold-blooded, systematic terrorism, not a strategy to win over hearts and minds.

One martyr to contra terrorism is Alejandro Espinosa, an agronomist in his mid-30s who worked as a government agricultural extension agent in the region around Estelí. Alejandro helped private coffee producers improve their farming practices, especially through better timing of weeding and fertilizing. Three times while riding in a jeep from farm to farm, he was ambushed by contra bands. The first time he escaped lightly wounded. The second time the contras put a pistol to his head, fired, and left him for dead. The bullet miraculously glanced off his skull bone. Two months later the jeep he was riding in was shot by contra snipers. The jeep crashed, and before Alejandro could escape a hand grenade was hurled through the broken front window, tearing him to pieces.

After the first two attacks, Alejandro's family and friends begged him to change jobs, at least to work in a region more secure from contra attacks. But he refused, saying that the whole point of the revolution is to bring services to people who never had them before. "If we're not going to do that because we're intimidated and terrorized, we might as well give up," he told his wife Lilys, an accountant in the agrarian-reform office in Matagalpa. Over 1,000 mourners came to his funeral, many of them small coffee farmers on their burros. For them, people like Alejandro Espinosa *are* the Sandinista revolution.

For the contras, the "crime" of Noel Rivera, a 52-year-old large coffee grower and cattle rancher in the Matagalpa region, was that he was a highly successful capitalist. He was investing and producing. Since the start of the revolution, he had expanded his coffee acreage and diversified by planting cocoa, beans, avocados, and mangos. He employed 80 farm-workers year-round and his payroll topped 200 during the harvest.

Politically, to be sure, Rivera was hardly a Sandinista. He belonged to none of the popular organizations identified with the revolution, such as UNAG and the CDS. While he found that he could do business with the Sandinista-led government, Noel Rivera thought of himself as "apolitical."

On July 19, 1984, the fifth anniversary of the defeat of Somoza's *Guardia,* a large band of contras kidnapped Noel Rivera about seven miles from his coffee farm. According to his wife Gladys, the peasants who witnessed the kidnapping didn't think the contras would really do anything to him since everyone knew Noel Rivera was not a supporter of the Sandinistas. But two days later some farmworkers saw the contras hack Rivera to pieces with machetes.

Targeting a politically neutral large producer like Noel Rivera was clearly intended to intimidate other large private growers and ranchers (and their families) who have chosen to produce. As Rivera's widow said, "The contras who killed Noel want to whip up discontent. They don't want us to bring the crops in. Then people would complain: 'Just look what's happening in Nicaragua.' We private producers are in a lot of danger from contra attacks in many areas. Our plantations are isolated and defenseless." Another producer in the region, Francisco Javier Saenz, commented, "Noel was an outstanding producer, and this was bad for the contras. They want to kill us not only with bullets; they want us to die from hunger."

Three years of attacks from contra bases in Honduras and Costa Rica have created fear in the Nicaraguan countryside. In 1983 alone, 811 farmworkers and peasants were murdered. Two Ecuadoran doctors working in Waslala, a small town 80 miles north of Matagalpa, report that, since a major contra attack in April 1984, "life has become a living nightmare for these people, thinking about contras in the mountains, wondering when the next attack will come and whether they will survive." Two young townspeople who lost their homes and loved ones in the attack now are being treated for clinical psychosis.

In the Matagalpa–Jinotega region the contras have assassinated more than 1,000 civilians. The unspeakable horrors committed against civilian and military victims alike are well-documented by international agencies. Girls and boys have not only been raped but their sex organs mutilated. In August 1984, two Canadians told us of how in a town they were visiting the contras had attacked and pulled a school teacher into the front yard of his home and tortured him in front of his wife, seven children, stepfather, and father-in-law. They cut of his ears and tongue and forced him to chew and swallow them. Then they cut off his penis and finally killed him. Young peasant men told us they feared being drafted into the Sandinista army because they have heard that if captured they will be forced to cut off their testicles and eat them. Eyes are gouged out while the victims are alive, a notorious trademark of Somoza's *Guardia.* U.S.-supplied bullets explode in the bodies of their victims, ripping them to pieces. Bodies commonly cannot be identified because their faces have been completely skinned and their heads cut off. Wives can identify their husbands, and husbands their wives, only by their clothes. Contrary to Nicaraguan custom, since mid-1984 the coffins of peasant militia members killed in combat have been soldered shut so that mothers cannot see what has been done to their children.

In some areas, the cooperative movement has been spurred forward by families who fear living in isolation. Coming together, they have formed "self-defense" cooperatives; men and women work the fields with guns slung across their backs. Three years ago when I asked small farmers what they most wanted the usual response was tractors. Now more often they answer guns—to defend their farms and homes.

But some families have become afraid to join cooperatives or even to receive land through the agrarian reform because they know the contras target the agrarian reform.

Most of the San Jeronimo's members seemed determined to rebuild the cooperative, although a few families remained camped out in Condega's high school, too terrorized to return home. When we were visiting San Jeronimo, agrarian-reform officials were there discussing members' immediate needs for new building materials. The families had decided to build their homes closer together and up on a hill. An army squad was now encamped on the hill to give an added sense of security to the cooperative.

In June 1984, it became national policy for the regions most affected by counterrevolutionary attacks and subversion to receive priority in allocation of all government resources. To win the war, every effort must be made to ensure that these areas experience the revolution concretely—schools, clinics, crop storage facilities, supply outlets, and better access roads.

To make certain this new priority exists not just on paper, a *comandante* has been assigned to head up the coordination of all programs and services of each of the war regions. *Comandantes* can see that decisions are taken and implemented swiftly, even when they involve serious changes in policy. This emergency development has further strained human resources at the agrarian reform's executive level: while Comandante Jaime Wheelock kept his post as Minister of Agriculture and Agrarian Reform (already more than a full-time job!), he was appointed the virtual governor of the Matagalpa–Jinotega region.

The north central highlands around Matagalpa and Jinotega have become an area of special concern for the Sandinistas. Some local campesinos have collaborated with the contras not only out of fear, but also because the remoteness and difficult terrain—or outright administrative incompetence—have meant delays in delivering the benefits of the revolution. The region is economically vital: it produces two-thirds of Nicaragua's coffee and thereby accounts for 20 percent of the nation's export earnings in recent years. But the region's mountainous slopes, so ideal for coffee cultivation, are also perfect for hiding contra guerrillas just as they hid Sandinista guerrillas only a few years before.

*　*　*　*

Visiting contra-attacked areas, I have often thought of the words of two Americans. The President of the United States in an address to Congress stated: "We Americans should be proud of what we have been trying to do in Central America." The other is Iowa Congressperson Berkley Bedell, widely thought of as "conservative." Upon his return from Nicaragua in April 1983, he reported, "If the American people could have talked with the common people of Nicaragua, whose women and children are indiscriminately kidnapped, tortured, and killed by terrorists financed by the American taxpayers, they would rise up in legitimate anger."

FIFTEEN

AGRARIAN REFORM IN DEFENSE OF A REVOLUTION

"THE SANDINISTAS ARE GOING TO TAKE away your land. They're communists, and they want to make the state the owner of everything." The powerful contra radio transmitter in Honduras beamed this message day in and day out in the northern half of Nicaragua.

"We're going to keep our promise that no Nicaraguan peasant will be left landless," vowed Comandante Jaime Wheelock, Minister of Agricultural Development and Agrarian Reform, as he handed 816 campesinos property titles for some 70,000 acres.

Land for the landless has been one of the most readily documented differences made by the Sandinista revolution. By the revolution's fifth anniversary, titles had been granted without charge for 2.4 million acres to 45,000 beneficiaries as family farmowners or members of farm cooperatives. This amounts to nearly 20 percent of Nicaragua's farmland—more than ten times all the land owned by poor peasants before the revolution. The beneficiaries and their families make up one-third of Nicaragua's campesinos.

The first agrarian-reform property titles were granted in October 1981. The implementation of Nicaragua's agrarian reform accelerated considerably following the escalation of the counterrevolutionary war in late 1982. In the 12 months before the war's escalation, some 6,500 small farmers and members of production cooperatives were given titles for approximately 200,000 acres. In the following year an additional 13,000 individual farmers and cooperative members received titles for 650,000 acres. By the fifth anniversary of the revolution on July 19, 1984—only nine months later—another 25,500 families had benefited from land titles handed out for 1.55 million acres.

In the three *weeks* leading up to the revolution's fifth anniversary, as many families received property titles as in the first two *years* of the land reform. The location of the new titles as well as the timing indicated the influence of the contra war: two-thirds of the titles were granted in the regions most affected by the contra attacks.

What Held Back the Land Reform

Throughout 1982 and well into 1983, many campesinos, farmworkers, the leaders of UNAG, and even staff and officials of the agrarian reform had become impatient with the slow pace with which the agrarian-reform law was being implemented. Since creating just and productive structures in the countryside had been a primary goal in overthrowing the Somoza dictatorship (see chapter 3), what had been holding back the pace of the revolution's land reform?

A Painstaking Process

The "conservative" nature of the Sandinista agrarian reform (see chapter 10) made implementation of the law painstaking and time-consuming. The Sandinista agrarian reform seeks not only to more equitably distribute economic resources, but also to promote production. The law is designed to motivate larger owners to produce with the guarantee that they can keep their land as long as they use it productively. Since the law places no limit on how much land anyone can own, case-by-case assessments have to be undertaken to determine whether a particular farm or ranch is being productively operated. These assessments require the involvement of local farmers and farmworkers who know, for example, how much weeding and fertilizing a particular coffee farm needs.

Once an owner is charged with not productively using a piece of agricultural property, an Agrarian Reform Council must rule on the accumulated evidence. Following the ruling, time must be allotted for a possible appeal to the Agrarian Reform Tribunal by an expropriated owner. The appeal process is no farce: about one-fourth of appeals have been decided in favor of the owners and their farms and ranches returned to them. As of July 1984, 20 government employees were serving prison sentences for abusive confiscations among other crimes.

Now a new set of problems arises. Who exactly is to receive land? And how much? Which campesinos have farms with soil too poor or too little land to earn a living for their families? The Ministry of Agricultural Development and Agrarian Reform (MIDINRA) must work closely with UNAG and the ATC (the national Sandinista-led farmworkers' union) to identify suitable beneficiaries. It is important to give land to people who are committed to farming and will not abandon the land if things prove tougher than imagined. In theory farmworker beneficiaries are to be identified who will morally agree to continue working in the export crop harvests (see chapter 9) even once they own their own land. Throughout 1982 and into 1983, the fear that once people could make a decent living from their own land they would no longer seek wage labor in the export harvests helped slow the pace of the land reform in regions with large export farms.

Each region requires research to determine quality of land and the suitable amount to be transferred for both immediate viability and longer-term economic development. A beneficiary should be granted neither too little nor too much land to make sure that the agrarian reform does not unfairly result in great advantages for some and guaranteed impoverishment for others.

These issues demand a tremendous amount of conceptual and technical work from any government—even more from a government with virtually no inherited administrative experience and reform and painfully stretched human and financial resources. Fortunately, key parts of the agrarian reform's implementation were decentralized and carried out by non-government organizations. In the fall of 1982, local organizations, especially affiliates of UNAG and ATC, were called upon to investigate local land utilization and to make detailed proposals for expropriation and redistribution of land in their communities.

Another factor slowing the land reform was the caution shown by the Sandinistas in dealing with the larger landowners. In the face of foreign aggression, the government emphasized fostering the broadest possible support for the revolution. Accordingly, the government initially attempted to limit expropriations to only the most blatant cases of decapitalizing landowners (see chapter 5), hoping other landowners would "see the light."

Conflicting Views

Perhaps the greatest factor in slowing the reform's initial pace was the existence of conflicting views of agrarian reform within the Sandinista leadership. Much of the internal debate centered on whether land redistribution should emphasize the creation of individually owned farms or cooperatives of collectively owned land and on the proper place of state farms in the agrarian reform.

Those reluctant to see land distributed in individual family farms feared repeating the experience of many reforms in Latin America and elsewhere. In these precedents, giving out acreage to every land-poor family initially appeared to be a sweeping democratization of the rural economy. But the problem of individuals getting ahead at the expense of others— even the impoverishment and enslavement of others—were never addressed. Competition, not pulling together, prevailed as the order of the day. It was not long before sharp inequalities—economic and therefore political—established themselves, the rich getting richer and the poor getting poorer. Urban and rural-based elites wound up asserting monopoly control over land, water, credit, and other economic resources that at best were nominally owned by the rural majority.

Opponents of family-farm redistribution argued that individual holdings inherently foster individualist consciousness. In one sense, they reasoned, farmworkers benefited from being landless: they thought of themselves as workers rather than as property owners. The insurrection had taught many that if they pursued their interests in common with fellow workers they could give political direction to the nation. Would not making them individual landowners be going backward by emphasizing individual rather than common interests?

According to this view, a countryside made up of hundreds of thousands of individual units makes poor economic sense. Larger units would allow economies of scale in providing technical assistance as well as health, educational, and other services. Given the nation's severely stretched resources, only a fraction would be helped if the rural economy consisted of a plethora of individual farms.

Critics of land distribution to individuals supported an agrarian reform that would focus on distributing land in the form of common property—cooperatives—and on the development of publicly owned state farms. Some advocates of cooperatives proposed a transitional form of cooperatives in which the members would share services and equipment but work individual parcels if they so chose.

Others countered that no matter how logical and attractive the grand design, agrarian reform should, above all, offer peasants and farmworkers a choice. While different forms of cooperative organization could be encouraged through subsidized services, lower interest rates for loans, and other incentives, joining cooperatives should not be made a condition for getting access to land. The voluntary approach, it was argued, was the essence of a popular revolution.

Proponents of state farms saw public ownership as the best hope for modernizing Nicaragua's agricultural economy. Calling state farms "dynamic poles of development," this current of opinion regarded the most important element of agricultural policy big-scale investments, often in new products (see chapter 19). Such heavy public investment in agriculture requires public ownership in this view. Its proponents were also reluctant to see any lands distributed before soil and water studies could be carried out to establish the best places for investments.

Opponents contended that state farms were proving to be too costly, as apparently they have been in other countries. This view argued that the state farms developed from the confiscation of the Somocista properties (see chapter 7) were already tying up far too much of the human and financial resources of the ministry and not resulting in widely perceived benefits.

Accelerating the Land Reform

Ultimately geography proved to be key. The contra attacks from their bases in Honduras and Costa Rica were concentrated in areas of the country dominated by peasants and medium-size producers. By 1983 this reality more than anything else was giving impetus and direction to the agrarian reform.

As the contra propaganda and military attacks intensified, the Sandinistas once again showed themselves flexible pragmatists capable of responding to political realities. They perceived that the defense of the revolution partly depended upon delivering its benefits in the areas under attack. Accordingly, they moved quickly to respond to the peasants' demand for land.

The speeded-up agrarian-reform program, in effect, legitimized individual land ownership. By September 1984, over 57 percent of the new land titles were distributed to individual peasant families. In the Matagalpa region, an area of heavy contra activity, the head of the MIDINRA office who had concentrated on the economic development of state farms and the larger private producers was transferred. Privately, Minister Wheelock has referred to his policies as "mistaken."

The high percentage of land transferred to individuals is in part explained by the decision to grant secure property titles to homesteaders who have been squatting for years on public lands in the "agricultural frontier"—the central interior of the country, which has been the center of much contra activity. By September 1984, over 50 percent of the land titled over by the Sandinista reform had already been farmed by the beneficiaries—without clear title—for years. This policy satisfied these peasants' long-term demand for land security and assured thousands in the war zones that the Sandinista revolution was not, as the contras charged, going to take their land from them and force them onto cooperatives or state farms.

Typically, the homesteaders were families who had been pushed off their coastal lands by land-grabbing cotton growers and cattle ranchers. Some were "beneficiaries" of Somoza's "land reform." Under heavy pressure from the Kennedy administration's "Alliance for Progress"—a response to the sweeping reforms in Cuba—the Somoza dictatorship in 1961 established a land-reform agency. Rather than expropriate lands from elites, this agency resettled impoverished peasants onto remote wilderness lands (generally of marginal quality and without services); but it never gave them the promised legal titles.

The political importance of the small and medium producers has been accompanied by a growing recognition of their economic importance by many MIDINRA officials. Some economists within the ministry contend that since the start of the revolution the small and medium producers have been one of the few groups investing in production. Admittedly, the investments are not as grand (or grandiose) as those of the state sector, but they tend to be highly productive, cost-effective, and often paid for out of savings. In visiting so much of the countryside, we have seen countless examples: two pigs instead of one, a row of windbreak trees, some fruit trees, a mule for getting to market. The recognition of this progress has strengthened the hand of those who argue that there has been an exaggerated notion of the economic importance of the large producers in comparison to the medium and small producers.

The acceleration of the agrarian reform has meant that the formation of cooperatives based on collective land ownership and production has been assigned a de facto lower priority. This policy shift reflects a strong commitment by the majority of Sandinistas to respect the will of the campesinos and, above all, to avoid coercion in the name of knowing what is best.

There is nonetheless a high-level commitment to the organization of producer cooperatives as a long-range vision. The goals of fostering public-minded consciousness and developing economies of scale in government economic and social services remain compelling for many. The widely shared hope among the Sandinistas is that the vast majority of individual recipients of land will move toward forming producer cooperatives through joining credit and services associations and participating in collective undertakings such as building grain-storage facilities or irrigation systems. The percentage of new cooperatives has been declining as the land redistribution has accelerated; still, by September 1984, 40 percent of the land granted through the agrarian reform had been in the form of production cooperatives (CAS).

The pace of land reform was accelerated by titling over land from the state sector and *not* by accelerating expropriations. In the first two years following passage of the August 1981 agrarian reform law, considerably more land was expropriated than was titled over (see chapter 10). But during 1983 almost 50 percent more land was titled over than expropriated. In 1984, the gap was expected to grow much wider, with the amount of land expropriated declining to less than a fifth of the amount expropriated in 1982 and a third of the 1983 figure. Nicaragua's percentage of agricultural land in the state sector peaked in 1982 at 20 percent. Since 1983 there has been a steady decline in the size of the state sector to 18 percent by mid-1984.

The Sandinistas hope that diminished reliance on expropriating large private holdings will quell large landowners' fears and foster national unity in the face of counterrevolutionary subversion and foreign aggression. In November 1983, Minister Wheelock went so far as to announce that the government would give certificates of "nonexpropriability" to private commercial producers who are using their lands productively. Of course, this announcement amounted to tactical reassurance rather than a change of policy since the agrarian reform law guarantees the right to private property as long as the owner puts it to productive use. (As of late 1984, whatever certificates the minister had in mind had not yet materialized.)

Proponents of state-farm development have traded-off increasing state-farm acreage for priority in investment capital (see chapter 19). The state sector is seen as being "consolidated": farms that are too small or too isolated to be efficiently centrally managed have been spun off into the private sector (generally to form cooperatives like San Jeronimo, but sometimes as family farms). Greater policymaking autonomy has been granted to each MIDINRA region, resulting in regional variations in state-farm practices. The Estelí region, for example, has been maintaining only those state farms that provide backup services (such as seed multiplication and livestock breeding) to small and medium private farms and cooperatives and state farms that are part of a few development projects, such as new tobacco farms, that require major investments.

In overall national practice, Sandinista agrarian policy is turning out to be two-tracked: private producer-based (individual small and medium producers and cooperatives) as well as state farm-based. Within MIDINRA it appears that two groups, each of a different mind, have compromised by dividing the turf and resources. Publicly there is no contradiction; privately each questions the other's sanity. On the one side, there has been a distinct ratification at the highest levels of a peasant property base to the Sandinista agrarian reform. But at the same time, as we will see, steep investments are being made in a distinctly centrally managed state-farm sector. It remains to be seen if the two-tracked approach attests to the wisdom of the Sandinistas or proves to be a luxury Nicaragua can ill afford.

SIXTEEN

GETTING OFF THE PESTICIDE TREADMILL

I N *FOOD FIRST* (CHAPTER 9), WE REPORTED on Nicaragua's "pesticide treadmill." The extensive monocultivation of cotton during the 1950s and 1960s created an environment ideal for pests, including cotton's most notable nemesis, the infamous boll weevil. Initially the growers got reassuring results using chemical pesticides, especially DDT and methyl parathion (a byproduct of chemical warfare research during World War II). Soon, however, they found themselves caught up in a vicious circle of dependency on more and more chemicals: Pests developed resistances to the chemicals and new pests emerged as the pesticides killed off their natural predators. Once on this "pesticide treadmill," growers wound up scheduling so many aerial sprayings of pesticide "cocktails" that the profitability of cotton production was threatened. By the late 1960s, Nicaragua had the dubious distinction of holding the world's record for the number of applications of pesticides on a single crop.

The environmental consequences—and the impact on human health and food production—were shocking. In the 1969–70 harvest season alone, 383 pesticide fatalities were reported. More than 3,000 acute poisonings a year were reported from 1962 to 1972. *Reported* figures, however, drastically understated reality. In Somoza's Nicaragua many poisoning victims would not seek medical attention because they were too poor or feared being fired if they missed work. Immediate fatalities and illnesses from pesticide exposure are only the tip of the iceberg. No one really knows the long-term consequences of decades of heavy pesticide use, especially since DDT and other pesticides in the organochlorine family remain in soil and water for years. What is known is certainly ominous: Hundreds of thousands of Nicaraguans have been found to carry extraordinary levels—16 times the world average—of DDT and other cancer-causing chemicals in their fatty tissues. Samples of mothers' milk were found to have 45 times the DDT maximum considered permissible by the World Health Organization. Pesticide "drift" has polluted water supplies and wreaked havoc on nearby food crops; it also set the stage for the resurgence of malaria, once the mosquitoes who carried the disease developed resistance to DDT.

In 1977 and 1978, cotton production costs exceeded export revenues. But the big growers were powerful enough to arrange for production subsidies by public borrowing from U.S. banks. The "hidden" costs were even greater: A 1977 United Nations investigation estimated that annual environmental and human health damage from pesticide use in Nicaragua added up to $200 million, while the foreign exchange generated from cotton never exceeded $141 million a year. On economic, environmental, and health grounds, the pesticide treadmill was monstrously irrational. But given the powerful economic and political interests behind it, it has literally taken a revolution to create the context to get Nicaragua off the treadmill.

From the start, the Sandinistas have understood agrarian reform to include improving working conditions in the countryside. Immediate steps were taken to reduce human poisonings and environmental contamination caused by excessive and improper application of pesticides. At the same time, the government moved toward the longer-range goal of sharply reducing the use of highly toxic and expensive pesticides without sacrificing production.

Since all pesticides but one used in Nicaragua were imported, the government used its control over imports to reduce and then eliminate (by 1981–82) the import of DDT, endrin, and dieldrin. (All three of these organochlorines had been banned or severely restricted in the United States for over a decade. Pesticide-formulating companies (licensees of multinationals) were pressured to substitute pesticides considered environmentally less harmful and less hazardous to humans. In 1980, the pesticide DBCP was banned after the chemical was found to cause sterility in production workers in California and to be a potent cancer-causing agent in laboratory tests. The pesticide is a favorite in banana production as well as in many other crops throughout the third world.

The government has promoted educational programs to illustrate the dangers of pesticides to factory and rural workers. The Ministry of Labor has organized over 4,000 safety classes since 1979. Safety inspectors have been trained to investigate every workplace in the country. A national commission, created in 1982, seeks to coordinate the efforts of the various ministries, labor unions, and producer associations (like the association of cotton growers) in addressing pesticide problems. In response to a proposal by the Sandinista-led farmworkers union (ATC), the commission has developed new regulations. Included is a system of simply worded, illustrated, and color-coded pesticide labels to provide information on hazards, personal protective measures, poisoning symptoms, first aid, and medical treatment. The national literacy campaign has helped make such measures effective among rural workers.

The progress achieved in the revolution's first three years is encouraging. A visitor still can come upon shockingly nonchalant handling of highly toxic chemicals, but a growing number of farm managers and workers, as well as peasant producers, now seem aware of pesticide hazards. Once again, however, the discouraging reality these days is Washington's war on Nicaragua.

As the contras stepped up their attack in 1983 and the U.S. invasion of Grenada in October set off nationwide alarm in Nicaragua, many projects came to a standstill. Mobilizations have drawn off many of those trained as health and safety inspectors. (Not surprisingly, a high proportion of volunteers for the defense mobilizations are those most actively involved in the revolution's new programs—they are Nicaragua's "best and brightest.") By the end of 1983, of Nicaragua's 40 inspectors, 13 had been mobilized to armed combat and five others to harvest coffee in regions where contra attacks contributed to the shortage of workers. Training courses have frequently been interrupted by defense mobilizations. Review of new pesticide regulations by the national commission was held up for nearly six months as key members were mobilized. Safety inspections and courses have been slowed by war-related transport problems. Imported tires and spare parts go on a priority basis to national defense. By the end of 1983, there were only two functioning vehicles for the 40 workplace inspectors. The inspectors who manage to get to the field, like other agricultural technicians, become prime targets of the contras.

U.S. aggression has also hampered Nicaragua's efforts to eliminate certain pesticides from use. Launched from a CIA ship off the coast, the October 1983 assault on the port of Corinto destroyed a major new shipment of pesticides on the docks. The attack coincided with the height of the boll weevil season. With the shipment of pesticides destroyed and shipping disrupted well into December, the government had no recourse but to reintroduce a number of banned pesticides locked away in warehouses.

Nonchemical Pest Control

The long-term reduction of pesticide use promises major economic as well as health benefits. Pesticides make up a third of the production costs in cotton growing, which accounts for 75 to 80 percent of all pesticide use in Nicaragua. Any significant reduction in their use would save millions of dollars. Despite subversion and sabotage, striking advances have been made toward the goal of sharply reducing pesticide use in cotton production. At the Institute for Food and Development Policy, we are pleased to have been associated with this work and have published a Food First Research Report called "Breaking the Circle of Poison" (see Resource Guide).

Practitioners of "integrated pest management" (IPM) have worked with the agricultural ministry on pesticide reduction. Advocates of reduced pesticide use invariably run up against the widely held assumption that environmental protection is at odds with production. IPM workers in Nicaragua have reduced pesticide use by developing alternative means of pest control, while demonstrating that output can be maintained and perhaps increased. IPM maximizes the use of naturally available nonchemical insect controls. In Nicaragua natural predators of pests have been introduced into cotton fields (with the help of technical assistance from the West German government). IPM also works to see that chemical pesticides are used only when careful scouting of the pest populations indicates they are needed. (Contrast that with the practice promoted by the multinational chemical companies of scheduled sprayings—"If it's Tuesday, it must be time to spray.")

But IPM's principal technique in Nicaragua has been "trap cropping." Trap cropping involves leaving four rows of cotton plants standing for every two acres of land when the rest of the plants have been plowed under after the harvest. These plants are the "trap" between seasons to which the boll weevils are attracted. Workers trained in safe techniques treat the trap crops daily with organophosphate pesticides, which, although extremely toxic unlike the organochlorines such as DDT, leave no lasting residues in the environment. Before planting the commercial crop, another trap is planted next to what remains of the existing one and treated until the commercial crop sets fruit. Trap cropping has been shown to postpone the need for pesticide treatments on the commercial cotton crop until much later in the season, greatly reducing the total amount applied.

In 1982 a pilot program in trap cropping was carried out on 41,000 acres, approximately one-sixth the area planted that year in cotton. The private and state farms in the program used only one-third the pesticides applied on farms outside the program, and produced slightly higher yields. Pest control costs were cut 63 percent, for a net savings of $2.14 million, even after figuring in additional labor and other costs. (To put that in perspective, the total earnings from cotton exports that year came to $87 million.)

This success went a long way toward combating the skepticism prevailing in the agricultural ministry and among private growers. The government expanded the program to cover three times the acreage in 1983. The national university in

León now offers a three-year masters program in integrated pest management mainly for technicians already employed on state and private cotton farms. At the university, IPM techniques are also being developed for controlling such health problems as malaria-bearing mosquitoes. This is of worldwide importance in the face of the resurgence throughout the third world of malaria from mosquitoes resistant to DDT and other chemical insecticides.

IPM practitioners emphasize that the agrarian reform makes it possible to ensure that all farms in a given area participate in the program. This coordinated approach is essential to successful implementation of biological pest controls. It also reinforces the Sandinistas' emphasis on local control and human resources development. Integrated pest management cannot be implemented by sweeping centralized decisions, but requires training numerous local managers and workers. The Ministry of Agriculture coordinates local weekly meetings of government and private pest-control technicians to evaluate area ecological conditions and to devise coordinated control tactics.

In many cotton-growing areas bean and corn production had been curtailed by the ecological disruption caused by the pesticide treadmill. With IPM in greater use, these staples can be reintroduced into the area. Thus, successfully reducing pesticide use in cotton production ultimately favors the agrarian reforms's goal of food self-reliance for Nicaragua.

SEVENTEEN

THE FOREIGN EXCHANGE BOTTLENECK

E VERY FRIDAY MORNING ON THE TOP FLOOR
of the government house, a high-level economic council
convenes to divvy up on a case-by-case basis Nicaragua's
exceedingly scarce foreign exchange. How much this week for
fuel, how much for fertilizer, how much for medicines, how
much for toilet paper, how much for cooking oil: all this will
be decided before noon.

The acute and worsening shortage of foreign exchange
overshadows every facet of Nicaragua's economic situation.
The crisis has "loomed" perhaps from the start. By 1981,
however, the crisis was overwhelming and all-pervasive: today
divisas (foreign exchange) is a household word even in rural
settings where a few years ago it hardly would have been
recognized.

The figures are alarming. So alarming for so long, they have
become numbing.

Nicaragua consistently spends far more on imports than it
earns from exports. In 1984, Nicaragua earned $386 million
from its exports (about 82 percent generated by agriculture).
Yet imports totaled $826 million.

Nicaragua will also have to lay out an additional $192
million for what economists charmingly call "invisibles." The
lion's share—$110 million—goes for interest and principal

167

payments on the foreign debt. (Debt "service" in 1984 would have been $180 million, but Nicaragua succeeded in negotiating part of the interest due into more debt.)

The $632 million total deficit (exports minus imports plus invisibles) in 1984 comes despite emergency austerity measures instituted in 1982 that slashed imports by 22 percent. At the start of 1984 imports were projected at $940 million, but by September the foreign-exchange shortage forced a further scaling down of imports. "We were cutting from what we had thought there was nothing left to cut from," commented one top government economist.

Lack of production is not the cause of the deficit: through 1984 Nicaragua has maintained and, in some cases, even boosted the volume of some of its key exports. In 1983, for instance, the total volume of exports—the tons of coffee, sugar, cotton—rose 10 percent compared to the previous year. But due to depressed international prices, Nicaragua received less than 1 percent additional revenue in exchange. Worse still, the prices for what Nicaragua imports have tended to rise. In 1983 Nicaragua had to export an average of 11 percent more just to buy the same goods it had imported the year before (see table 12). At 1978 prices, 1984 imports would cost only an estimated $500 million, somewhat in line with the country's export earnings.

The 1984 balance-of-payments gap comes on top of deficits almost as great each previous year of the revolution (see table 12). Yearly borrowing to cover the deficit has racked up an ever more crushing debt. By the close of 1983, the foreign debt stood at two-and-one-half times what it had been just after the overthrow of Somoza. (Interestingly, half of the new debt was to other third-world countries.) Total foreign debt will approach $4 billion by the end of 1984.

Snowballing debt makes the goal of narrowing the balance-of-payments gap ever more elusive. In 1982, 48 cents out of every dollar Nicaragua earned went to foreign creditors. In 1983, Nicaragua gained precious breathing space by convincing some of its creditors to convert the interest on short-term debt into medium- and long-term loans. While the Reagan administration has done all in its power to isolate Nicaragua from Western financial sources, private U.S. banks have agreed to reschedule their loans to Nicaragua. This is not as surprising as it might at first seem. Since third-world default ranks as nightmare *número uno* for many banks, they undoubtedly prefer to reschedule payments.

Ominously, in 1985 Nicaragua is scheduled to commence larger repayments on the Somoza debt, owed in great part to U.S. banks. The weakness of Nicaragua's position is underscored because much of the interest is pegged to the U.S. prime rate. A 1-percent hike in the U.S. prime rate ups the annual interest on Nicaragua's foreign debt by an amount greater than the total earnings from its record 1981–82 sugar harvest.

The deteriorating terms of trade, the balance-of-payment deficits, and the accumulating debt come on top of an unknown amount of capital flight (see table 14 and chapter 5); and the estimated $380 million the contra war had cost Nicaragua by the end of 1984 — much of it in foreign exchange.

If sizeable foreign-exchange shortfalls are nothing new for the Nicaraguan revolution, what is new is the much tougher scramble to get new loans to cover the deficits. Borrowing came easy during the relatively halcyon days of the revolutions' first two years, coinciding with the Carter administration. Nicaragua's two principal lenders then were those bastions of international capitalism, the World Bank and the Inter-American Development Bank. Perhaps borrowing was *too* easy. One of the most frequent self-criticisms of the Sandinista leadership is that early in the revolution the government "normalized" the economy rather than imposing austerity measures from the start. Credits in the first couple of years flowed in so abundantly from a sympathetic world that Nicaragua lacked sufficient "absorption capacity." (This proved a blessing-in-disguise when these credits, in some cases two and three years old, served to cover part of the trade deficits in 1982 and 1983.

But once an overtly hostile administration in Washington came to power, the United States began using its leverage and veto power in the World Bank and the Inter-American Development Bank to block virtually all loans to Nicaragua and even to freeze some funds in the "pipeline" from previously authorized loans.

The denial of additional loans by official international agencies and private banks can be attributed in part to Nicaragua's cloudy repayment prospects. But the real barriers are the political decisions of U.S. foreign policymakers. Nicaragua hardly stands alone mired in economic crisis and over its head in foreign debt. Neighboring Costa Rica is in even greater per-capita debt and in an economic crisis worse than Nicaragua's, with even fewer longer-term economic development hopes to cling to. But because U.S. policymakers have decided that Costa Rica cannot be allowed to go under and have assigned it the role of staging ground for counterrevolutionary commandos, it continues to receive extraordinary loans from the very sources now closed to Nicaragua. In El Salvador, where the economy is in shambles, the United States makes even more blatant the political criterion for lending and throws good money after bad, even though U.S. government investigations attest that much of it winds up in the Miami bank accounts of the Salvadoran elite. In Chile, with the highest per-capita debt in Latin America, poor economic prospects, and a notorious human-rights record, the Pinochet dictatorship has obtained the Reagan administration's support for $1.2 billion in new loans from the official international lending agencies, even in violation of U.S. law prohibiting aid to gross and consistent violators of human rights.

For the foreseeable future, Nicaragua's economy will continue to depend greatly on continued international support. This is a worrisome prospect, since the Reagan administration has been hard at work discrediting the Nicaraguan revolution in the eyes of sympathetic governments and political parties in Western Europe and Latin America. The administration is reported to have pressured NATO allies and Mexico, Venezuela, and Brazil to cut off aid. By late 1984, West Germany all but ended direct aid to Nicaragua. West Germany had been an important source of loans and grants to Nicaragua.

Assistance from Eastern Europe and the Soviet Union has proven to be of limited economic value. Nicaragua's technological and cultural ties to the United States and Western Europe run deep. Only dollar or dollar-convertible loans that can be freely applied enable Nicaragua to keep existing machinery running (needed replacement parts are seldom compatible with those made in the Soviet-allied countries), to import familiar consumer goods, and to make payments on its outstanding foreign debt. In 1983 Nicaragua was still getting almost 20 percent of its imports from the United States. What has been forthcoming from the East has been not dollárs but "tied" aid—loans good only for purchasing commodities from the lending country.

What is the impact of the foreign exchange crisis?

There is much less available to buy in Nicaragua these days. During the first three years of the revolution, I recall many foreign visitors marveling, even a bit scandalized, at the abundance of U.S.-produced nonessentials—from California wines to Fisher-Price toys—in Managua's *supermercados*. Rich and middle-class Nicaraguans, like their counterparts in other third-world countries, have consumer aspirations straight from Madison Avenue. Accordingly, most of what they desire must be imported. For as long as possible the Sandinistas consciously opted to try to maintain their consumption levels while seeking advances in nutrition, health, and education for the majority of Nicaraguans. This was understood as part of the price of maintaining as much national unity as possible in the face of Washington's hostility to the revolution. By mid-1982, economic and military war, combined with unprecedented flooding and a crop-destroying drought, made such coddling no longer affordable. (Some had always thought it excessive or at least ultimately futile.) The reductions in imported consumer goods were fairly sweeping. By 1984, only 35 consumer items were available for every 100 items before the revolution.

Most of us, I suspect, would never cry over Nicaragua having to stop the importation of "luxury" goods. But drawing the line is complicated. Much of what we in North America and Western Europe take for granted is ever more likely in Nicaragua to count as a luxury import—toilet paper, toothpaste, over-the-counter medications, baby articles. Even pencils. By 1984, office staff in MIDINRA were allotted only one pencil a month; but as one MIDINRA economist joked, there's usually no paper to write on anyway. Thus, austerity can wear down many middle-class urban Nicaraguans. Even peasants and farmworkers, who in the first years of the revolution became familiar with consumer items they had never before used, now complain when they are hard to obtain. The shortages created opportunities for those who would propagandize against any society attempting the necessary changes to make the majority able to meet their basic needs.

Cutting consumer imports also undermines incentives for producers. Hardest-hit have been large commercial agricultural growers and ranchers. Their tastes run to cars, video recorders, stereos, stylish clothing, and shopping trips to Miami. But many more modest consumer items—radios, lighters, handmills, baking powder—desired by peasant and farmworker families must also be imported and are now being curtailed.

Nicaragua's foreign-exchange and borrowing crunch has a severe impact on the acquisition of productive inputs and machinery—fertilizers, seeds, pesticides, tractors, spare parts, lubricants, etc.—and not just for the "modern" sector. In the first couple years of the revolution it was commonplace for advisors to suggest that, if the foreign-exchange picture got rough, campesino producers, in contrast to modernized producers, would not require much in the way of imported inputs. Give them their machetes and mules and they'll keep on producing—that was the basic idea. It turns out that the machetes are imported (and the campesinos want *curved* machetes from El Salvador, not straight ones from Columbia!) as are nails for shoeing for the mule. In fact, in September 1984 I was shown an incredibly long list of imported supplies Nicaraguan campesinos consider vital. Some items that stick in my memory are resin for machete handles, pills to set cheese, and needles. We, the advisors, had simply failed to appreciate how fundamental import-dependence is to the Nicaraguan economy.

Much of what Nicaragua can still import is tied to specific credits determining what and where it can buy. A loan from, say, Spain is now unlikely to be a blank check to shop, even in Spain. Credits tend to be specified for "big ticket" items, such as an electronic pivot-irrigation system (manufactured in Spain by the Nebraska-based Valley Irrigation, Inc.). These are often newly developed items for which the lending country wishes to develop its overseas market. One is not likely to get credits for wire, machetes, spare parts, boots, veterinary supplies—the small, unexciting items that are crucial to maintaining production. For those, one needs cash.

This problem was brought home for me in June 1984, when I was interviewing medium and large private producers of chickens and eggs. The industry's output was stagnating in their estimation but not because of a lack of know-how or producer unwillingness. There were good profits to be made, even before recent hikes in the government-regulated prices for chickens and eggs. Several of the producers wished to expand their operations.

The producers were finding that they couldn't get essential inputs, almost all of which must be imported—hens, fertile eggs, day-old chicks, balanced feed, antibiotics. The largest egg producer in the country, whose production was seriously down, had not been able to buy new laying hens since October. The average age of the hens exceeded the recommended maximum age; without new hens, productivity soon would plummet. Furthermore, many of the hens had gotten out of their cages and were running wild (and thus laying virtually no eggs) because the nearby Santiago volcano had released into the atmosphere sulfuric acid, which was eating away the wire on the hens' cages. Wire is not manufactured in Nicaragua. There were no foreign credits for chicken wire and it simply wasn't being imported. The only antibiotics another major producer had been able to obtain came as a donation from the Wisconsin Partners Program. The boxes bore expiration dates three months past. Interestingly, none of the producers thought the state poultry farms were getting favored access to inputs. As the general manager of the largest egg farm told me, "Things are tough for everyone. We all share the same scarcity."

Without the customary flow of imported inputs, the revolution's advances in agricultural production are jeopardized. This syndrome is, of course, a vicious circle: the more agricultural output drops, the less foreign exchange is generated and the more production is crippled.

Inadequate foreign exchange had left spare parts for farm

machinery and vehicles in short supply, causing increasing, seemingly irrational, drains on production. One agricultural ministry official was telling me of his frustration at not being able to get the foreign exchange to import a few small parts needed for a combine while a new combine was obtained on credit from an Eastern European country. On many large farms, machines are being "cannibalized"—taken apart to create parts to get other machines rolling again. In one region every ministry jeep must be shared by five agricultural extension agents, exacerbating the shortage of technicians.

Importing only from countries that extend credits also means that Nicaragua will wind up with a patchwork of agricultural machinery. One state farm we visited in 1984 had tractors from the United States (Ford and International Harvester), the German Democratic Republic (Fortshritt), Italy, the Soviet Union, Spain, Brazil, and Mexico, and some were expected from Bulgaria. Maintenance problems in the third world are difficult enough without having a hodgepodge of a dozen different types of tractors, all with their idiosyncratic designs and spare parts. Even cannibalizing is made more difficult. I could not help but wonder how many of the tractors would still be operating on our next visit.

* * *

My experience (confirmed by a nationwide opinion survey carried out in June 1983) suggests that most Nicaraguans do not blame the *divisas* crisis on their government. Instead they view the crisis as part of what they have come to refer to as "Washington's war of attrition." With the re-election of President Reagan, an end to that war of attrition—and to Nicaragua's mounting economic woes—was nowhere in sight.

EIGHTEEN
THE
LABOR CRISIS

I N 1983–84, COTTON FELL TO THE GROUND unharvested for want of workers in the cotton fields. This labor shortage would have been even worse had International Harvester and John Deere cotton combines not harvested over one-quarter of Nicaragua's cotton acreage. The harvesters had been imported over the previous three years at the cost of millions of dollars. For coffee, there were so few regular workers that one-third of those participating in the harvest were volunteers (Nicaraguan and foreigners). They worked at an estimated one-quarter efficiency of professionals and some unwittingly damaged the trees, thus harming future production. Lack of workers resulted in a late sugar cane harvest (fortunately possible because the rainy season started late), but a late harvest means lower yields and higher costs.

One reason for the serious shortage of workers in Nicaragua's export agriculture is historical. There have consistently not been enough Nicaraguans for the harvests since the rapid expansion of export crops in the early 1950s. Migrant workers used to enter Nicaragua from Honduras and El Salvador. Now this source of labor has been shut off because of the war and because payments in Nicaraguan córdobas can no longer be converted into dollars.

In some areas the agrarian reform's distribution of farmland to landless farmworkers has resulted to some extent in the feared falloff in the number of persons seeking work in the harvests, despite their "moral commitment" when they received the land. In those areas, Minister Jaime Wheelock talks of establishing belts of cooperatives around the state farms. The cooperative members' greater organization and commitment to the revolution is likely to make them more readily available for employment when they are needed.

Defense mobilizations for the army and the volunteer militia have taken many workers away from the fields. The fear of contra attacks has further reduced the labor force available for the coffee harvest in northern Nicaragua. During Christmas 1982 a contra band descended on a coffee farm at Wambuco near the Honduran border. They kidnapped several coffee pickers whom they took by force to their military camp. Among those kidnapped were Felipe and Maria Eugenia Barreda. A married couple from Estelí, the Barredas were highly esteemed for their deep Christian commitment and had volunteered to help with the harvest. According to witnesses who had also been kidnapped and later escaped, the Barredas were cruelly tortured, then murdered, and their bodies mutilated. In the 1983–84 harvest alone 180 workers belonging to the ATC were killed.

Inadequate Wages

A more troubling reason, however, why it is ever more difficult to find enough workers for the harvests—and even for year-round farm work—is increasingly unattractive wages.

True, before the revolution, the official minimum wage was seldom paid to agricultural workers, especially women. One has to be careful, therefore, not simply to compare the official minimum agricultural wage before the revolution and in, say, 1984. For now the minimum wage is enforced—largely because workers are no longer afraid to speak up and are widely organized in unions. Furthermore, workers have successfully demanded free and improved workday meals. In some places (but in our experience by no means all) living conditions have also been improved.

It is true as well that workers' declining purchasing power has been offset by a "social wage" in the form of free health and educational services. Fringe benefits probably covered the decline in purchasing power from 1980 through 1982. Since then inflation has started to erode its effect. More alarming, the government-provided benefits are increasingly threatened by the economic crisis precipitated by foreign aggression. Defense spending represented less than 7 percent of the national budget in 1980 and 1981. But it increased to 13 percent in 1982, 19 percent in 1983, and 25 percent in 1984, and would have been higher were it not for foreign grants of defense material. These increases have forced cutbacks in spending on health and education. As of July 1984, the government had frozen any planned new projects in health and education facilities. The cutbacks decrease the "social wage" of all workers, agricultural and otherwise. The effects, however, are more sharply felt in the countryside where cash earnings tend to be much lower.

It is also true that the government has sought to offset declining wages by making some of the most basic consumer goods available at low, subsidized prices (see chapter 13). But as the economic crisis has worsened, finding essential groceries and other basics at the official prices has become easier said than done in many places. And not all the items in the basic "basket" of goods every working-class family needs are included in the official controlled price program. (More on government efforts to keep prices in line with working-family incomes in chapters 22 and 23.)

Agricultural wages that buy less and less not only do not attract workers but also tend to erode the incentive for better worker productivity. As a result, more workers are needed to do the same amount of work, exacerbating the labor shortage. During the time in which two rows used to be planted, a government economist told us, only one gets planted now. For many the length of the workday has officially and unofficially been shortened. (A Chilean dairy technician who manages a large state farm first complained to us about the low productivity of the workers; then he shrugged his shoulders and added, "But what can you expect when their wages are so miserably low?")

The government continued through 1983 to officially hold the line in wage hikes for all workers. Its position was that until Nicaragua could afford to import more goods, wage and salary increases would be "demagogic" since more money in the hands of workers would just heat up inflation and leave the workers no better off. Comandante Wheelock and other Sandinista leaders have personally continued to try to convince workers that, justified as they are, their wage demands simply cannot now be met satisfactorily.

The right to strike was suspended as one of the emergency measures taken in 1982. The measures came in response to the bombing of two vital bridges—shortly after disclosure by the *Washington Post* that President Reagan had authorized CIA covert destabilization operations in Nicaragua, including the bombing of bridges. The suspension of the right to strike has been highly controversial among many Sandinistas and their supporters. It has also provided occasion for *La Prensa* and other right-wing elements to take opportunistic advantage. In my opinion the suspension was ill-considered. Only a revolutionary leadership lacking in self-confidence resorts to an authoritarian infringement of one of the workers' most sacred rights—one systematically denied to Nicaraguan workers under the Somoza dictatorship. Of course, I am once again painfully aware how my government deliberately seeks to pressure the Nicaraguan government to restrict freedoms. In August 1984, as part of the pre-election lifting of various aspects of the emergency decree, the legal right to strike was restored. In November 1984, I was told by Isodoro Tellez, a leader of Nicaragua's Marxist-Leninist labor union that had been virtually banned by the Sandinista-led government, that since July the union has been "absolutely free" to organize. In the fall of 1984 we found that government planners were anticipating a wave of strikes and were worried about the impact on the country's fragile economy.

Even when the strike ban was in effect there were strikes. Both non-Sandinista and Sandinista labor unions organized stoppages over poor working conditions, management behavior, and low wages. One of the most notable of these "stoppages," as they were called, occurred at the San Antonio sugar refinery, the largest agroindustrial plant in the country.

In no case was military or police force used by the government, as invariably happened during the Somoza dictatorship when workers were sometimes killed for striking. The Sandinistas understood that once strikes were declared illegal, they became prime vehicles for counterrevolutionary provocation. Repression by the Sandinistas would be a shot heard around the world. Therefore, the Sandinista government's response to strikes and stoppages, one government insider told me, has been publicly to talk tough and quietly to make quick concessions.

Despite its good theoretical reasons for not doing so, the government submitted to political "realism" and by mid-1983 initiated steps to raise wages. The first step was to finalize plans to revamp the wage and salary scale. The plan was to institute the principle of equal pay for equal work, as a prelude to raising the minimum. Over the years people doing one type of work on one farm wound up getting paid significantly more than someone on another farm doing the same work. The plan would have gone into effect in October but was delayed because of the nationwide, spontaneous alarm produced by the U.S. invasion of Grenada. When the plan finally went into effect over a seven-month period in 1984, we found widespread discontent especially among office workers. It seems that most people assumed that any wage and salary reform would mean that their earnings would go up. Of course, not everyone's did. Only 60 percent of workers got a nominal increase.

Not surprisingly, government policymakers are especially interested in raising wages for productive work in agriculture. Before the 1984–85 export-crop harvests, the agricultural minimum daily wage was raised a substantial 57 percent. Since much harvest labor is paid according to the amount collected, piece rates were similarly increased. The payment per can of coffee picked, for instance, was hiked from 14 to 21 córdobas. Under consideration is an ATC proposal that the amount paid per unit harvested increase the more one harvests, as a way to reward greater worker productivity.

Another type of labor problem facing Nicaraguan agriculture is that agricultural technicians and administrators, in short supply, can be lured away from government to private employment, and away from Nicaragua to abroad. By mid-1984, the salary of a state-farm administrator had fallen to the equivalent of $60 a month, taking the black market rate for córdoba exchanges. (On one hand, the dollar equivalency is misleading, since living expenses would be in córdobas, not dollars; on the other hand, with the shortages, someone of the administrator's social class is likely to desire to shop in Costa Rica and that requires dollars.) An administrator's salary on a comparable private farm would be several times greater. One vice minister of agriculture, who before the revolution was a prosperous agricultural producer ("everything from sugar cane to race horses") and a clandestine collaborator with the Sandinistas, told us in June 1984 that he had lost six top assistants to multinational agribusiness companies and U.S. universities. "It's another form of aggression," he commented.

Some have suggested that on balance Nicaragua is better off without technicians who quit for higher salaries or the wonders of life abroad since their attitudes often go against the grain of what the revolution is about. "They treat the workers like peons. The last thing they'd do is help a worker learn anything," one Basque veterinarian working on a large state dairy farm told me.

Picking Versus Selling

Perhaps the knottiest problem involving agricultural wage policy is that more and more Nicaraguans are finding that they can earn much more in commercial activity, so-called non-productive work. For example, a person who can put together a rough-hewn cart, buy a block of ice and get some sweetened fruit colorings to sell snow cones at a Sunday afternoon baseball game in Managua, can make more money in one day than from three weeks' work on a coffee estate. Even more profitable is reselling toothpaste and toilet paper smuggled in from Costa Rica. Selling coconut milk or flowers at traffic intersections is probably more lucrative than even skilled agricultural labor. One woman in her 30s told me that she had worked in cotton harvests since she was 15, but now she was making "much, much more" selling cold Coke across the street from an army barracks.

Such "informal" activities, to use the economists' term, constitute Nicaragua's biggest and fastest-growing source of employment. Over one-third of the economically active population of Managua (a vastly oversized city for such a slightly populated country) is engaged in buying and reselling. From the individual's point of view (and the customer's) it might seem all to the good. But from the point of view of the national economy, things look quite different. Nicaragua's underdeveloped, export-dependent economy sinks or floats on its production of cotton, coffee, and sugar. When exports fall because of insufficient labor power, that's a problem that sooner or later affects everyone's well-being. Selling and re-selling, while perhaps fulfilling some needed services, not only don't generate foreign exchange, but invariably consume it. (Even blocks of ice are made with electricity generated with imported oil.) The problem is not the existence of a service sector but its great size and expansion out of proportion to the "productive" sector. This deep-rooted distortion is ironic: economic activity that is most important for the nation's survival tends to be the least financially rewarding for the individual.

One approach toward a solution that the government has halfheartedly pursued is to mechanize agriculture. To many, this sounds anathema. Why would the Sandinistas, of all people, be interested in big equipment manufactured by multinational agribusiness giants? The Sandinista planners reason that without mechanization what one worker produces is not worth enough on the world market to pay wages that would attract anyone to agricultural work. With mechaniza-tion, however, output per worker would jump significantly, making higher wages feasible. Machinery should also make work less backbreaking as well as attracting to agriculture more young people who now have opportunities for training as machinery operators and mechanics.

By both reducing the total number of workers required and making agricultural work more attractive, the mechanization approach holds out promise for easing the agricultural labor shortage at least in the cotton and sugar cane harvests, which are more readily mechanized than coffee. But in the face of military and economic aggression, Nicaragua's capacity to afford and to get spare parts for imported machinery is a big question. (In June 1984 several time bombs were found hidden inside a shipment of cotton harvesters coming overland from Honduras.)

* * *

Nicaragua shares its labor crisis with many third-world countries. In seeking to maintain a free-market economy, Nicaragua has avoided the "Cuban solution." Rather than outlawing private selling and making employment obligatory for adult males, as Cuba did in the late 1960s, Nicaragua is seeking noncoercive, market-based solutions to a difficult problem of national development. Many third-world countries could benefit from Nicaragua's experience. But since it is war more than anything else that undermines Nicaragua's supply of goods and makes smuggling and speculative commerce so lucrative, headway toward a solution is unlikely unless the military and economic war on Nicaragua is stopped.

NINETEEN

LOOKING AHEAD: IS THERE A WAY OUT?

IT IS EASY TO BE DEPRESSED ABOUT THE economic prospects of most third-world nations. Nicaragua is certainly no exception. Nicaragua exports raw commodities—bales of cotton, sacks of coffee beans, boat-loads of sugar, sides of beef—to other countries where the processors and final marketers make most of the profits. All the commodities are readily obtainable elsewhere; Nicaragua is in no position to hold out for a better deal. Most countries competing with Nicaragua, in fact, are willing to exploit their workers far more than Nicaragua. With no oil and little industrial production, Nicaragua finds itself importing much more than it exports; and import prices are rising faster than export prices (see table 11). At the same time its citizens have rising expectations for more industrial consumer goods. Not surprisingly, indebtedness mounts; the interest alone could soon outstrip export earnings. A vicious circle sets in: Foreign exchange is so tight that cutbacks have to be made even of imported inputs that are needed for production of exports to earn foreign exchange. Sustaining many of the revolution's advances in health and education increasingly depends on foreign charity. As we said, the big picture can be depressing.

In most countries facing such a crisis today, those who control the wealth and economic decisions are scrambling for a way out—for themselves. They're disinvesting, liquidating whatever they can in order to transfer as much wealth as possible into foreign bank accounts and investments. There is no vision of a way out for the nation.

But Nicaragua is different, and clearly it is the revolution that has made the difference possible. The Nicaraguan government is investing heavily in a series of calculated-risk, large-scale projects. Some of the country's planners and economic advisors think that these long-term projects could be the *salida*, the way out for the Nicaraguan economy.

The vision of the *salida* goes something like this:

—Nicaragua is investing in its first Atlantic coast deep-water port and a railroad to connect it to the Pacific coast deep-water ports. By the late 1990s, Nicaragua would export to Europe, the Middle East, and the Atlantic Coast of North America without the expensive and delay-fraught passage through the Panama Canal. Also, offering the world an "overland canal" would generate significant income for Nicaragua. At the same time, the port and rail network would facilitate the development of the country's entire Atlantic coast.

—With financing from Spain, Nicaragua is building a new railroad to link the Pacific port of Corinto with Managua. Transferring the cargo that passes through Corinto from truck to rail will save an estimated $15 to $20 million a year in diesel fuel imports.

—Nicaragua is putting one-quarter of its investment budget into several geothermal power and hydroelectric schemes. The short-term goal is to replace the present oil-fired electricity-generating plants with geothermal ones by the end of the decade. In 1982, Nicaragua spent $25 million importing 1 million barrels of oil for generating electricity. The first geothermal plant, at the base of picturesque Momotombo Volcano, already came on line in 1983. It produces 35 megawatts of electricity from a huge turbine driven by the force of naturally generated steam. The geothermal technology is from Japanese and Italian corporations. Momotombo is but the first in a planned series of geothermal energy projects. Short-term hydroelectric investments include new dams to increase the output of existing turbines. In the longer term, the Soviet Union will assist in the construction of two massive dams in the Atlantic Coast region. By the 1990s, Nicaragua would be a major surplus generator of electricity, selling it to its Central American neighbors through the already existent Central American power grid.

—Abundant electricity from renewable sources would favor the development of a textile industry. Nicaragua would no longer export raw cotton, and import cloth and clothing. Nicaragua has started construction of its *first* thread plant, scheduled to open in 1986.

—Abundant electricity from renewable sources would help make economically feasible a steel mill built with aid from North Korea and using scrap metal inexpensively brought in over both oceans.

—Abundant, inexpensive electricity would aid in pumping underground water for irrigation of much of the fertile Pacific coastal plains. Irrigation would allow for an extra crop, such as corn or beans, during the dry season in rotation with cotton.

—Nicaragua is investing in the largest and most efficient sugar plantation and mill in Central America, with financing and credit from Cuba and Spain. Sugar would be produced at the lowest cost in Latin America. The mill's boilers would also generate electricity from the combustion of cane waste products and fast-growing trees between cane harvests. Sugar refining would also produce 70,000 tons of molasses a year as a by-product. A top-notch cattle feed, the molasses could be used to increase beef production for domestic consumption and profitable exports to North America and Japan. Under consideration, with possible financing from Brazil to import Brazilian technology, is producing gasohol from sugar to replace about 35 percent of the gasoline consumed in Nicaragua and make the country less dependent on imported oil.

—Nicaragua is investing in a 10,000-acre tobacco project with financing from Bulgaria. In a joint venture with the giant multinational British American Tobacco and the Bulgarian government, cigarettes will be rolled in Bulgaria and eventually in Nicaragua for BAT brands to be marketed in Eastern Europe (described by BAT as the "last great untapped cigarette market"). Negotiations are underway, I am told, to sell the leaf tobacco to Miami-based Cuban cigar companies ("business is business"). Rosy projections put tobacco revenue in 1990 at $80 million a year. Tobacco cultivation and curing are expected to generate a large number of jobs.

—Nicaragua is investing, with financing from Holland, in African oil palm schemes to generate employment in zones not suitable for tilled agriculture. Palm oil would supply much of the nation's consumption of cooking oil; current levels of cottonseed output have been inadequate to meet rising demand. Palm oil could also provide a high-grade machine oil and another possible substitute for gasoline.

—Nicaragua is investing, with financing from Bulgaria, in a major vegetable and fruit producing and processing project. Not only would local availability improve, but Nicaragua would become an exporter of everything from canned tomatoes to canned pineapples for Eastern Europe, the Middle East, the Central American Common Market, and the Caribbean. The steel milling plant mentioned on the previous page would reduce the need for imported canning materials.

—Nicaragua is investing in a rubber tree scheme. Rubber could be used for retreading tires. If world petroleum prices soar again in the 1990s, natural rubber prices would boom.

—Nicaragua is investing, with credits and technical assistance from Brazil, in cocoa plantations to be cooperatively owned by Miskitu Indians. A processing plant to be built on the Atlantic coast will generate employment, eliminate chocolate imports, and open the way for a new export.

—Nicaragua is investing in two enormous dairy schemes with improved irrigated pastures. There are plans for 21,000 cows in the "smaller" scheme—and seven times that in the other! In the 1990s, Nicaragua will aim at consuming much more milk and cheese without the need to import, a formidable achievement in the tropics.

—In the long term—and with an estimated $1.4 billion in 1980 dollars—Nicaragua could develop the 500-million-barrel oil field thought to lie off its Pacific coast.

Nowhere else in the Caribbean Basin, a region mired in an economic crisis worse than the 1930s depression, is there so much public investment in the future. Between 1978 and 1982, imports of machinery and other capital goods for agriculture shot up 400 percent as a percentage of the GNP in Nicaragua, while they fell 60 percent in Guatemala and 75 percent in Costa Rica. For agricultural and agroindustrial projects, Nicaragua is using or counting on credit lines and loans from Japan, Argentina, Spain, Cuba, France, Sweden, Holland, Brazil, Bulgaria, Mexico, Yugoslavia, West Germany, Libya, Italy, and East Germany.

Will It Work?

Of course, chickens should never be counted before the eggs are hatched. Most of the projects are high risk—and maybe all are, given Nicaragua's circumstances. It remains to be seen whether they will pay off. If they fail, they will leave the country hopelessly in debt.

Frankly, the agricultural projects I have visited have left me queasy—and for reasons I fear may be equally true for at least some of the nonagricultural projects.

First off, I have been struck by what often appears to be an overbelief in high technology. This seeming naivete about the technical, economic, and social pitfalls in green revolution-type technology is often reinforced by advisors and aid agencies, including those from socialist countries. (If anything, technofascination seems more alive and well in the ag schools in Moscow, Havana, and Sofia than in their counterparts in the United States, Canada, and Western Europe.)

The high-tech approach is especially disconcerting when less capital-intensive and import-dependent alternatives seem available, even for the same project. The Chiltepe dairy scheme, for example, includes a giant electrically powered pivot-irrigation system to draw up underground water for the pastures. Chiltepe, however, would seem ideal for windmills.

Also, Chiltepe borders the shore of the large Lake Managua, offering an alternative to depleting the underground water supply. The Chiltepe project includes constructing milking parlors (for the latest Swedish electric milkers) fully out of concrete (using imported cement), when wooden ones (perhaps made from the trees being torn down for the pastures) would do just as well in Nicaragua's climate. The cows are purebreds flown in from Canada, which may have difficulty adjusting to Nicaragua's climatic conditions.

And what about labor-intensive, peasant-based alternatives to the whole project? Within the highest levels of the ministry it has been suggested that with a modicum of technical assistance peasant farmers with one or two cows giving a single liter of milk a day could double their cow's production. While an extra liter of milk might not sound like much, when multiplied by the hundreds of thousands of such cows, the increased output could easily equal the total milk produced by an enormous capital-intensive scheme aiming to boost several thousand cows' output five or six liters each.* And the added income for tens of thousands of poor farmers would surely result in increased support for the revolution.

The high-tech approach is also disconcerting in a country with few technicians and a working class generally with little technical experience. As a result, such projects tend to be centrally controlled. Centralization runs counter to the goal of democratizing access to and control over economic resources. At the same time, the workers' lack of experience with machinery leads to new problems. These include: shoddy maintenance (on one new state farm we saw dozens of expensive tractors and combines without any shelter, exposed to torrential downpours); obliviousness to the importance of technical data (on the same farm we were told that workers supposedly recording data from the electronically controlled pumps would write it on the backs of their hands and more than once lose it all in washing up); and improper use of equipment (not cleaning the cows' teats before attaching the milker, for instance—the state-farm manager commented that it was hard to ask them to do such things since the

---

* Chiltepe's milk, of course, can more easily be marketed in Managua. Without refrigeration, many peasant farmers turn their cows milk into cheese, a staple in the Nicaraguan diet.

workers themselves lived in such foul barracks).

. With the country's technically qualified human resources stretched to the hilt (especially with the war), Nicaragua seems in some cases to be rushing headlong into projects without the time or capacity for feasibility studies or pilot projects. In June 1984, we visited San Ramón, a new high-tech state farm created to rotate irrigated corn with cotton. Located in a particularly hot, arid zone, it is a virgin farm, part of the emergency food production plan. (We will look at the emergency plan—and San Ramón—in detail in chapter 21.) There is a bevy of unknowns: Will it really be possible to harvest one crop in time to plant the other? What will pest problems be like with large-scale continuous cropping? What are the underground water resources and where is it best to drill? What will production costs be like and does the venture make financial sense? Would it be better to rotate the cotton with something other than corn (such as beans)? Not only were these and many other problems not studied (or only in the most sketchy fashion), but the first planting of corn was done not on a pilot basis but on a full 3,500 acres.

One also cannot help but question the wisdom of large-scale projects completely dependent upon machinery and inputs that must be imported. Foreign exchange is ever more difficult to come by. Foreign economic aggression at times—such as when the CIA mines harbors—is tantamount to a blockade. My nightmares include a Nicaragua a few years from now with dozens of projects uncompleted and abandoned, fields of rusting machinery and half-completed buildings. Another nightmare is that after the giant new sugar mill is completed, it will be bombed by contras. Already in 1984 some cane fields as well as some of the new tobacco sheds were set afire by contras.

Since the new sugar complex—which has been highly controversial within the agricultural ministry—alone accounts for more than half the total funds in agroindustrial investments, this venture merits our special attention. It is hard not to be concerned about the prospects for sugar. World sugar prices have always been erratic. For the past few years they have been considerably lower than production costs even for efficient producers. World sugar output has significantly outstripped world consumption during this period. Even more alarming, large industrial users, such as food-processing and soft drink companies in the United States, have been switching their plants to high fructose corn sweetener—not to mention the trend to "diet" drinks. For those who look to using sugar for producing alcohol for "gasohol," Brazil's mixed experience is a sobering warning. Proponents of the gigantic sugar project stress that burning cane stalk after processing the sugar and fast-growing trees outside the cane-harvest season will generate electricity. But how useful will that be if the geothermal and hydrothermal projects are successful and make Nicaragua, as already noted, a surplus producer of electricity? Perhaps the most economically attractive aspect of the project is the production of molasses for cattle feed.

With the sugar complex and other large-scale, capital-intensive projects, one final concern is how much administrative, technical, and financial resources they tie up. Especially in a country with limitations like Nicaragua's, a choice to do one thing is a choice not to do something else. Supporters argue that these projects do not use up financial resources because they generate special-purpose loans and credits otherwise unlikely to be available. Spain would give credit for pivot irrigation not for windmills, I am told. Libya wanted to finance something big and flashy. But this perspective seems shortsighted. Not only do the projects deplete the nation's financial resources by greatly increasing foreign indebtedness, they tie up scarce human resources, urgently needed to improve peasant productivity.

This issue came into focus for me when we met a veterinarian assigned to one of the big state dairy farms. He told us of his frustration at being tied down to a single farm when he could be working through the national small and medium producers' organization helping thousands of farmers better their animal breeding and care practices. "This farm is supposed to be a model breeding center to eventually improve the quality of the national herd and to be a center for farmers to come and learn from. But the real-life conditions of the small farmers and even perhaps of the cooperatives are so different from what we have here. I question how useful this showcase ever will be. At best, results will take many, many years. Meanwhile only a handful of Nicaraguans will be aware of

what we are doing here and the revolution misses the chance
to bring small but felt improvements to many thousands, with
far, far less dollar cost."

* * * *

These are important and difficult issues of national development and are ones that few Americans ever hear about. It is
sad that Washington's deliberate fabrication of false issues
about the Nicaraguan revolution deprives the world from
learning about the serious debates and experiments in development issues being conducted in Nicaragua. (If anything,
Washington should be delighted with the investment orientation of the Sandinista revolution; Nicaragua has never been a
better potential customer for capital goods from the United
States and U.S. multinationals.) A major frustration for me in
speaking around the United States and Canada about Nicaragua is that seldom, even in university settings, do I feel I can
share the knotty and fascinating questions raised, or that
should be raised, about the Nicaraguan experience. For all the
time is instead taken up responding for the umpteenth time to
Washington allegations, mostly made, I am convinced, in bad
faith.

Criticizing Nicaragua's development strategies should
never lead us to forget that Washington is Nicaragua's real
problem. Without that problem, I am convinced Nicaraguans
in due course could successfully deal with all these concerns.
And perhaps the essence of the revolution is that Nicaraguans
have earned the right to make their own mistakes.

TWENTY

FOOD FIRST: POLICIES AND RESULTS

"GOD MADE THIS LAND FOR CORN!" exclaims Victorina Sanchez, hands on her hips, looking with satisfaction at the long rows of green, cob-laden stalks. Along with fifteen other former tenant farmers and farmworkers, Victorina, a robust, barefoot peasant, is now part owner of a cooperative farm on the bank of the Gallo River in northern Chinandega. "Before," she tells us, "this farm belonged to a *Somocista*. He let the rich soil grow over with weeds and kept only a small herd of cattle to prevent the likes of us from planting on it." When the owner abandoned the property in the final weeks of the dictatorship, it was first made into a state farm and then, in the spring of 1982, turned over to Victorina and her fellow cooperative members. "All this went to waste before. Now it produces enough grain to feed our 15 families and dozens more. This is the way things were meant to be."

Growing more corn—and beans and rice and all the other foods Nicaraguans need—lies at the heart of the Sandinista revolution. Transforming Nicaragua into a country that would produce harvests bountiful enough for everyone was a primary goal of those who made the revolution. With the triumph over the Somoza dictatorship, realization of that goal quickly became vital to the success of the revolution itself.

As we recounted in the first edition of this book, the insurrection against Somoza severely disrupted Nicaragua's food production, leaving the country more dependent than ever on food imports. In 1979 and 1980, concern that food shortages would hit the poor hardest led the new government to allocate more than 100 million scarce dollars to import food, principally from the United States. At the same time, the government strove to promote domestic production in the hope of rapidly reducing food imports. It extended credit liberally to food-producing campesinos (something virtually unheard of before), set a low maximum rent for land cultivated with food crops, and trucked seeds, fertilizers, and tools into the food-producing interior. Groups of landless farmworkers, eager to work off-season growing their own food crops, were lent, free of charge, unused land on farms expropriated from the *Somocistas.*

In 1981 the arrival of the overtly hostile Reagan administration made achieving national food security more urgent than ever. Soon after inauguration, President Reagan cut off U.S. credits to Nicaragua for wheat imports. His move left no doubt that Nicaragua's aspirations for national self-determination necessitated food self-reliance. Never again could the food well-being of Nicaraguans be left to the mercy of political or market forces outside Nicaragua.

The Promise of PAN

The Sandinista response to Washington's saber-rattling was to launch in April 1981 the National Food Program or PAN (see chapter 12). A "priority program of the revolution," PAN's ambitious mission was to coordinate government agencies as well as private producers and marketers in stepped-up efforts to improve food production and distribution.

The wide variety of PAN measures to boost food production included:

—**Price incentives for food producers.** Government-guaranteed producer prices for corn, beans, rice, and sorghum have been hiked before each planting season. Between 1981 and mid-1984, the government tripled its guaranteed price for corn and raised the price for beans 78 percent. Producer prices for rice and sorghum were tripled and doubled, respectively.

—**Low-interest credit to small-to-medium farmers and to peasant cooperatives.** In the wake of the mixed results of the 1980 credit "spilling" (see chapter 6), lending leveled off and expanded much more gradually thereafter. Nevertheless, in 1984 small- and medium-size independent farmers and cooperative members obtained official bank credit to plant 632,900 acres of corn, beans, and other staple crops. This contrasts sharply with a peak of 34,000 acres before the revolution. In some areas efforts have been made to supply credit in the form of farm inputs such as seeds, tools, and fertilizers since cash loans appeared to play a large part in the peasant credit problems in 1980.

—**New farm-to-market roads.** For generations, Nicaragua's peasants, the backbone of the nation's food production, were pushed off the Pacific coastal plains into the interior highlands. This shifted much of the nation's food cultivation to areas where roads are poor or nonexistent. Delivery of farm inputs, as well as consumer goods (important to help motivate producers), is consequently extremely difficult and costly—as is getting harvests out to market.

A road-building project in such food-producing areas was part of a $7.4 million grant to PAN from the European Economic Community. Alejandro Benavides of the Santa Teresa cooperative described to us the difference a simple road included in that project has made: "Before this year, the only way we could get fertilizer for our corn was to make a two-day muleback trip into Somotillo [the nearest town]. We could bring back only a few bags at a time. But now there's a new road passing right by our cooperative. Last month MIDINRA [Ministry of Agriculture] trucks brought us all the fertilizer and seeds we need. All in one trip! And the ministry's agricultural technicians have already driven out twice to look at our beans since the road was completed."

—**Peasant training.** New Cooperative Development centers have been set up by MIDINRA and UNAG in each of the country's regions. These centers offer workshops and weekly classes in improved farming techniques and cooperative enterprise self-management. Another program, funded in part by an Oxfam America grant, conducts similar nine-month, three-days-a-month training courses for UNAG.

—**Improving and expanding grain-storage capacity.** Traditionally, most peasant producers store their corn crop on the stalk or piled up in the corners of their dirt-floor homes. Postharvest spoilage and birds, rats, and other pests have regularly reduced such supplies by a third or more. Training courses have been given to producers in grain drying (to prevent spoilage) and short-term storage before marketing. In addition, by mid-1984, new grain silos and warehouses built by ENABAS had expanded national storage capacity by one-third over 1979. It is estimated—rather generously we suspect—that from 1980 through 1983 improved storage had already reduced postharvest corn losses by a cumulative total of 300,000 tons, equivalent to an entire year's national consumption.

—**Coordinating and more efficiently allocating scarce transport resources.** Transportation bottlenecks have prevented much farm produce from reaching urban markets. In one case, a private trucking firm had to keep almost half of its vehicles off the road for lack of foreign exchange to import parts and tires. At the same time, ENABAS had an allotment of foreign exchange but was desperately short on trucks to get newly harvested beans and corn to market. PAN brokered a contract by which the transport company got its spare parts and tires while ENABAS got its grain hauled. As the PAN director at that time, Julio Castillo told us, "It isn't in the interest of the government, private truckers, or the Nicaraguan people for trucks to stand idle. Our job is to help get everyone working together, which is in the interest of all."

As the transport crisis has worsened, PAN has sought to coordinate trucking schedules for both state and private firms, pushing to get the most out of existing vehicles. The idea is that a truck carrying, say, sugar from a Chinandega mill to a warehouse in Matagalpa will return loaded with beans from the ENABAS storage center there.

—**Giving idle and underused lands to landless and land-poor farmworkers and peasants.** Many advocates of increased food procution saw the land reform as a means to boost food-crop productivity. Peasant families such as Victorina Sanchez's have been relocated on lands often more fertile than those to which they had historically been restricted.

Efforts to boost food production have not been limited to corn, beans, and the other staples. Agricultural and marketing studies of different fruits and vegetables have been carried out with aims of expanding their cultivation for domestic consumption. At the same time, PAN has pushed for greater government support for small-scale horticulturalists. Credit—channeled primarily toward small farms and cooperatives—for fruit and vegetable production expanded steadily between 1979 and 1984. The hope has been to improve both nutritional well-being and rural incomes.

The state-farm sector has emerged as an important supplier of perishable produce. Some former Somocista lands—immense, and immensely underproductive, cattle ranches on the fertile Pacific coast—have been turned into lush, irrigated fields for vegetables and fruit orchards. PAN also has promoted regional state vegetable farms. Every foreign visitor has seen the 68 acres of squash, tomatoes, watermelon, cucumbers, and other fruits and vegetables planted next to the huge 19th of July Plaza in the heart of Managua. Consumers reap an added advantage from the state-farm role in production: vegetables and fruits from state farms are likely to reach retail markets at the low, official prices.

But PAN has not relied exclusively on state-farm efforts in produce. One high-visibility PAN program has been the Popular Mobilization for Food Self-Sufficiency. The program aims to ensure a year-round supply of fruits and vegetables at affordable prices. Playing the role of coordinator in a decentralized program, PAN has sought to involve every conceivable government agency and popular organization: the Ministry of Agriculture, the National Development Bank, local government councils, and mass-membership organizations such as the National Women's Association (AMNLAE), the urban neighborhood committees (CDS), the UNAG, and the ATC. Since the program was initiated in mid-1983, several thousand backyard, neighborhood, and school gardens have been planted. While government ministries and factories were also slated to start up gardens, we have seen no evidence of them.

Local self-provisioning in perishable produce lowers transport costs, cuts losses due to the lack of storage facilities, and undercuts commercial intermediaries and speculators, who would drive prices beyond the reach of many households. The program has urged farmers to sign production contracts with MIDINRA in hopes of cutting out intermediaries. Those who sign up are promised adequate supplies of seeds, fertilizers and pesticides, spare parts, credit, and technical assistance and are paid stable prices for their crops by the government. Along with state-farm output, the ministry sells the produce directly to the *expendios populares* (people's outlets) and Managua's supermarkets at official prices.

The mass-member organizations have popularized the National Mobilization program in rural areas. Working with the mass media, they disseminate gardening information, nutritional education and even cooking tips (why *pipian* is a terrific veggie for you, easy to grow, and how on earth you make it into a dish that will wow the family). A colorful billboard advertising the benefits for farmers who join the program is now a common sight in the countryside. Technical pamphlets, written in plain language and colorfully illustrated, have been put together for farmers.

In addition, regional training centers, with some eleven hundred farmer alumni by mid-1984, offer hands-on courses on growing techniques, nutrition, and ways to preserve fruit and vegetables. The trainees, it is hoped, return to their communities to spread their newly acquired skills in small-scale horticulture among fellow farmers.

Planting a Future

In the lush, hilly Carazo region, we visited Los Patios ("The Yards"), a project begun in 1983 through local initiative and later coordinated with the national Popular Mobilization for Food Self-Sufficiency. The impetus for Los Patios was that hundreds of peasant families were growing coffee on tiny hillside plots that, due to coffee rust, outmoded cultivation techniques and the lack of funds to modernize, were no longer productive or profitable.

Los Patios aimed to help these scattered small farmers get out of coffee farming and into the more profitable cultivation of vegetables and fruits. By 1984, 620 families had joined the program, more than half forming credit and services associations and production cooperatives. As with other projects in the Popular Mobilization Program, local government institutions joined with branches of the mass-based organizations to provide technical, financial, and organizational support. Los Patios has already become an important source of cabbage, squash, and various tropical fruits for consumers in the neighboring towns, as well as for the producers themselves. Within a few years, its avocado and citrus trees should begin to bear fruit. These perishables sell well on the local market and offer the chance for good profit, even when sold to the government marketing agency at official prices. For the small farmers and cooperative members of this region, Los Patios represents an escape from dead-end coffee production and the road to higher incomes and improved production of nutritious and varied foods.

Disappointments

As of mid-1984, despite real achievements in food production, PAN's overall performance has been disappointing.

PAN has never succeeded in "cracking heads"—in getting everyone to pull together to make food production a priority. Despite gushes of rhetoric, PAN has not benefited from the full Sandinista push that went with, for example, the literacy campaign. In theory, PAN was to be a priority coordinator for a whole gamut of ministries and agencies. In practice, it has been stuck in a bureaucratic limbo, remaining understaffed and lacking a director with the clout necessary to coordinate. (Government ministries and agencies in Nicaragua, as in so many countries, are notorious for operating as competing fiefdoms. They even pirate personnel one from another, which results in a high turnover that compounds inexperience.)

A second area of disappointment is producer prices. Official producer prices have never been high enough to be a strong incentive for most producers. Despite annual increases, prices often have not even covered rising costs, especially for peasant producers getting only a few hundred pounds of corn off an acre. In September 1984, UNAG was publicly complaining more strongly than ever that government prices for corn and beans were below average production costs. †

Inadequate price increases have been one reason why corn supplies have remained tight. Small producers have switched from growing corn for market to other crops they find more profitable. In one area several families who received land through the agrarian reform told us that after two seasons of corn they were now planting sesame. (Sesame production has more than doubled since before the revolution.) Some producers with low corn yields have been making their corn more valuable by feeding it to pigs and chickens and then marketing the animals.

Why has the government been so conservative in raising producer prices? Probably more than anything else, it is because it has felt constrained by mounting national-budget deficits. Every producer price hike translates into bigger deficits and, therefore, higher inflation. Early on, the Sandinista-led government opted to freeze consumer prices for staples (see chapter 13), out of a commitment to making essential foods affordable for the poor majority and to maintain broad urban support for the revolution. The government picked up the tab for the widening gap between the prices paid by consumers

---

† In October 1984 government policymakers *doubled* the producer bean price. This late effort, however, is unfortunately partially undermined by accelerating inflation. By late 1984, the country's emerging inflation has become a planner's nightmare: a new price is likely to be outmoded by the time it goes into effect.

and those offered to producers by ENABAS, the government wholesaler. In addition, the government absorbed all the considerable costs of storing, transporting, processing, and packaging.

An untried alternative would have been to raise official consumer prices gradually from the start to cover at least part of the cost increases. In this way, higher prices could have been offered to farmers to stimulate production without inflating the budget deficit to unmanageable proportions.

Low government-subsidized consumer prices have also undercut production by tempting some farmers simply to buy the corn and beans they need for their own consumption rather than growing them. This "changing hats" phenomenon—producers becoming consumers—has been particularly significant on large coffee and other nongrain farms. Traditionally, these farms set aside land to grow food for their permanent and seasonal workers. But these acreages have in many cases been taken out of grain production since it became cheaper to buy food from ENABAS. By 1983, this disconcerting situation was prevalent enough even on state farms (!) that the government had to direct them to produce food for their workers.

A third disappointment with PAN's performance has been that technical assistance to peasant producers has been woefully inappropriate. Deciding what technical assistance Nicaragua's peasant producers could use has been based on insufficient in-the-field experience with peasants to determine the concrete agricultural constraints they must cope with. (The research arm of the agricultural ministry has done better at getting a true grasp on social and economic constraints on production.) There has been all too much rushing in with a recipe-book mentality of modern technological fixes accompanied by widespread belittling of any effort to develop appropriate techniques.

Here we can hardly single out Nicaragua for criticism. The fact is that in most of the world agricultural research is carried out under ideal conditions. Technical assistance is understood as "extending" a "package" developed by researchers to peasant producers whose soil, water, and drainage situation is invariably less than ideal. "Green revolution" packages of "high-response" (hybrid) seeds and fertilizers (see Food First,

Part IV) have been pushed here and there in Nicaragua. These packages are inappropriate agronomically, and therefore financially, since their considerable additional costs cannot be justified by increased yields, if in fact there are any. (The high-tech approaches brought in from outside also run the risk of total failure; there have been reports that hybrid seeds brought into Nicaragua from Mexico and other places have failed even to germinate—setting off suspicions about what the CIA is up to.) The majority of Nicaragua's food producers labor with such primitive traditional technology— machetes and planting sticks—that much more basic improvements in tools and cultivation practices would probably increase yields appreciably enough, at modest financial cost and without risk of crop failure.

Instead of focusing on the real-life agricultural problems of peasant corn and bean producers, PAN has concentrated on getting Nicaragua's modernized food producers—the rice growers and the sorghum producers—agricultural inputs and machinery spare parts. Not surprisingly, productions of both rice and sorghum more than doubled prerevolutionary levels by 1983–84 (up 113 and 139 percent respectively). During the same period, bean and corn productions were barely keeping ahead of population growth (up 37 and 21 percent over 1977– 78 respectively), although we should not forget that the war is concentrated in major bean and corn zones (see table 7).

A fourth problem with PAN has been that, even though credit for food producers is considered crucial, each year the National Development Bank has been reluctant to lend (see chapter 6). Under pressure from UNAG and MIDINRA, the bankers have eventually come around, but—and this is a big "but" in farming—often very late, resulting in smaller harvests. Low prices in relation to yields, bad weather, and other factors have made it difficult for many food producers to repay loans. With the fiscal crisis mounting, the bank has balked at calls for stepped-up lending to increase food production. For its part, UNAG has repeatedly and publicly accused the "bureaucracy" of the bank of being "disordered" and inefficient, resulting in untimely delivery of credit.

Finally, land redistribution moved too slowly to boost food output appreciably. A core part of the PAN concept was that the agrarian reform itself would boost the nation's food supply. Underutilized lands given to peasants would be more fertile, easily farmed, and market-accessible than the marginal interior lands onto which land-grabbing elites had historically pushed them. Idle land put into working hands was exactly what happened to Victorina Sanchez and her fellow cooperative members—but for too long there were too few such cases. By the time the agrarian reform was stepped up, the accumulating problems with PAN, combined with the military and economic war against Nicaragua, made it impossible to realize the impact on food production hoped for from land redistribution.

The Results

No one can say for sure if Nicaragua would have achieved national food self-reliance were it not under military and economic siege by the world's greatest power. Certainly, the rapid recovery of most food crops after the devastating war against the Somoza dictatorship was promising. Overall food production figures, even through 1983–84 (see table 7), are respectable enough, especially if we keep in mind the 1982 natural disaster. (In May of that year, tropical storm Aleta washed away tens of thousands of acres of newly planted food crops as well as rural roads and bridges. Unprecedented flooding was followed by a severe drought, which badly damaged the replanted crops as well as pasture-lands for dairy cows and beef cattle.)

Despite big increases in national consumption of rice and beans, production advances in 1982 and 1983 allowed Nicaragua to do away with imports of these two staples of the national diet. Rice output more than doubled between 1977–78 (the last "normal" Somoza year before the insurrectionary war) and 1983–84. Bean output went up a more modest 37 percent over the same period.

Corn imports were substantially reduced in 1981 and 1982 from record imports in the aftermath of the war. While corn output has notched upward, it has continued to be disappointing. Corn imports shot up sharply in 1983, costing the nation some $20 million in scarce foreign exchange. Increased corn imports were needed in part because of a shortfall in 1982 sorghum production for livestock and poultry feed.

Sorghum is a key ingredient in feeds used by large-scale poultry producers. Its importance in Nicaragua's food supply is underscored because chicken and eggs are critical to improving the diet of the poor majority—especially since the slow rebuilding of the national cattle herd has resulted in speculative beef prices on local markets. Sorghum production more than doubled between 1977 and 1981. In 1982, however, output plummeted because of the Aleta floods and the government's reluctance to raise the producer price. Before the 1983 planting season the Ministry of Agriculture held several rounds of heated negotiations with the Sorghum Growers' Association (mostly large and medium producers with modern technology). The government raised the price once, but still the producers balked. Then Minister Wheelock himself entered into the negotiations, and the price was raised further to 60 percent over the 1982 price. When the sorghum growers went back to work, production hit an all-time record level.

The showdown with the Sorghum Growers' Association prompted some in the Sandinista leadership to question whether some state farms should produce sorghum so that a vital link in the nation's food system would not be at the mercy of a small group of elite producers. (Perhaps they also should have questioned the logic of expanding large-scale poultry production dependent on sorghum, corn, and soya feed, part of which is likely to have to be imported and with dollars; grass-fed beef, though an export item, might make more economic sense than dollar-fed poultry.)

Cotton is Nicaragua's only crop whose output has consistently remained significantly below prerevolutionary levels. Cotton's best year since the revolution, the 1983–84 season, represented a recovery to only 75 percent of the output in 1977–78. While most of us think of cotton as a nonedible export crop, for Nicaragua cottonseed is the main source of cooking oil (and Nicaraguans, especially urban Nicaraguans, don't eat anything, even rice, unless they can fry it). In the longer run, the Ministry of Agriculture is banking on the new state-owned African palm oil projects on the Atlantic Coast and, to a lesser extent, promotion of soybean production to cover for the drop in cottonseed output.

Chicken production has steadily increased since the revolution, with commercial production up 84 percent by 1984. Eggs are up a phenomenal 364 percent over 1977–78. Pork production has increased 86 percent. But domestic beef supplies have remained insufficient, with total beef output still 19 percent below 1977–78 levels, giving rise to speculative prices. The cattle industry, which has a much longer reproduction cycle than the chicken and hog industries, has not yet fully recovered from the massive and indiscriminate slaughter and rustling of cattle into Honduras during and shortly after the insurrectionary war.

Milk output, in part for the same reasons as beef production, is sharply down and way below rising demand, especially in Managua. Fresh milk has been in short supply also because many dispersed farmers owning only a few cows have no way to market fresh milk and either consume it themselves or make farm cheese (requiring no refrigeration). Cheese also fetches a considerably higher price than the government-controlled milk price. Thanks to powdered milk donations from abroad, however, supplies of reconstituted milk have increased.

Fruit and vegetable production, as we have seen, is one of the big success stories of PAN. Even though consumption has gone up, imports of the five most important perishables in the Nicaraguan diet—tomatoes, onions, cabbage, potatoes, and plantains—have been reduced from $22.1 million in 1980 to only $1.2 million in 1983. By mid-1984, the nation was virtually self-sufficient in tomatoes, cabbage, and potatoes and was already exporting a modest amount of onions. These successes suggest what might be achieved were it not for the war: most perishables are grown near major urban areas and in other areas not directly affected by the war.

*   *   *

By far the greatest obstacle to what had been Nicaragua's good prospects for achieving national food security has been Washington's military and economic aggression.

One fact alone readily suggests the grave consequences of the military aggression for food production. Over 70 percent of Nicaragua's corn and beans are cultivated in the mountainous northern zones hit hardest by contra terrorist attacks. The contras have burned thousands of acres of crops. By 1984, more than 120,000 peasants in the war zones have fled contra raids, abandoning their homes and fields. Thousands who stayed behind have joined local militias to defend their farms. The heavy drain of peasant farmers from the fields has severely crippled food production as have the mining of roads and ports, the bombing of bridges and farm supply warehouses, and the assassination of agricultural technicians. Efforts to raise fish production, increasingly a substitute for beef, were dealt a blow by the mining of the ports in March 1983, which cost the fishing industry $9.1 million in damages to boats and cargo.

The external economic strangulation of Nicaragua has also taken a heavy toll on food production. The Reagan administration's blocking of loans from the World Bank and other international financial agencies, coming on top of the depressed world market prices for Nicaragua's exports (see chapter 17), have thwarted repair of the war-damaged economic infrastructure and the import of essential farm supplies.

Foreign military and economic aggression so overshadows all internal errors, shortcomings, and other setbacks that it has become impossible to weigh the importance of these internal factors alone. It has also become increasingly difficult to take corrective measures.

In thinking of Nicaragua's short-term food prospects, I remember what Santos, a peasant member of a cooperative in northern Madriz province, told us in the summer of 1984: "Newly planted corn is very delicate. Too much or too little rain, insects, diseases, cows on the loose—all kinds of problems can come up and ruin your crop. It's the same with our baby revolution. Too many attacks on our cooperatives, too many workers taken out of production for defense, not enough food for our people; . . . this war could wipe out everything we've been working for. Like that corn out there, we need peace in order to grow."

TWENTY ONE

THE GRAIN CRISIS: AN EMERGENCY PLAN

By 1983, NICARAGUA WAS FACING A NATIONAL food crisis. For the foreseeable future, most small and medium producers were unlikely to significantly improve their yields of beans and especially of corn. The vulnerability of Nicaragua's corn production to weather had been highlighted by the 1982 flooding and drought. The resurgence of costly imports of corn and beans—just when it had seemed the country was well on the road to food self-reliance—was disheartening. Official forecasts were predicting mounting shortfalls. And the need to resume these multimillion-dollar food imports came at a time when foreign exchange could no longer be counted on.

Also by 1983, as we saw in the last chapter, the war had started seriously to undermine production. The war also brought a new dimension to national food security: at all costs, Nicaragua would have to have a secure domestic source of food for its defense forces.

The Emergency Grain Plan

Months of internal discussion of proposals and counterproposals on how to deal with the gathering food crisis resulted in the "Emergency Plan." In a nutshell, the Emergency Plan aims at rapidly expanding corn acreage in areas relatively secure from military attack, and aims at pushing yields several times higher than the national average. The plan calls for irrigating large tracts of fertile Pacific Coast cotton lands so that each year a crop of hybrid corn could be rotated with cotton.

By May 1984, when we took a firsthand look at what had been accomplished under the plan, some 24,000 acres had already been irrigated and planted in corn (and to a lesser extent, sorghum) on state, cooperative, and large private farms. In just its first year, then, the plan more than doubled the grain acreage under irrigation compared to the peak acreage before the revolution.

Indicative of the go-for-broke spirit in which the Emergency Plan was conceived and implemented, planners ambitiously intend to bring an additional 17,000 acres of cropland under irrigation every year for the next ten years. To better understand the economic, social, and environmental implications of such a large-scale expansion of irrigation, experts from around the world were being invited to a conference in Managua on irrigation issues funded by the Ford Foundation. Unfortunately, the project will be well under way by the time of the conference.

The Emergency Plan's agribusiness-style technology and sweeping scale set it off from the small- and medium-producer-centered efforts to increase corn output that had been key to the original PAN concept. The irrigation equipment is state-of-the-art: giant, mobile pivot-sprinklers manufactured in Spain by a U.S. multinational corporation (Valley Irrigation). Each unit automatically rotates an 800-foot long sprinkler pipe on 20-foot high "stilts" and waters a square kilometer of corn with each full turn.

In addition, the project has imported a fleet of new tractors, harvesters, and agricultural equipment from Italy, Austria, West Germany, the Soviet Union, and the United States. (Once again, much of the machinery had to be imported from wherever credits could be obtained. As a vice minister of agriculture told us, "If you weren't aware of that, you'd think we were crazy having such a mixture of machinery.") The project also requires large quantities of imported fertilizers and other chemicals of "technified" farming. Even the electrical lines necessary to extend the power grid an additional 100 miles to the irrigation pumps had to be purchased abroad. In all, slightly more than half of the project's 1984 first-stage costs—some $30 million—must be paid in foreign exchange.

Proponents of the project admit that it will continue to be highly dependent on imported machinery and inputs. They argue, however, that much of the foreign-exchange costs will be covered by the export of cotton produced on the same land. Cotton productivity too will be boosted by irrigation. In fact, the decision to continue to cultivate cotton, in order to offset the foreign exchange needs of the project, was taken despite the fact that corn and cotton do not make for an optimal crop rotation since they deplete the same nutrients from the soil. The additional fertilizers necessitated by soil depletion further increase foreign-input costs. Nitrogen-fixing beans, for instance, might be a better rotation with corn.

Proponents point out that if the projected average yield for the first (1984) stage—50 quintales per manzana (3.2 metric tons per hectare)—is achieved, the project will produce roughly 15 percent of Nicaragua's annual corn consumption. For such an important production increase, proponents argue, the initial import costs are worth it. They emphasize that the site of production, the fertile Pacific plains, is an area outside the contra attack zones and with comparatively good roads.

Finally, a goodly part of the start-up foreign-exchange costs of at least one of the state farms in the plan (San Ramon) are covered by Libya through a coinvestment agreement in which Libya has agreed to reinvest any profits in Nicaragua. (Khadafi has been notably generous toward Nicaragua with untied dollar grants and loans; I have been told he likes the Sandinistas because they are devoutly religious, not like the atheist Cubans.)

The Critics

The Emergency Plan, however, is not without its critics. Opposition can be found at the top levels of the Ministry of

Agriculture and throughout the rest of the government. (Only those who are fooled by Mr. Reagan's caricature of Nicaragua as a "totalitarian monolith" will be surprised to learn that in Nicaragua there are contending visions and ongoing debates in which criticisms are expressed without fear.) Many of these criticisms speak to the general problems with Nicaragua's high-tech investments we outlined in chapter 19. These problems include ignoring more appropriate "low-tech" alternatives, a shortage of technicians, a technically unskilled labor force, the failure to make more adequate feasibility assessments, and dependency on imported inputs. Here we'll take a more in-depth look at how these problems manifest themselves in the specific case of the Emergency Plan.

The most commonly expressed criticism is that the plan defeats its own purpose—to ensure Nicaragua's food supply—by tying grain production to high levels of imported inputs. As one resident foreign advisor to the ministry put it, "It's just weird for a country with a big foreign-exchange bottleneck to seek to guarantee its food supply through methods that depend so heavily on foreign exchange." Given the project's high initial foreign-exchange costs—albeit with some foreign credits and assistance—and its built-in, unending dependence upon imported spare parts and agricultural inputs, wouldn't it be cheaper simply to import corn?

Given not only the imported-input dependency but also the external threats to Nicaragua's commerce for the foreseeable future, is the Emergency Plan a way to food security? The CIA mining of Nicaragua's harbors in early 1984 gave ample proof that the plan's technified farms were hardly beyond reach of foreign aggression. On one visit to the plan's San Ramon state farm, for instance, we learned that tractors and plows had to be rented for the first planting because the harbor mining had delayed delivery of the farm's own imported machinery. This forced operating costs up 30 percent in the first season. Moreover, while the contra attacks have been concentrated in the interior highlands, a direct U.S. invasion would almost certainly center on the Pacific Coast where the plan is centered. Thus, contend the critics, the plan neither saves foreign exchange nor safeguards Nicaragua's grain production from Washington's war.

Though immensely impressive to the casual observer, note

some of the critics, the mammoth pivot-irrigation systems have already been fraught with problems. Many units arrived with factory defects and have had to be replaced (all the way from Spain, through the time-consuming Panama Canal). The sprinkler systems demand large amounts of electricity and stand idle whenever there is a power failure (which is increasingly often as the war of attrition grinds on). Since this is the first time pivot sprinklers have been used in Nicaragua, costly delays have been caused by the shortage of trained technicians to install and repair them.

At the San Ramon state farm, the first wave of corn planting in February 1984 was seriously damaged by lack of water due to power failures, pump breakdown, and a shortage of service technicians. Yields of high-tech farming, especially in relation to costs, can be much worse than those of traditional agriculture when something goes wrong. In a May visit to San Ramon these first fields of corn looked extremely bad, indeed, the most stunted, withered, cobless corn we've seen in Nicaragua. Later we were told that they salvaged 35 quintales per manzana (well below the projected 50 quintales). Even if they did, it must be some of the most expensive corn going.

It is also troubling that serious feasibility studies and pilot projects have not been carried out. Obviously, this is due to the sense of emergency and the defense effort that is stretching the country's technically qualified human resources to the limit. Yet there are far too many unknowns. Even the manager of a state farm in the plan told us that the plan was a case of "trying too much too quickly," and that experiments should have been conducted on a pilot basis before launching such a costly endeavor on 24,000 acres.

Many argue that Nicaragua's agricultural development requires a fundamental shift in land use. As we saw in chapter 1, generations of development carried out under the control of a tiny elite has led to an irrational pattern of employing natural resources. In the country's hilly interior, corn yields seldom climb above 16 quintales per manzana (1.1 tons per hectare) and till farming is rapidly leveling the forests and eroding the thin topsoil. At the same time, much of the country's most fertile and flat lands along the Pacific coast are left to extensive and inefficient cattle grazing.

The agricultural ministry's long-term redevelopment

strategy calls for shifting the locus of production of corn and other basic food crops from the ill-suited lands in the interior to the Pacific Coast where irrigation, greater technification, and intensive double-cropping is possible. Cattle ranching would be relocated from the Pacific plains to the interior highland more appropriate for grazing than plowing. The cost of transporting low-value grains to urban markets would thus be greatly lowered. At the same time, the small-scale, low-yield grain producer of the interior are to be helped to switch into tree crops, such as cacao, mangos, and citrus, as well as animal husbandry. Such a switch would not only be more ecologically sound, but through higher value production, bring an improved standard of living to farmers of the interior, historically among Nicaragua's poorest citizens.

But the tragic element in this major food-production program is that Washington's aggression is rapidly narrowing Nicaragua's space to experiment. For the real problem is not errors that might be made but the external aggression that prevents new departures from being fully tested and learned from. Already the haste imposed on Nicaragua is severely truncating the Emergency Plan's latitude to forge an approach toward a long-term agricultural "redevelopment" strategy.

TWENTY TWO

EXPANDING DEMAND, SABOTAGED SUPPLY

I N MANY THIRD-WORLD COUNTRIES (AND also in the United States), people go hungry not because there is not enough food, but because they are deprived of the economic resources they need either to grow or to buy food. Often farmers complain about mounting surpluses and shop-keepers tell of food thrown out because no one buys it. In economists' terms, the problem is *effective* demand, not supply.

In Nicaragua, by contrast, the effective demand for food has greatly increased since the revolution. The reason is simple: many more Nicaraguans now have the money to buy food. Nicaragua's food crisis is rooted precisely in the country's increased demand for food. The increased demand has become ever more difficult to meet due to the serious food-production obstacles we outlined in the previous chapter.

In addition to setting low controlled prices for staple foods, the revolution increased effective demand through a number of early measures we described in chapter 13. These included: interventions in wholesaling and marketing by ENABAS, the National Basics Food Corporation, steeply subsidizing consumer food prices, establishing a "guaranty card" system, opening thousands of workplace commissaries and cafeterias, and establishing special nutrition programs for the most vulnerable Nicaraguans.

Let's take a look at how these measures have fared over the past two years.

ENABAS. ENABAS has attempted to guarantee low food prices by undermining speculation on shortages. The goal is to maintain reliable stocks of whatever basics might be in short supply even if imports become necessary. The Sandinistas hoped to use ENABAS to avoid direct government control of marketing.

In the past two years the government has become increasingly active in wholesaling. Expanded storage facilities, the wider use of production contracts (whereby farmers are guaranteed seeds, fertilizers, etc., if they sell to ENABAS), and higher producer prices helped ENABAS "capture" an ever greater share of each harvest of the staple food crops. In 1983, ENABAS purchased 23 percent of the corn crop, 60 percent of the beans, and 95 percent of the rice and sorghum. (Because rice and sorghum are large-scale, highly mechanized crops with few producers, it is relatively easy for the government to coordinate their purchase and marketing. This contrasts with corn and beans, which are produced on as many as 90,000 individual farms and cooperatives.) Taking into account substantial corn imports in 1983, ENABAS controlled 60 percent of the wholesale corn market.

ENABAS also expanded its "network" of stores to over 8,500 by 1984. Almost half are the privately owned *expendios populares* (people's outlets), neighborhood stores that agree to sell the controlled basic goods at official retail prices in return for a guaranteed supply from ENABAS at official wholesale prices. That so much of the network is privately owned speaks to the continued efforts of the Sandinista-led government to work with the private sector (and benefit from small merchants' know-how).

We talked with Doña Mercedes, one such "franchised" store owner in Ciudad Sandino, in March 1984. She was glad the CDS approved her shop being in the ENABAS network. "It's an honor because it means my neighbors think I'm honest." She also thought her ENABAS contract would mean good business. As the basics become increasingly scarce, her store would become the most popular place to shop for everything, including some noncontrolled items. "A guaranteed, though modest, profit is something. Empty shelves don't make a profit."

Subsidized food prices. As noted in chapter 20, the government froze most official food prices throughout 1982 and 1983. While overall inflation rose to an annual rate of 40 percent in 1983, prices for salt, cooking oil, sugar, rice, beans, corn, and milk were the same as in 1981 at supermarkets and other official distribution outlets. In 1983, ENABAS was buying corn from local producers for 1.80 córdobas per pound (and paying dollars for imported corn), yet selling it to consumers for 1.00 córdoba per pound. The government absorbed the entire difference in addition to all the costs of drying, packaging, storing, and transporting. Official prices for some other foods, such as eggs, chicken, cheese, and pork, were raised somewhat but much less than rising costs. Subsidized food prices, of course, helped make it possible for many Nicaraguans to afford more food. (And controlled, subsidized prices for many nonfood basics, ranging from soap to public transportation, left Nicaragua's poor majority with more to spend on food.)

The "guaranty card" system. The idea behind the guaranty card was to ensure everyone's right to the food he or she needed. The card offered each Nicaraguan who so desired a formal guarantee of a monthly quota of particular staples at the affordable official prices.

Guaranty cards were introduced in early 1982 in order to distribute sugar more equitably. Previously, spot shortages of sugar, an important food to Nicaraguans, had touched off widespread hoarding and speculation. Then, in the aftermath of the severe flooding caused by tropical storm Aleta in May 1982, a wave of speculation—and widespread outcries against it—convinced government leadership that the guaranty card system should be expanded. The Ministry of Internal Commerce (MICOIN) added rice, cooking oil, and soap to the card in early 1983.

As with sugar, households received their cards from their CDS neighborhood organization. Guaranty cards entitled each household to purchase up to official monthly limits of each item: four pounds of sugar and rice, one liter of cooking oil, and two large bars of laundry soap for each member. The expansion of the guaranty-card system appreciably undercut speculation and regularized the sale of these key goods at official prices, most importantly in low-income neighborhoods.

The government emphasized without qualification that no one need belong to a neighborhood CDS organization to obtain a guaranty card; furthermore, to deny anyone a card for his or her views is a punishable offense. Those who wish to paint a picture of Nicaragua as a "totalitarian dungeon" (to cite a phrase from President Reagan) have claimed that the guaranty cards are used to force political compliance. We have been close to this situation—Paul Rice has lived in a lower-middle-class Managua neighborhood—and have found no credible evidence to support these charges.

Beans and corn were not brought onto the card at this point because producers are so numerous and scattered that it would be exceedingly difficult to organize and control their marketing. Also corn is a special case since most Nicaraguans consume their daily corn in the form of tortillas, which they buy ready-made from thousands of small-scale tortilla makers. It is these corn processors, often among those very poor people the revolution most wants to help, and not the final consumers, who most need to have a reliable and stably priced supply of corn.

In many isolated rural areas, a guaranteed supply of refined sugar and cooking oil tended to increase consumption of these products. In fact, before the guaranty-card system, such industrially processed foods had never been available. In some places they were seen for the first time during the 1980 literacy campaign when middle- and upper-class urban youths and their visiting parents brought them. This difference in the countryside escapes the notice of many of the better-off residents of Managua and of all those journalists whose knowledge of Nicaragua comes from "Western diplomatic sources."

In Managua and the other urban areas, the guaranty-card system expanded effective demand, rather than curbing it as a rationing system might have. Those in jeopardy of being cut out by speculators' prices generally had their minimal consumption needs protected by the guaranty card. At the same time these four items could still be purchased in unlimited quantities, although at much higher prices, on the "parallel" or black market. While shopping on the black market was technically illegal, no buyers, as far as we know, have ever been arrested.

Of course, these goods—cooking oil, sugar, rice, and soap—come from a handful of factories either owned by the government or supposedly selling all their production to it. How could these staples end up for sale on the black market? This was a question raised in some CDS neighborhood meetings in Ciudad Sandino. It seems the sources of free-floating goods varied. Much was secretly siphoned off at the production site and sold illegally on the side. In some cases, goods were "leaked" by corrupt MICOIN officials out for some quick money. At other times, MICOIN actually distributed the controlled items, usually sugar, to small vendors for resale on the black market—a political decision taken to improve the livelihoods of the small vendors and to allay the grumblings of sweet-toothed consumers for whom the official quota (1 pound per person per week) was not enough.

Commissaries. Workplace commissaries were set up to sell the food staples and the other basic items to workers at official prices. These outlets were primarily located in factories, government agencies, and on the large farms. We heard frequent complaints about shortages and the limited variety of goods in many of the commissaries.

Workplace cafeterias. By 1984, almost 2,000 *comedores populares* were providing substantially subsidized hot lunches in state-owned farms and factories as well as in some private enterprises.

Nutrition programs. In 1982 the Ministry of Health began providing weekly allotments of milk, flour, cooking oil, and other products to some 60,000 preschool children and pregnant and lactating women throughout the nation. The same year the Ministry of Education started sponsoring a program providing primary-school children a morning glass of milk and noontime meal free of charge. Initially serving 30,000 thousand children in two provinces, the program was expanded throughout the country, despite—or perhaps because of—the deepening economic crisis. Partly as a result of these programs, healthworkers have suggested that the revolution's greatest nutritional improvements have been made by low-income mothers and infants.

In addition to these policies that *directly* concern food distribution, other factors have resulted in increased demand for food. Among them are wage hikes and enforcement of minimum-wage regulations, as well as expanded free health services and other items in the "social wage." Government policies have led to a greater number of people employed and mushrooming public expenditures, putting more money into more people's hands. The amount of money in circulation more than doubled in the first five years.

Another factor, often overlooked, is that Nicaragua's population has been growing at a very rapid rate. Although the birth rate has been high for years and good statistics are hard to come by, there is a widespread sense that the revolution has triggered a baby boom—as well as a significant decline in infant mortality. Rough calculations suggest that by the revolution's fifth anniversary there were over a half million more Nicaraguans than in 1979—a 22 percent increase. This is a legion of new consumers who are, needless to say, too young to produce or pay for their own food. The baby boom also brings an increased demand for special foods, notably powdered milk. Postrevolutionary Nicaragua has also seen an appreciable and steadily growing influx of foreign visitors. Before the revolution, Nicaragua was never a tourist mecca. There have also been tens of thousands of resident "internationalists" working in Nicaragua. Unquestionably foreigners up the effective demand for food. (Yes, the Intercontinental Hotel's world-class, all-you-can-eat buffet mentioned in the first edition has continued.)

Food Supply: Not Keeping Up

Nicaragua's heightened demand for food makes for a volatile mix with its deepening food-supply problems. The country's mounting difficulties in food production were discussed in chapter 21. By 1983, major obstacles such as the war and the foreign-exchange crisis were also starting to have a negative impact on getting food supplies to market.

By the end of 1983, one-third of the ENABAS fleet of

grain-transport trucks were paralyzed for lack of spare parts. More than half the trucks used to transport food in and out of Matagalpa were off the road for lack of tires. The defense effort required the mobilization of scores of civilian trucks, which aggravated an already serious shortage of vehicles needed for the delivery of farm inputs and the marketing of farm produce.

Even when trucks were available, deliveries to the cities were held up by the mining of northern country roads, the bombing of bridges, and attacks on trucks hauling food by contra commandos. It was not long before ENABAS found it difficult to find drivers willing to transport farm produce from the war zones. In June 1984 Minister of Internal Commerce Dionisio Marenco told the Council of State: "Right now, the beans that are being eaten all over Nicaragua came from the winter harvest of Neuva Guinea. It cost the lives of six compañeros to get those beans out of the mountains. It is very common now to talk about the war and its effects on the food supply and so forth. But when you have to go to the house of a dead man's mother and say, 'Here, I've brought your son's body. He died driving a truck to bring beans to the people,' it's a more painful and difficult task, which brings the whole security question down to earth."

The contras, recognizing the importance of food supplies, have targeted storage facilities wherever they attack. In 1983 alone, they rendered useless 8 percent of the national grain storage capacity. In June 1984 contra commandos attacked the northern town of Ocotal, destroying all six of the region's main grain silos. Twelve hundred tons of rice, corn, beans, and sorghum were set afire, and four workers were killed. American Maryknoll sisters living in Ocotal told us that the next day the townspeople sifted through the charred rubble gleaning whatever grain they could.

The severity of the military war's impact on basic food supplies really sank in when a top official told us in September 1984 that the government had just cut in half its estimates for the year of how much corn and beans ENABAS would be able to buy from producers in the northern provinces. Moreover, he commented, the food situation will be even more critical next year. He anticipated that the war will make it impossible next spring to bring out anything from the winter harvests in

Nueva Guinea and much of the rest of northern Nicaragua.

The Reagan administration's economic warfare, by exacerbating the foreign-exchange shortage, has seriously sabotaged
Nicaragua's food distribution. Key items such as cooking oil
and powdered milk, even when produced from local sources,
are processed and packaged with materials that must be
imported. Understandably, priority in the allocation of foreign exchange has gone to agricultural inputs. Yet the lack of
enough foreign exchange to also import such items as waxed
cartons and tin sheets for cans and bottlecaps has increasingly
resulted in food-supply bottlenecks. There is plenty of wheat,
donated by a wide political range of countries (too much in
fact, leaving no room to store the sorghum crop). But no one
donates yeast, and Nicaragua has a hard time coming up with
the money to import it. There is also a shortage of plastic bags
for selling flour.

The Managua Problem

As U.S.-supported counterrevolutionary offensives grew ever
more fierce and frequent, the government was forced to shift
its long-standing priority favoring Managua in the distribution
of consumer goods. In order to bolster civilian morale in the
face of enemy attacks and efforts at internal subversion,
Nicaragua's supply priorities now favor the defense forces and
the war regions. In mid-1984, the Sandinistas launched an
educational campaign on the supply crisis in Managua with
the slogan: "Everything for the combatants, everything for the
war fronts!"

Managua, with somewhat less than a third of the national
population, has long been accustomed to consuming more
than half the country's food. The capital has taken an even
greater share of processed foods. In the past, more than 70
percent of canned powdered milk—a much-sought-after item
in Nicaragua, especially with the baby boom—was sold in
Managua; in 1984, less than 30 percent. And there is less
powdered milk produced, period. (In September 1984 we were
told powdered-milk production would plummet still further:
in addition to the shortage of milk and of tin cans, half of the
personnel of the factory had been mobilized for combat.)

To many in Managua, the war is unreal: there has been no combat, no sound of mortar fire, no schools burned to the ground. Foreign visitors are often struck that their anticipated sense of militarization is absent fom the capital. Yet at the same time Managua is increasingly pressed by the war's economic brunt. As an agricultural technician in Jinotega put it, "Up north, you don't have to remind people that there's a war going on. They see it, hear it, breathe it, in some places every day. In Managua it's very different. People grumble and grumble because they're only told about the war. Some even think the war is just the government's excuse."

The "Managua problem," as one top government strategist referred to frustrated consumer demand, is exacerbated by Nicaragua's daily doses of U.S.-style consumption messages. People in Managua can receive radio and television broadcasts from Costa Rica. In the north they get it from Honduras. And it seems every Nicaraguan family has relatives abroad—Los Angeles, Miami, San Francisco, Panama, Mexico. "Everyone knows what the latest is and they want it," commented the government strategist.

Many of us might at first take a certain satisfaction in learning of a country where the tables are reversed—where the countryside gets priority in consumption over the capital city. But the deteriorating level of consumer goods in Managua undoubtedly portends a growing political handicap for the revolution.

TWENTY THREE
CONFRONTING SHORTAGE

"**W**E HAVE TO PREPARE OURSELVES FOR some hard times in Nicaragua. I don't see any way of overcoming the shortage problems in less than five years.... We'll be happy if we can guarantee just rice and beans," announced a somber Minister of Internal Commerce in August 1984.

By mid-1984, shortages and irregular supplies of many foods and other basic goods had become commonplace. Although nobody could complain about the low official prices for more than 50 basic items, actually finding them for sale at those prices had grown increasingly problematic. Working-class families in Managua found themselves making repeated trips to the local *expendio popular* in order to get their share of the basics at the official prices. At the supermarkets, lines before morning and afternoon openings grew longer and longer, with runs on the stores whenever news of a delivery spread by word of mouth.

Many—at least those who could afford to do so—resorted to the black market, centered in Managua's Eastern Market, where they paid two, three, even ten times the official price for the most basic goods—chicken, powdered milk, cooking oil, toothpaste, toilet paper. Even beans, Nicaraguans' thrice-daily fare, became hard to find at anything near the official price. In June 1984 Nicaragua imported 4,300 tons of beans, the first beans imported since 1981. In July, black-market vendors were still taking advantage of the preharvest scarcity, hawking one-pound plastic bags of beans, officially priced at 2.8 córdobas, for 21 córdobas.

The "Hunger Speculators"

For an economy still as market-dominated as Nicaragua's, dwindling and unstable supply compounded by excess demand can fuel wild rumors of shortages. The rumors trigger a vicious circle: speculators and those who can afford to hoard buy up goods and create greater shortages and wilder rumors.

In late 1983 toothpaste was a classic instance. One day it was officially announced that imports of toothpaste tubes would be temporarily halted because of the foreign-exchange crisis. Everyone knew toothpaste output would soon fall since Nicaragua produces its own paste but has to import the empty tubes. Immediately professional speculators went into action. They paid droves of poor people to descend upon government stores to buy up existing inventories at the official price of 16 córdobas per tube. From then on "Dentex" could be found only in the Eastern Market and for 50 to 60 córdobas. (A half year later the price was up to 135 córdobas—a day's wage for many urban workers.) One government official mentioned to us that he has learned to get many more brushings out of a tube than he had ever dreamed possible.

Speculators have gone to considerable lengths to buy up stocks of scarce commodities for resale. During the dry season in 1983, a slack period for slaughterhouses when beef supplies are at their tightest, people slept out all night on the sidewalks in front of Managua's price-controlled butcher shops to be the first in line the next day to buy beef at low prices. With ten pounds of fresh meat, peddled in the Eastern Market or door-to-door in the better-off neighborhoods, they could easily net 250 córdobas in a day, more than five times the minimum wage for an agricultural laborer. Naturally, such speculation made beef exceedingly hard to come by for ordinary families. Similarly, eggs, powdered milk, light bulbs, and toilet paper became hot items of speculation, selling in the Eastern Market for several times their official prices.

To prevent hoarding, scarce products began to be informally rationed in 1984. Price-controlled stores sold them only in limited quantities upon presentation of the family guaranty card. Customer hoarding and speculator reselling of imported powdered milk prompted supermarket managers to restrict the sale to two one-pound boxes per child per week. Buyers were required to show their children's vaccine cards as proof of legitimate need for the milk, and cashiers noted all purchases on the families' guaranty cards. The supermarkets also imposed a limit of two pounds of beef each purchase per person. Speculators, however, got around this restriction by hiring "shoppers" to make repeated beef purchases at the official price. Once the supermarkets ran out of beef for the day—which didn't take long—the speculators would resell the morning's catch for three or more times as much on the black market.

The popular response to the shortages and uncertainties has been to blame hoarders and speculators. The media that are progovernment have carried regular stories about those who "speculate on hunger." A weekly program on Sandinista television focused on problems with a particular product. One week, for example, we watched an episode with the unlikely title, *"Que pasa con el papel higienico?"* (What's Happening with Toilet Paper?) At one point, the program zeroed in on a vendor in the Eastern Market selling a mound of toilet paper rolls. When asked where she had gotten them, she replied that she had bought them from an official of MICOIN.

Understandably, many working-class and even middle-class Nicaraguans were outraged at such profiteering—and dismayed that the government seemed to be doing little to put a halt to it. Neighborhood committees, which are organized mainly in the poorer and working-class barrios, demanded stricter government controls on food marketing and an "iron fist" against the hoarders and "hunger speculators." Prices, *"bandido"* speculators, and where to find this or that item became daily conversation topics. Opposition parties sought to make political hay of the growing supply crisis, blaming it all on the Sandinistas. Liberal Party presidential candidate Virgilio

Godoy, who had been Minister of Labor up until the electoral campaign, spoke openly on the campaign trail of Nicaragua as becoming the "country of '*no hay*'" ("there isn't any").

Angered by hoarders and speculators, many Nicaraguans were asking when "their" government would finally do something about such opportunists. We'll never forget one angry working-class mother who spoke up at her neighborhood CDS meeting in Ciudad Sandino: "We understand that shortages will be created by the war. We know that priority has to go to the war front. I don't mind tightening my belt for the defense of the nation as long as everyone else tightens along with me. But, my God, why can you still find everything that you can't get in the ENABAS store abundantly available in the Eastern Market but at outrageous prices?"

The widespread chorus of protest against the "hunger speculators" rose to a high pitch in the spring of 1984, convincing the Sandinista leadership that the majority of Nicaraguans were ready for a new policy.

To Ration or Not to Ration?

One knowledgeable source has told us, "Food supply, and rationing in particular, has been the single most debated issue at the top level of the Sandinistas." In 1983, a National Supply Commission had been set up to formulate short- and long-term policies and to monitor the food-supply situation. The commission was no ordinary study committee but a cabinet-level body that made a difference you could feel. It brought together the various ministries and was chaired by Minister Jaime Wheelock. Representatives of private and government-owned industry, organized labor, and the popular organizations also participated.

Since its formation, the commission has met weekly to discuss the status of production, marketing, transport, and a host of other supply questions. Working committees investigated specific problems, such as what to do with Managua's Eastern Market. As the supply crisis deepened in the second half of 1983, the commission took on the role of food-crisis troubleshooting.

But it was clear to everyone concerned that the commission's troubleshooting solutions—deciding what import to sacrifice in order to import beans from Argentina, of raising the producer price for eggs, or arranging a donation of powdered milk from the Soviet Union—were only stopgap measures. At the same time, therefore, work proceeded on designing a system of rationing—to give, as one CDS national leader put it, "the best response to a bad situation."

Many issues needed to be studied and thrashed out to create a food-rationing system appropriate for Nicaragua. There was keen interest in the food-rationing systems in other countries. (Having just completed our five-year-long study of Cuba's food situation at the Institute for Food and Development Policy, I was asked to do a high-level seminar on the realities of Cuba's food rationing.) One fundamental issue hotly contested at the highest level was whether scarce items should be equally distributed to everyone across-the-board or prioritized for workers and peasants, leaving the elite minority to fend for themselves. (The decision was that everyone should get the same.) What quantities of the foods to be rationed should be guaranteed—or, more pivotally, *could* be guaranteed? (Failing to deliver on the amount guaranteed on a ration card could be a political disaster; it was crucial to assess as realistically as possible—thus pessimistically—the likely supply situation.) What should be done with restaurants and the thousands of street vendors and people selling noonday meals out of their homes? (For the time being it was decided to make no substantial changes.) Should the prices of staples continue to be subsidized at the cost of massive deficit spending by the government? What should be the role of the popular organizations, particularly the neighborhood CDSs, in the new stage? Should the rationed goods be sold through government stores only? What should be done with the commissaries in the workplaces?

In the second half of 1983, the commission wisely initiated a pilot project in Region IV (Carazo, Granada, Masaya, and Rivas provinces). There the guaranty card was expanded to cover eight basic items, which were sold through a network of some 1,750 outlets, mostly privately owned. The commission appointed Ramon Cabrales, a popular commander from the liberation war, to shepherd the experiment. Caliche Barrios, a young Sandinista leader in this area known to readers of another Institute for Food and Development Policy book, *Now We Can Speak,* had been pushing for just such a program. When we spoke to him and others living in this area in June, 1984, all agreed that things were running remarkably smoothly and that speculators had definitely been undermined. Some zones in the region had even raised the per-person guaranteed quota for some items when surpluses began to accumulate, probably due to the curb in hoarding.

By June 1, 1984, enough groundwork had been carried out for a new Law of Consumer Protection. In essence, the law, debated and passed by the Council of State, stipulated that:

—Eight basic products are to be sold only under the control of the Ministry of Internal Commerce (MICOIN): sugar, cooking oil, rice, laundry soap, beans, salt, corn, and sorghum. More items could be added to the list if the government judged it to be in the interest of consumers.

—Every household is to be issued a card guaranteeing a fixed quota of these basic products (except corn, which would be allocated to tortilla makers, and sorghum to animal feed industries). Viewed one way, this meant that only beans and salt were being added to the existing guaranty-card system. But the significant change was that the new law strictly prohibits the sale of these products in the Eastern Market or anywhere else. Every household now will need a guaranty card. This is, then, as MICOIN chief Dionisio Marenco told us, "rationing—make no mistake about it."

—Every household is to be assigned to a particular neighborhood store for buying its quota of the six rationed basics. This will require a careful household census carried out by the CDS neighborhood organizations.

—The mushrooming government food subsidy is to be sharply cut back, to half of the projected 1.2 billion córdobas following the April 1984 hikes in producer prices. For most of the basics the government will no longer cover the gap between consumer prices and official consumer prices. Even if consumer prices run higher than current levels, they would still remain below prices on the black market, where the shortages have forced many consumers to do their shopping. Price subsidies are to be maintained only on milk and sugar. The government will continue, however, to absorb the costs of processing, storing, and transporting all the staples.

—In July consumer prices were raised according to the new formula. But in October 1984, the government backed away from sticking to the new pricing policy. In response to months of vocal calls for higher producer prices from the Sandinista-led small and medium farmers' association (UNAG), the government dramatically doubled the price paid to producers for beans. According to the new pricing policy, this move should have automatically doubled the retail price of beans—surely a heavy and sudden blow to the purchasing power of the poor majority. Instead, the government held retail beans at 4 córdobas a pound, putting itself back in the position of subsidizing a major producer-consumer price gap. As some commented, perhaps the imminent elections influenced this sudden and publicly unexplained policy reversal.

—In addition to the six guaranteed items on the card, 18 other "priority products," including toothpaste, eggs, toilet paper, powdered milk, and deodorant (the tropical climate!) would be sold only through the same network. For these products, the economic crisis and Washington's war made the government wary of guaranteeing supplies. All that could be promised was that whenever items were available, they would be marketed in a more planned and equitable manner. The defense forces and the civilians in the war zones would receive priority in allocating scarce supplies, as would areas with exceptional need for a particular item. Rubber boots, for example, would first be put on sale in the rainy mountainous regions of the interior where they are most in demand.

A telling feature of the new policy is that no private stores are to be nationalized and no new government stores are to be opened. The 6,000 outlets in the new program are all mom-and-pop stores. Dionisio Marenco commented to us, "If we created a network of government stores, we'd be creating such a bureaucratic apparatus that we'd only be complicating distribution problems." (Such talk—and deeds—from a ranking Sandinista official shatters any illusion of the Sandinistas as would-be totalitarian statists.) Stores selected by the neighborhood organizations and MICOIN are eligible for government financing and various other forms of organizational support.

But the private middlemen—wholesale marketers—*are* cut out of the picture, at least for the eight basic goods. The new law gives MICOIN the exclusive authority for wholesaling the basics. (The role of ENABAS was cut back to commodity collection and processing.) To facilitate and decentralize wholesale distribution, construction immediately started on new MICOIN warehouses in each region of the country, with more than half completed by July.

MICOIN itself needed to be seriously overhauled for its tremendous, new responsibilities. Inadequate staffing, internal disorganization, inefficiencies, and even corruption had contributed to distribution problems in the past. (At a February 1983 closed-door seminar, Dionisio Marenco jokingly complained that the staff of CIERA, the research arm of the Ministry of Agriculture and Agrarian reform, was larger than the entire Ministry of Internal Commerce.) New supervisory measures were established to clean up the "leakage" of controlled goods through the ministry, backed by no-nonsense punishments for all forms of official corruption. Procedures were set up to punish those taking privileges they might think built into the new system; supermarket employees, for example, were prohibited from buying more than the quota of goods allowed to any shopper. A number of MICOIN employees found guilty of corruption and bureaucratic workstyles were fired. (We should keep in mind that extensive corruption was a way of life in Nicaraguan officialdom for generations and that many in the middle and lower echelons of the Nicaraguan government today were in the Somoza government; in addition, relatively low government pay in the face of skyrocketing prices probably put pressure on many. But the widely shared impression, even of a World Bank study mission, is that corruption no longer *characterizes* the government and definitely not the top leaders.)

In order to assist MICOIN in identifying problems and policy alternatives, the National Supply Commission is being duplicated at the regional level throughout the country and the formation of similar committees in each zone and locality is planned for the future. The point of regionalizing the commission is to facilitate the flow of information about food problems from all corners of the nation to MICOIN and the various other ministries. Regional and local committees should also provide a forum for the mass organizations to apply greater pressure on the government to live up to its promises to guarantee equitable distribution of basic necessities.

At the same time, the commission is conducting monthly nationwide household surveys on complaints and suggestions about the supply situation. The households selected represent a wide range of income and classes. This too has been organized in close collaboration with the CDS neighborhood organizations.

Enforcement

The new law will be meaningless, of course, unless it is seriously enforced. Stiff penalties have been written into the law against unauthorized sale of six of the eight products on the guaranty card. (Corn and beans may still be sold privately by the tens of thousands of producers but only at official prices.) Penalties range from fines to prison sentences for anyone caught hoarding or reselling the six basic necessities.

MICOIN officials told us that the fines previously levied againt professional speculators were a joke; their profits were great enough that a fine of several thousand córdobas amounted to nothing more than the proverbial slap on the wrist. Minister Marenco spoke of his readiness to be tough. A truck driver, for instance, who buys up beans from peasants and transports them for sale at the Eastern Market will now know that he runs the risk of having his goods and even his truck confiscated. The tough talk and stiff penalties apply to anyone who breaks the law, including the Eastern Market's thousands of small-time speculators; but these penalties are especially aimed at closing down the big dealers and middlemen.

There are political costs both abroad and at home attached to a strict enforcement of the law. Internationally, a crackdown on profiteering merchants could be twisted into "government repression" and "human rights abuses" by those who cared neither before nor now about the hungry. Domestically, facing an election, the Sandinistas risked alienating tens of thousands of small and basically poor vendors, many of them women supporting children, for whom buying and reselling is their only livelihood. As of this writing, however, we have seen sales openly going ahead in the Eastern Market. This suggested to us that the Sandinista leadership was having second thoughts about how "tough" it was prudent to be with small speculators at this time. One high ranking MICOIN official told the *Los Angeles Times* in November 1984 that "tough actions in the Eastern Market might be seen as persecution of the thousands of people who work there."

But there has been no backing off from the promise to crack down on the large-scale middlemen and the "food mafia." When the new policy first went into effect in early August, police and MICOIN inspectors set up nighttime roadblocks on all highways leading into Managua and stopped transport vehicles to inspect their cargo. Those carrying large amounts of food products illegally, that is, without a license or official receipts, had their produce confiscated. Similar operations were carried out in the provinces, with daily reports in the newspapers of hundreds of tons of illegally acquired produce confiscated and later resold to consumers through the MICOIN-franchised stores at official prices.

The task of enforcing the law does not rest only with MICOIN inspectors and local police officers, it also depends upon organized consumers. Neighborhood CDS committees play a watchdog role, making sure their local MICOIN-authorized outlets post official price lists and stick to them. Each barrio has recruited a number of volunteer "people's inspectors," ordinary citizens chosen by their neighbors at public meetings to help monitor the operation of each outlet.

The participation of ordinary citizens at the community level was also essential in setting up the new food distribution apparatus. Before the new guaranty cards could be issued, CDS committees nationwide conducted a household-by-household census in every barrio and community. This not only enabled gathering the necessary data for issuing cards, assigning households to stores, and planning the delivery of supplies, it also provided the opportunity for neighborhood committees to explain the new law and answer questions.

Through their CDS committees, the residents of each barrio also controlled the selection of their own official distribution outlets from among the local stores. In exceptionally well-attended public meetings, neighbors discussed the service histories of all the stores in the area, noting which ones had, for example, given interest-free credit; which had speculated in times of scarcity; and which had generally served their customers well. Committee members talked with store owners and gathered information about the stability of each enterprise, its sales capacity, and its willingness to work in cooperation with the new distribution system. One neighborhood CDS committee activist commented to us, "In the selection of a 'secure' store, we are not necessarily looking for a Sandinista but simply someone with the disposition to serve our neighborhood well." In a few neighborhoods where suitable stores could not be found, CDS committee members stepped forward to volunteer their own homes as distribution points for the basic goods.

Throughout June and July, the national CDS network also organized hundreds of neighborhood consumer assemblies to discuss and clarify the new distribution law. We talked to people who attended these meetings and went to some ourselves. Frequently, community members at the meetings expressed worries about the pending increases in consumer prices. Another concern was whether the quotas would really be enough. (These worries—and the general anxiety—led people to line up to stock up on basic goods before the new law went into effect.) Some criticized MICOIN for poor organization and delayed deliveries. On the other side, many people demanded that the government adopt stricter measures against hoarders and price speculators and called for the inclusion of other foods and basic items on the new guaranty cards. The results of all the neighborhood meetings were passed up to the national CDS headquarters, which formulated recommendations for modifications in the proposed law.

Displaced Sellers

The shop owners who are in the new MICOIN network stand to do well. Orfilio Vega, the owner of a small shop in Managua's Santa Rosa barrio, put it this way: "We believe the measures are good for both us and the consumers. If I have to buy at high prices from the intermediaries, I have no choice but to sell to people at high prices, right? But now the limits are clear. I know I can expect to make a reasonable profit and yet sell to my customers at prices they can afford. I'm ready to go to work."

But not all of Nicaragua's existing grocery stores and market stands will be able to join the new distribution network. In June 1984, Managua alone had some 18,000 grocery stores and market stands, several times more than were needed for selling the six products on the guaranty card to the city's 800,000 residents. Many of these stores had sufficient sales of other goods to make losses on the controlled items marginal. (Without peace, however, these goods too are likely to become more scarce.) But for others, particularly vendors at small, open-market stalls, the economic loss is potentially substantial. Many of these people have been making more money than ever before in their lives speculating on scarce goods. Not surprisingly, they are among those outspokenly hostile toward the new policy. In the weeks following the announcement of the new law, the tension in Managua's Eastern Market was unmistakable; many vendors were suspicious of any curious outsiders (although some were ready enough to be interviewed by foreign journalists). Some even declared war on MICOIN or vowed to "go underground." (One such vendor showed a U.S. journalist we know a trap door for concealing illegal goods whenever an inspector was thought near.)

Anticipating the market vendors' response, MICOIN and the vendors' CDS committees sought to dispel rumors and directly address vendors' anxieties and criticisms by convening information assemblies in each of the capital's markets. MICOIN and the committees explained the new policy in detail. The presentations we heard emphasized that the only "targets" were big-time speculators and middlemen. As one marketplace CDS organizer and shopkeeper Olga Orozco told us, "We want to reassure the small retailers, many of whom are poor and quite patriotic, that they are and will continue to be important sellers of goods to the people. The poor people of this country have suffered enough from this war, and it'd be absurd to make honest *pulperos* (mom-and-pop store owners) the next casualty."

Efforts are underway to provide alternative livelihoods to those hurt by the new measures. Huembes market in Managua is one of the new markets where the CDS has been especially well-organized. The Huembes CDS committee helped form an association of cloth retailers among the basic foods vendors not contracted by MICOIN to sell the rationed products. Aided by a loan from the National Development Bank, the association signed a contract with a government-owned textiles factory to market a steady supply of cloth at official prices, ensuring a reasonable livelihood for its members. MICOIN is helping to set up similar retail cooperatives for sellers displaced by the new system in markets throughout the country. Efforts like these have undoubtedly helped ease the worries of some small vendors. But it is clear this group will remain highly skeptical of the revolution—and perhaps a source of trouble—until the full effects of the new system are fully known.

Rationing in Action:
Early Problems and Prospects

Problems are sure to arise in the application of any new food policy on a national scale, and they certainly have with this one.

In the first weeks and months following announcement of the new policy, newspapers were full of exposes of speculators and stories of arrests and confiscations. Neighborhood rumors abounded and expectations ran high. Complaints were heard on all sides. Consumers grumbled about uneven service at some of the new outlets, long lines, and continued shortages of some of the items people had been told were "guaranteed." Never were complaints greater than in October, when MICOIN started using the supermarkets to sell scarce products that, like powdered milk, were often not available through the outlets. But the supermarket prices were virtually as high as those in the Eastern Market. We fully supported a friend who is a Sandinista coordinator for one region near Managua. He told a people's assembly that he would "not defend an indefensible policy."

At the same time, affiliated store owners argued they needed greater help with bank loans and in resolving transportation difficulties. One reputable neighborhood store owner in Ciudad Sandino told us in November that she had given up being an official outlet. Many items arrived at her store short-weighted; the bottoms of cooking-oil drums contained several inches of water. The store owner found she was losing money. She suspected truck drivers contracted by MICOIN. (We wondered if the drivers had been reading the CIA manual on economic destabilization.) Many store owners, consumers, and truck owners criticized MICOIN's implementation of the law as slow and disorderly, suffering from bureaucratic tie-ups. Many working-class citizens criticized MICOIN for its seeming reluctance to come down hard on the speculators in the Eastern Market. MICOIN, for its part, found itself unprepared to meet its July 1 announced start-up date. Numerous details had to be rethought in light of criticisms and suggestions gathered on all levels; it was not until August that the authorized outlets officially commenced operation.

Nonetheless, the sense of most consumers is that the system is necessary: limiting the sale of scarce items to an equitable card system is probably the best way to counter those who would speculate on people's needs in the face of the shortfalls of war and economic crisis. For most, the new stage represents a logical way to deal with a bad situation fundamentally caused by foreign aggression. At the same time, it is doubtful that any of the proponents of the new stage either in or outside the government see the guaranty cards and "secure" stores as a panacea for the shortage problem. A Sandinista official involved in the pilot program in Region IV emphasized this point: "As long as the war continues, cutting into production and demanding more food and other resources for the fronts, consumption will be limited for the rest of us. What our experience in Region IV shows is that what little we have can be shared with fairness. But ultimately, everything depends upon halting the aggression against our country and improving our capacity to produce."

Our own view is that the new measures are likely to particularly benefit Nicaragua's poor majority, precisely because the poorer barrios tend to be more highly self-organized than others. (There is virtually no neighborhood organization, including CDS, in the higher-income neighborhoods, which resemble U.S. suburbs in their individualism.) Relying on communities' self-organization to solve food distribution problems should strengthen the capacity of popular interests in Nicaragua to take control in dealing with future problems. Greater self-organization may be another good brought out of a bad situation. The greatest worry about the program seems to us the possibility of the system failing to deliver on the guaranteed quotas. This situation would seriously undermine confidence in the mass organizations and their leadership.

A War of Attrition

It would be difficult to find a poor Nicaraguan—and we should never forget that the majority of Nicaraguans are poor—who could not recount personal experiences of malnourishment and not having enough to eat before the revolution.

It would be difficult to find a poor Nicaraguan who could not tell you about changes since the start of the revolution bringing a better diet and the hope of never again going hungry, of never again watching a hunger-weakened child die.

But it would also be difficult now to find a poor Nicaraguan who could not tell you of the mounting difficulties in obtaining food—long lines, empty shelves, speculators' prices, and genuine uncertainty about what will be lacking next. Indeed, by the revolution's fifth anniversary, military and economic aggression were generating so many material problems in everyday life that—even with the new efforts at equitably sharing the necessities—five years of notable advances by the majority of Nicaraguans stood gravely threatened. Nicaragua in late 1984 was on the brink of being plunged into a war economy of serious hardship.

Without doubt, throughout the world there would be great,

perhaps unparalleled, protests against a direct military invasion of Nicaragua. The Reagan administration appears to know this.

But while maintaining in readiness the direct military option, the Reagan administration is also waging a war few are aware of and few protest—a war of attrition. The war of attrition bleeds Nicaragua's economy and threatens to do the same to the spirit of the people. The war of attrition is the most difficult war to mobilize a nation against, since it tends to wear people down, divide them against themselves and even sap their will to struggle. At the same time, the war of attrition undermines every material advance achieved by and for Nicaragua's poor majority—the people who constitute the revolution's broadest base of support. The war of attrition is also the most difficult against which to mobilize international resistance because it is silent, surrogate, and billed simply as "pressure."

Is Rationing Inevitable?

In its sixth year the Sandinista revolution has responded to the worsening effects of aggression with rationing. We can be sure that Washington ideologues will seize upon food rationing as proof that revolution "inevitably" results in deprivation and a suppression of freedom of the marketplace. (They will conveniently forget that such capitalist bulwarks as Britain and the United States turned to rationing in World War II or that many called for gasoline rationing during the oil crisis of 1973.) Sadly, much of the mass media and others readily fall into such sophistry.

There is nothing inevitable about rationing for a society that strives to build an equitable social order. In the case of Nicaragua, we have seen that the policies of the first years of the revolution increased most food production, including export crops, to record levels (see table 7, the years 1979–80 and 1981–82). Per-capita food consumption, despite a considerable population increase, demonstrated solid progress through 1982 (see table 8, comparing the annual averages during the period 1980–82 and 1976–78). Unlike in most countries, where per-capita food consumption statistics mask sharp differences between well-off elites and an impoverished majority, the *distribution* of basic foods was improving by all accounts. Greater production *and* enabling more Nicaraguans to share in the produced wealth, not rationing, were the hallmarks of the Sandinista revolution at the completion of the first edition of our account of the revolution.

It was not until 1983 that spot shortages of certain basic foods began. At this writing, most indications are that production and supply problems are getting worse with little prospect of improvement in this decade. We have seen that Nicaragua shares the causes of many of these problems with other third-world nations: an economy long ago structured to be excessively dependent on imports and geared to production for export rather than local needs; generations of enforced technical backwardness; depressed prices for commodity exports and declining terms of trade; soaring interest rates; and a crushing inherited debt. Still we have not shied away, as the Sandinistas and most Nicaraguans have not, from pointing out errors, misconceptions, and concerns about the wisdom embodied in specific policies and practices. But whatever these internal deficiencies, we have found the overwhelming obstacle to be outside military and economic aggression. Hypocritically erected in the name of concern for the people of Nicaragua, this obstacle makes the correction of most internal problems more difficult and more costly.

Rationing is not a good in itself. It is administratively cumbersome and costly and enforces a considerable degree of uniformity in tastes and desires. Although the Sandinistas have tried to learn from rationing experiences elsewhere (and therefore, for instance, have opted for a largely nongovernment distribution network), they still view food rationing as an emergency response to severe national economic hardship, not as a goal. Many countries today, with even worse economic crises and more widespread shortages than Nicaragua, do not have rationing—except highly inequitable rationing by income. Equitable rationing, we would suggest, is the hallmark of a society where there is a government with a keen commitment to fairness and a strong reverence for the life of all its citizens.

Far from being experienced by most citizens as a suppression of the freedom of the marketplace, food rationing in Nicaragua came to be *demanded* by most Nicaraguans in order to be free from those who would profit on hunger in the name of "freedom." For the majority, the revolution means that whenever there is scarcity they have the right to see it shared equitably. Attempting equitable distribution of limited staples through rationing—despite the international and internal (especially in an electoral year) political costs—is evidence of the Sandinista leadership's commitment to the interests of the poor majority, those who traditionally suffer most in times of war and economic crisis.

Is rationing inevitable? One might say instead that if anything seems inevitable in the process of a society striving to build an equitable social order, it is not so much rationing as a counterrevolution sponsored by a foreign power. For, to the leadership and most of the people in Nicaragua today, it seems that no matter how cautiously and legally they move, no matter what compromises they are willing to make, they must suffer again and again open and lawless intervention from the United States working through the overthrown elite of the old order. What has been proven is merely that the most powerful nation in the hemisphere can exact a very high price from the people of one of the hemisphere's smallest and most economically vulnerable countries.

Unless this utter defiance of all norms of civilized conduct is protested and resisted by more citizens of the United States and its allies, the world is in great danger of once again being deprived—as it was in Guatemala, in Brazil, in Chile, in Grenada—of knowing not what *is* "inevitable" but what *could* be.

TWENTY FOUR

1985–1986: RESETTING PRIORITIES

"ANY NICARAGUAN WHO STILL HAS PROP-erty here and has not lost it is going to lose it because this is the system, the ideology, and the doctrine of those who govern this country." These words, broadcasted around the world on June 18, 1985 by the major media (I woke up to them on National Public Radio's *Morning Edition*), were those of Enrique Bolaños, who, as president of the Higher Council of Private Enterprise (COSEP), has been a prominent opponent of the revolution. Along with a number of other large, private cotton growers, he just recently had much of his actively worked farmland near Masaya expropriated. Bolaños's words—and he is fluent in English—could only have been music to the ears of the Reagan administration. A "private-sector martyr" is born.

The international mass media tended to present the "Bolaños story" as unlawful revenge by the Sandinistas against an outspoken political opponent. It seemed to fit perfectly with a preconceived idea of Nicaragua as on the road to a totalitarian society in which the state would own everything.

What is the truth behind the Bolaños expropriation? For one thing, his land was not turned over to the government; it was not made into state farms. For the most part, it went to individual private producers — "family farmers." However much this may have displeased Sr. Bolaños, it was hardly, as we shall see, an attack on private property. What's more, it demonstrated that the flexible, nondogmatic quality of the Sandinista leadership we noted from the earliest days of the revolution was still operative. The process of popular, democratic actions by many campesinos, which brought the Sandinista leadership around to this policy — a policy running counter to previously held notions of many Sandinistas — is worth looking at in some detail.

First, the key factors behind the Masaya expropriations. The department of Masaya lies immediately southwest of Managua. It is by far the most densely populated rural area in Nicaragua, with only 1 acre per resident, in contrast to a national average of almost 13 acres per rural resident. Before the revolution, the contrast between relatively few wealthy producers and thousands of impoverished campesino families with too little or no land was even sharper in the Masaya area than in the rest of the nation.

After the victory over Somoza, many Masayan campesinos had high hopes. Carlos ("Caliche") Barrios, a young Sandinista leader in the area, told Frances Lappé and me in early 1982* that local campesinos had thought the revolution meant land for them. After all, Carlos Fonseca, the founder of the Sandinistas, and who was assassinated by Somoza, had vowed, "In Nicaragua no campesino will be without land." Hundreds of poor Masayan campesinos participated during the insurrectionary period in farm takeovers, which totaled some 3,500 acres.

Understandably, these campesinos were not pleased, Caliche recalled, with the first results of the revolution: farms that could not be proven to be owned by Somocistas were taken from campesinos and handed back to their owners; and farms that had belonged to Somoza and his cronies were made into state farms (see chapter 7). Respect for the Sandinistas led most campesinos to acquiesce. But when I visited three

---

*Frances Moore Lappé and Joseph Collins, *Now We Can Speak*, pp. 9 f.

state farms in the area during that period, it became clear to me that they were less than enthusiastic about their newly assigned role as workers for the state farms. A month before my visit, in February 1980, thousands of Masayan campesinos marched on MIDINRA's Managua headquarters demanding land.

By mid-1985, the protests had little practical affect. The Sandinistas agrarian reform had distributed land to only 15 percent of the 8,730 landless and land-poor families— considerably less than the national average of 22 percent. What was holding back land reform in an area crying for it? In addition to the general factors we discussed in chapters 9 and 15*, even most of the wealthy owners' farms in the Masaya area were under 850 acres and were arguably well exploited. The conservative Agrarian Reform Law, however, called for the expropriation only of farms that were bigger than 850 acres and were not being used productively. "Here in Masaya," land-hungry campesinos complained, "the Agrarian Reform Law doesn't touch anybody; it simply passes through the clouds."

What land was distributed in Masaya (largely from state farms in an effort to streamline their administration) was allotted in the form of cooperatives. Many agrarian reform officials felt cooperatives were inherently more in line with the socialist goals of the revolution and could more easily receive technical assistance than could a myriad of individual plots (see chapters 11 and 15). This ran counter to the strong desire of many campesinos for private plots.

But if the revolution had not given land to most of Masaya's poor campesinos, it had fostered in them a sense of their right to productive resources. It also freed them from the fear of

---

*The concern of the Sandinista leaders that land expropriations would undermine a multiclass national unity in the face of foreign aggression; their fear that large-scale land distribution to campesinos, who generally favor food crop production, would diminish export crop acreage as well as create an acute shortage of manual labor on the remaining agro-export farms, thus reducing vital foreign exchange earnings for the nation; and the urban technocratic bias of many of the Sandinista leaders that resulted in a lack of confidence in traditional peasant farming techniques.

speaking out against the government—a fear that had charac-
terized the Somoza dictatorship. As a result, the Sandinista
leadership was to become painfully aware that land-poor
Masayan campesinos viewed the land reform as insufficient
(too little land expropriated) and inappropriate (too centered
on state farms and cooperatives).

Their mounting discontent was expressed in many ways. As
Caliche told us, every April, when the year's first rains normally fall, the campesinos "smell the moist earth [and] begin
to think of planting corn and beans. And when the peasants
think of planting, they think of getting land." So every April,
thousands of Masaya's rural poor crowded into government
offices to solicit land from state farms or to seek government
help with conflicts with large landowners who would not rent
them land to grow corn and beans. (I recall paying a visit to
the area in February 1980 with an agrarian reform technician.
There was a freak early rain that afternoon; my companion
looked up at the sky and said, "Ay! The campesinos will knock
down our office walls this year!")

Then there were the assemblies and demonstrations. In
August 1981, shortly after the passage of the Agrarian Reform
Law, some 2,000 campesinos marched on the government
offices in the city of Masaya, protesting that the new law did
not meet their needs. Toward the end of 1982, 1,200 campesino families from 23 communities in the area organized a
protest rally to demand the expropriation of a number of large
private farms, including Bolaños's, in order to distribute land
to the landless.

As with earlier demonstrations, the government turned a
deaf ear to demands for expropriations, opting to defend the
large owners' interests in order to try to maintain national
unity in the face of U.S. aggression. In contrast, the desti-
tution of Masayan campesinos as well as their geographic
distance from the zones of military attacks by the U.S.-backed
contras made it difficult for them to understand why the
Nicaraguan revolution had to be guided by foreign demands
rather than domestic needs.

In the national elections in November 1984, only 40 percent of the registered voters in the Masaya department cast
their ballots for the Sandinista slate. Although this per-

centage put it ahead of all other political parties, the margin of victory was considerably below the national average. Opposition parties were especially strong in communitiès where less than 10 percent of the population had received land through the agrarian reform. While the Reagan administration prejudged Nicaragua's elections as a farce, the Sandinista leadership took them very seriously as a barometer of support for its policies.

In the subsequent months, Masayan campesinos expressed their waning enthusiasm for the Sandinistas by not participating in UNAG (the Sandinista-affiliated small farmers' association), evading the military draft, and not turning out for Sandinista political ceremonies. This "political strike" was viewed as a serious problem by the Sandinista leadership. The tide was turning. The campesinos triumphed when their discontent made the Sandinista government rethink the question of agrarian and national unity: after adhering to a policy of guarantees to the wealthy private producers to maintain their support in the face of expected foreign aggression, by 1985 UNAG officials and many other local Sandinista leaders in the Masaya area thought that they now needed to *regain* campesino support. The national Sandinista leadership decided that the overall "project" of the revolution no longer could afford to postpone the demand of some of the nation's poorest campesinos for land. And, if most of them wanted individual farms, so be it.

The first step, taken in late May, was to distribute much of the remaining state-farm land. Since there was insufficient state land in the department of Masaya to meet the needs of land-poor campesinos, negotiations were opened with the larger private producers for the purchase of land.

The entire process was strictly legal under a clause in the Agrarian Reform Law empowering the government to declare "agrarian reform zones" where a change in land ownership was deemed necessary to solve special problems or promote development projects of major national importance (see chapter 10). In many nations, including the United States, such authority is a constitutionally vested right of the government under the rubric of "eminent domain." (Indeed, to create the huge Timal sugar plantation mill and project, this clause was used to expropriate the farms of an entire peasant community.)

MIDINRA offered the large producers from whom land was to be expropriated reasonable cash payment or land elsewhere of equivalent size and quality. The government thus hoped that it would be seen as keeping its fundamental promise to the large private producers—to guarantee a law-and-order framework in which they could do business—and yet acceding to campesino pressure. Even at this point the ministry displayed a degree of flexibility that would startle anyone following the Nicaraguan government through the U.S. mass media's parroting of "White House charges." Campesinos prematurely occupied one farm to be expropriated; the government, over loud protests, demanded that the campesinos quit the property so the owner could harvest his 1,200 acres of cotton before turning the land over to the new owners.

All the expropriated landowners agreed to the negotiations. All but one, of course. Bolaños even turned down the government's proposal of 2 acres of similar quality in a cotton-producing area near León for every 1 acre of his in Masaya. Having refused all offers, his principal cotton estates were confiscated.* "In the end," MIDINRA's first Vice Minister, Salvador Mayorga, commented to me, "we had to choose between Enrique Bolaños and 8,000 campesino families. We had no trouble making up our minds."

Through UNAG the government made it clear that it was not going to insist on or even push for the distribution of the expropriated lands on a collective basis. The campesinos were told that, in effect, *they* would basically have to work out how the lands were to be parceled. Reportedly, Minister Jaime Wheelock shrugged his shoulders and told one community of campesinos, "Obviously, we don't know how to do these things, so it's up to you."

In 1985, the Sandinistas, far from eliminating the private sector, were expanding it.

---

*Bolaños's nearby dairy farm was not confiscated. He is owner or part-owner of several other farms in the area.

Privatization

Developments in the agrarian reform in Masaya in 1985 were but an intense case of what was happening nationally. At the core was the Sandinista leadership's critical reappraisal of the agrarian reform, provoked by the erosion of campesino support for the existing agrarian reform and therefore for the revolution. Increasingly, the leadership realized that it had erred by giving priority in the first years of the revolution to state farms and, after 1982, to production cooperatives. Excluded were the many campesinos who simply did not want to farm collectively and were not willing to accept land if this were the condition. Effectively, agrarian reform policy in many regions was playing into the hands of the counter-revolution.

In 1985, new agrarian reform titles for the year totaled over 1 million acres. (This high figure is especially noteworthy as 70 percent of the land consisted of *redistributions* and not just secure titles for small farmers to lands they previously held without legal titles.) By the start of 1986, 86,556 families, or some 60 percent of the nation's campesinos, had received land titles (51,971 actually received redistributed land) to almost 4.5 million acres, or one-third of the nation's farmland. Before the revolution, all of the nation's poor campesinos had a total of less than 300,000 acres.

Land, of course, is not all that campesinos expect of an agrarian reform. Now that a significant number of new landowners have been created, the government will increasingly be measured in terms of the farm inputs, the machinery, and the services the agrarian reform makes available to them. Distributing land can be viewed as the easy part of the agrarian reform because land is an internal resource and Nicaragua has abundant farmland. Washington's military and economic war on Nicaragua, however, will continue to make it especially difficult to meet campesino expectations for productive goods, many of which have to be imported.

MIDINRA's mid-year plan for land distribution for the remaining months of 1985 called for a tripling of the amount of land given to individuals, compared to what had been distributed to individuals since the passage of the Agrarian

Reform Law four years before. According to this plan, farm land to be parceled out to individual farmers would account for 26 percent of all land distributed during 1985, up from only 2.5 percent in the 1981–84 period.

Much of the land distributed to individual campesinos in 1985 was taken from the state-farm sector. In the war torn Region I (Estelí) bordering on Honduras (which has always been in the vanguard in reducing the area in state farms), so many state farms had been given to land-poor campesinos that by the end of 1985 the state-farm sector had been reduced to only 6 percent of total land area in the region. The experience of the region has been that both land and labor productivity have generally increased when state farms have been broken up and worked by small farmers either cooperatively or individually. Breaking up state farms also reduced the risk of contra attacks since state farms were a prime contra target. In the Carazo area bordering on Masaya, where campesino pressure for land has also erupted, almost all state-farm land was turned over to campesinos in 1984–1985.

Where state-farm land is insufficient to satisfy campesino needs, as in the Masaya area, MIDINRA negotiates with large private producers to buy their land at a mutually agreed upon price and with payment in cash or kind (state land in other areas). (Keeping its pledge in this way, to respect private property, will undoubtedly cost billions of córdobas and significantly run up the already massive budget deficit, and thereby further fuel runaway inflation.)

Pressure to expropriate efficiently run large farms should be relieved and more land made available to land-poor campesinos through the first-ever modification of the Agrarian Reform Law in January 1986. No longer is an unproductive farm exempt if it is less than a minimum size (850 or 1,700 acres, depending on the region). The bottom line of the reform continues to be productive efficiency, only now extended to all producers without exception.

By 1986, the direction of policy thinking was that the appropriate role of government was not to farm (by and large, the government has achieved less than spectacular results in direct production) but to use state enterprises to provide private cooperatives and individual producers with support services, from planting to marketing. Many of these private producers, as they themselves will often tell you, could be producing much more if they could buy machetes, seeds, and other inputs; obtain *timely* credit; rely on technical advice if they need it; and have access to transport and centers for selling their harvests.

Ironically, the model cited by the proponents of such a state role is the contract farming mode of the multinational agribusinesses operating in the area, TANIC (British American Tobacco) and PROLACSA (Nestlé). Both companies provide a complete "package" of credit, inputs, and technical assistance. These farmers produce for the companies' processing facilities, thereby assuring them of a market. Operating in a similar way with producers of coffee, cattle, and basic grains, state enterprises, it is argued, could boost output in the mountainous hinterland. At the same time, state agroindustries would be helped to capture an ever greater portion of production, and therefore greater control over distribution.

Redefining the role of the state sector is not without its vocal critics. Strong opposition often comes from managers and technicians of MIDINRA's enterprises (a typical "enterprise" groups 30–40 separate state farms). Many enterprises have borrowed heavily to improve installations and equipment (barns, irrigation, machinery) on farms now being handed over to campesinos free of charge. The debts incurred nonetheless stay with the "mother" enterprise since most campesinos would not accept a farm if it came heavily mortgaged from the start. Debt repayments for many MIDINRA enterprises have become so steep that future social investments (housing, day-care, clinics) seem remote, if not impossible — and that tends to undercut worker and manager productivity in such enterprises. A manager of the Estelí-based Filemón Rivera enterprise commented that he was "quite unhappy" about the privatization thrust. In 1982–83, the enterprise had approximately 40 percent of its total holdings (or 40,000 acres) taken from it with no relief from its sizeable debts. The manager planned to appeal to Wheelock to pass the debt on to the new owners; he thought, however, that he had little chance of success.

MIDINRA enterprise administrators also tend to argue that splitting up state enterprises sacrifices advantages that result from planning capital investments and allocating labor, natural resources, and other inputs over a large number of farms. As resources in a wartime economy become ever more scarce, they argue, more rather than less state planning is required to ensure that the national interests are served.

Despite such critics, we can expect in 1986 a more decentralized, privatized, campesino-based strategy to take ever greater priority in the wartorn interior regions. In the important Pacific regions (Chinandega, León, Managua), however, the state farm model is holding its own. There, supporters of this model argue that the local conditions and needs are different. The Sandinista agrarian policy is likely to continue its two-tracked approach.

Going Against the Grain Plan

1985 also saw a critical re-evaluation of the Emergency Grain Plan and of the thinking behind it. As set forth in chapter 21, the plan is essentially a large-scale, high-tech, capital-intensive approach to solving Nicaragua's grain crisis, characteristic of one major current of opinion within MIDINRA on development strategies and food security. The plan drew fire because of its extreme import dependency (in a nation so lacking in foreign exchange); its high vulnerability to power failures and other technical foul-ups, not to mention direct sabotage; and its de facto diversion of resources away from campesino-based strategies. UNAG leaders were particularly influential in their outspoken criticisms of the plan (and also of the high-tech dairy schemes like Chiltepe, discussed in chapter 19).

Toward the close of 1984, a high-level MIDINRA planning session evaluated the Emergency Plan's first-year performance. Costs had been high, and output had fallen far short of projections. Some at the session labeled the Emergency Plan a "technocratic vision" of development—and starry-eyed at that. Not surprisingly, the Emergency Plan was significantly downgraded in MIDINRA's food security strategy for the coming year. The plan's big high-tech farms were to be maintained, and even expanded, but at a much slower pace than previously projected. In addition, because of the increasingly

serious national grain shortages and technical problems encountered in rotating corn and cotton within a single year,
many of the Emergency Plan's irrigated farms had dropped
cotton cultivation altogether and opted for two crops of corn a
year. In 1985, this double-cropping helped push up the Emergency Grain Plan's share of national corn output to 15 percent.

MIDINRA's 1985 revamped food security strategy projected a broader, more diversified, and more campesino-
oriented strategy than the earlier Emergency Plan. The shift
to this new approach was summarized by Reynaldo Tremenio,
National Director of MIDINRA's Division of Agricultural
Production. He commented to us in December 1985: "We
thought the Pacific Coast was paradise. Now we see that
Nicaragua has to develop the rich potential of its peasant base
in the nation's hinterland. This is a much cheaper and, in the
long run, much more reliable, source of food security." Two
new programs were launched to boost output as quickly and
cheaply as possible by building on the foundation of campesino production in the mountainous hinterland.

One of the programs, the Directed Technical Assistance
Program (*directed* is the key word) provides "technical
packages"—credit, improved seeds, fertilizers, mechaniza-
tion services, and technical assistance—to campesino producers with strong underrealized productive potential. Such a
program, given the war and the resulting scarce resources, will
be difficult to carry out. In 1985, nonetheless, some 107,000
acres of campesino-grown beans and grain were included in
the program, with yield increases projected at 20 to 30 percent. In August 1985, in one northern fertile mountain valley,
La Vigia (where Paul Rice was working on a MIDINRA
project), two U.S. agronomists working in Nicaragua and I
visited campesinos participating in the program. They showed
us what we agreed was the best corn we had seen growing
anywhere in the country. They proudly anticipated yields that
should easily surpass those on the high-tech farms of the
Emergency Plan and at a fraction of the foreign exchange
cost—provided, of course, their crops were not burned to the
ground by marauding contras. (These campesinos, by the way,
had been resettled in La Vigia earlier in the year by the army.
They had been evacuated from their mountain homes and

much poorer quality fields in wartorn and contra-infested areas close to the Honduran border. While the evacuation was mandatory, the campesinos were given cooperative and individual titles to rich valley lands that had been state farms.)

The other major campesino-oriented program initiated in 1985 called for bringing into production virgin lands primarily in zones dominated by small farmers in the north-central interior of the country. These lands had been covered with marshes, forests, and natural pastures. The program targets areas that with small government investments in drainage, clearing, and soil conservation could become highly productive corn, bean, and sorghum farms run cooperatively and individually. In 1985, some 6,000 acres were brought under cultivation through this program; 17,000 additional acres have been targeted for 1986.

Washington's Toll

Throughout 1985, Washington's war on Nicaragua continued to cut seriously into agricultural production in both direct and indirect ways. Every line of agricultural production suffered in some way:

—**Coffee.** Some 59 farms were burned by the contras during the 1984–85 season; more than 200 coffee pickers were murdered in ambushes and nighttime raids; and more than 20,000 acres of coffee, valued at $69 million (over one-fifth of what Nicaragua earned in foreign exchange that year!), were abandoned because entire zones were simply too dangerous for pickers to enter.

—**Tobacco.** Because tobacco-growing is centered in the wartorn Nueva Segovia and Estelí regions, over half of all full-time tobacco farmworkers were mobilized into local militias for defense against contra attacks. As a consequence, the growers' labor costs soared because producers are required to pay for replacement workers on top of paying the mobilized workers' salaries. The quality of the tobacco also declined because of the inexperience of the newly hired, largely early adolescent, even child, labor force. In 1980, 65 percent of Nicaragua's tobacco was of export quality; by 1985, only 42 percent.

—**Beans.** Output increased slightly in 1984, but the destruction of storage facilities by the contras and the continued difficulty of getting the harvests out of the war zones meant that in 1985 the government agency ENABAS was able to collect only 70 percent of what it had the year before. As a result, beans were at times in short supply in the cities. Bean imports jumped from virtually none in 1983 to 24 million pounds in 1984, with even greater amounts projected for 1985 and 1986. At least 25 percent of the corn and bean production in the war zones was destroyed by the war in 1984, requiring some $14 million in imports to fill in the gap.

Prioritizing Production

A leading concern in 1985 was to adopt policies to confront the war's heavy toll on production. The thrust has been to formulate financial incentives for both owners and workers. (From the start of the revolution, the Sandinistas—in contrast to Ché Guevara and other early leaders of the Cuban revolution—have eschewed purely idealistic exhortation to motivate more and better work, and instead have sought to find effective material incentives.)

The government tripled prices paid to coffee producers for the 1985–86 harvest. Moreover, the córdoba-dollar exchange rate used to pay part of the price and additional bonuses for export-grade beans was raised to the lofty "parallel" rate (900 to 1 in early 1986). The government's incentives for boosting coffee output took note of the likelihood of a 1986 upswing in world coffee prices because of drought in Brazil.

As the coffee harvest approached in late 1985, the Sandinista-affiliated farmworkers' association, the ATC, organized a series of assemblies throughout the coffee regions to work out recommendations (which were adopted by MIDINRA) for better wage incentives for coffee pickers. In addition to a hefty boost in the rate per can, a 40 percent bonus was set for each can of coffee beans harvested over the norm of five cans per day. (This two-tiered approach had long been recommended by the ATC leadership as a way to boost worker productivity and not just total output.)

With this new wage scale, a typical, experienced picker (not to be confused with a North American or other foreign volunteer!) could earn 15,000 to 20,000 córdobas a month, comparable to a skilled industrial worker's wage in Managua. This narrowing of the rural-urban wage gap, it was hoped, would be attractive enough to draw many new pickers into the 1985–86 harvest, and would help ease the previous year's estimated labor deficit of 20,000 pickers.

With the slogan "Not a single bean unharvested," the ATC also organized special brigades of highly experienced farm-workers to "retake" those coffee plantations that went unharvested in 1984 because of the war. Big bonuses and partial payment in U.S. dollars were offered to attract volunteer pickers, while the army geared up to provide a protective shield of some 7,00 soldiers and militia members.

As the harvest season got under way in November 1985, coffee growers and workers alike expressed enthusiasm for the new package of incentives.

Bonuses for better quality products and increased worker productivity were also offered in the 1985–86 cotton and sugar cane harvests. State tobacco farms even implemented a pilot program that gave newly formed farmworkers' cooperatives control over production on selected parcels of the farms. In response to the increased reliance on young people's labor with the deepening of the war, state tobacco farms in the northern valley of Jalapa started offering free milk and shoes to children and youths who regularly showed up for work as well as an afternoon school.

Export plantation owners and farmworkers were not the only ones offered sizeable incentives in 1985. Grain farmers were offered greatly increased producer prices by ENABAS. Between 1984 and 1985, the price offered for all food crops increased: corn and beans tripled, rice almost doubled, and sorghum quadrupled. Of course, with general inflation for 1985 thought to be running at 250 percent, the gain in real terms for these producers was much less.

In a major policy turnaround last year, the government dropped all official marketing restrictions for producers of corn and beans in the country's war zones, and allowed farmers to seek their own buyers and to sell at the best prices they could find. Through conversations with small grain producers I found them eager to take advantage of the new free-marketing policy, especially those in the more remote, mountainous areas where ENABAS collection points had commonly been a two-day mule ride away. With the significant shortfall in bean production in 1985, farmers could get from private dealers as much as twice the ENABAS price for good quality beans. Predictably, ENABAS was having a tough time purchasing any beans at all in late 1985. In an effort to cope, ENABAS devised special arrangements with some producers. For example, in the Jalapa Valley, cooperatives signed contracts to sell 80 percent of their bean harvests to ENABAS in exchange for a guaranteed supply of machetes, fertilizers, and other inputs.

There is good reason to believe that the government's new free-market tack will succeed in boosting both production *and marketing* of corn and beans in the mountainous interior—and help win (and in some areas regain) the political support of the campesinos. Nevertheless, these efforts mean greater difficulties and increasing costs to guarantee reasonably priced staples for low-income, urban Nicaraguans.

Changing Distribution Patterns

The policy of enhanced financial incentives for production is logically linked to new measures to improve consumption for certain sectors of workers. Early in 1985, Worker Supply Centers were opened in the cities in what had been state-run supermarkets. They carried a wide variety of low-priced consumer items not covered by the guaranty card (see chapter 22) exclusively for factory and office workers, who had to show special I.D. cards to get in. The idea was to give an economic advantage to those people doing productive work over those in commerce and the informal sector (see chapter 18), in an effort to arrest the flight of skilled workers from factories and offices to the more lucrative work in petty commerce and speculation.

Serious problems plagued the new Worker Supply Centers at the outset. Shoppers frequently complained of long lines to enter the stores, and of high prices and spot shortages of many items. Some were angry about falsification of I.D. cards and speculation by some workers on goods they had purchased in the stores at low prices. As more stores of this kind were opened and more experience was gained in their operation, some of these problems were brought under control. In October 1985, the Sandinista-affiliated trade unions strongly and publicly criticized prices in the centers; shortly thereafter, the prices for many items were lowered by 10 to 15 percent.

Nevertheless, with an ever tighter foreign exchange bottleneck (see chapter 17), galloping inflation, and such austerity measures as cutbacks in consumer subsidies, the basic consumer problems of high prices and shortages remained unsolved. Only with an end to the military and economic warfare could Nicaragua hope to come out of what was increasingly referred to in 1985 as the "survival economy."

The new policy of giving priority to productive workers in the distribution of scarce goods was also applied to campesinos and farmworkers, especially those producing key exports like coffee and cotton. In the weeks just before the annual harvest season, the government imported and made available to coffee producers tons of tires, car batteries, and spare parts for coffee mills, as well as truckloads of rice, beans, and corn for the tens of thousands of seasonal pickers who would soon (hopefully) arrive. In what might seem bizarre in most countries, some imported goods were more available in the hinterlands than in the capital. The ATC set up new workers' commissaries on dozens of state coffee estates, and ENABAS added several new trucks to its fleet of mobile commissaries serving the smaller and more remote coffee farms.

At the same time, following a critical reappraisal of its attempts to set up and operate a rural distribution network, the government decided to pass the wholesale distribution of many basic consumer goods back into private hands. In the northern Segovia mountain range bordering on Honduras, for example, the government's wholesale marketing corporation, CORCOSE, was transferred to a private marketing cooperative in early 1985. It did quite well in its first year under private control.

Also in 1985, UNAG started its first agricultural-inputs distribution cooperative in the Matagalpa and Chontales/ Boaco regions, vowing to do better than government agencies had in making agricultural supplies and tools as well as some consumer items available to its members. A top economic advisor of the government commented that if this initiative proved successful the government might turn the business of national marketing to private rural producers over to UNAG.

Despite these hopeful efforts at better distribution of scarce goods in the hinterlands, until the ever darkening foreign exchange picture clears, no one expects an easing in the fundamental scarcity of essential producer and consumer goods in the countryside.* One future-oriented, albeit partial, solution is for Nicaragua to produce its own basic farm implements (machetes, files, axes, corn grinders, horseshoe nails, barbed wire, etc.). In 1985, East Germany started to help build a metallurgical plant in Managua to produce agricultural implements, spare parts, and simple machinery. But this plant will not come on line for several more years. In the meantime, farmers will have to return—and they are—to older methods (hollowed gourds in place of plastic containers, the lining of a calf's stomach instead of imported rennet pills to curdle milk for making cheese) and old-fashioned ingenuity.

Tackling the Oriental

In 1985, the government finally decided to get tough with the flagrant speculation on food and other basic goods in Managua's infamous Eastern Market (*Mercado Oriental*). Long seemingly untouchable (see chapters 13 and 23), the sprawling Eastern Market had grown to more than twice the size it was before the revolution, thriving as a haven for hoarders and speculators—where you could find whatever you wanted and couldn't find elsewhere, but usually at outrageous prices. According to a 1985 census, more than half of the market's 30,000 (!) vendors were operating without commercial licenses.

-----

*In January 1986, the People's Republic of China offered Nicaragua interest-free credits to import Chinese goods. This could help ease the acute tool shortage in the countryside since China produces machetes, horseshoe nails, and other basic goods that Nicaragua's farmers need and that France, Sweden, Spain, and the other Western European nations offering Nicaragua credits simply do not produce. Nicaragua, which had active diplomatic, aid, and trade ties with Taiwan during the first six years of the revolution, established diplomatic relations with China for the first time in December 1985.

The "cleanup" started in earnest in late 1985. Some 12,000 legal vendors were issued new permits; the rest were either relocated to the capital's other markets or told to seek productive employment. The remaining licensed vendors were organized into CDS committees, which, among other things, should facilitate vigilance about what is sold and at what prices. Physically, the largely outdoor market underwent a face lift. Vendors were grouped in different sections according to the type of product they sold; old stalls and carts that had choked walkways were cleared out; and commercial activities were prohibited in the surrounding residential areas that had been overrun by vendors in recent years. In all, the market was compacted in size from an unbelievable 35 city blocks to 5 city blocks.

The long-term success of the new crackdown on speculation quite possibly will depend more on the viable alternatives provided in the productive sector for the thousands of redundant vendors. One program to provide a new source of productive work for capital city dwellers—while also boosting food production—is called the Managua Plan. Started in mid-1985 by MIDINRA and PAN, the Managua Plan in its first year gave out almost 2,000 acres of idle land in and around the city for planting by newly formed cooperatives and individual small farmers. In 1986, more areas around the city were being identified for distribution. CDSs and other urban community organizations began encouraging families with no stable income to apply to MIDINRA for land through the Managua Plan.

Another alternative for some vendors shut down by the crackdown on speculation was to migrate back to their rural communities to look for work. According to local, knowledgeable people, the return of landless campesinos who had been forced out of the Eastern Market to the Carazo Plateau (bordering on the department of Masaya) was directly related to an upsurge in militant demands for land in this area at the end of 1985. This added factor in the longstanding pressure for land by the Masaya-Carazo region helped push MIDINRA to distribute some 27,000 acres of state-farm, abandoned, and government-purchased private land in individual holdings to some 4,000 campesino families.

In general, MIDINRA officials are hoping that the reorientation of the agrarian reform in the direction of creating many more small farmers, combined with greater producer incentives and priority to the rural areas in marketing basic goods, will reverse the deterioration of the "terms of trade" between the city and the countryside, and slow the large-scale migration of the rural poor to the cities.

* * *

In 1985–86, with an ever sharper focus on economic and political *survival*, the Sandinista revolution has passed into a major period of self-criticism and resetting of priorities. Agrarian reform and farm policy are now to emphasize the majority of producers in the countryside over not only the elite private producers but also the state farms. Priority is off importing high-tech solutions to food crisis and is on improving traditional farmers' methods. Distribution is to be not according to need but according to one's contribution to production.

External aggression, predictably, "radicalizes" revolutions in the third world. The Sandinista revolution is no exception. However, unlike so many revolutions—notably Cuba's—rather than turn to greater state ownership, the Sandinista revolution has moved toward greater democratization and expanded privatization of production and services. President Reagan seems not to have taken notice.

Postscript

WORLD HUNGER AND THE NICARAGUAN REVOLUTION

For more than a decade, we at the Institute for Food and Development Policy have probed the roots of world hunger— through research, field work, and the work of colleagues living in the third world.

While many countries do not enjoy the rich agricultural potential of Nicaragua, we have learned that in virtually no country with chronic hunger is the scarcity of resources the primary obstacle. The obstacle instead is that the hungry, often the hungry *majority*, have been dispossessed—deprived of control over the resources rightfully theirs, which they need to free themselves from hunger.

Thus roots of hunger run deep, very deep. More than a problem of food or land, hunger is a problem of power. Hunger

Editorial Note: Joseph Collins and Frances Moore Lappé coauthored this postscript. Since assisting with the first edition of this book, Frances has focused on Nicaragua's political process, the debate over "democracy" and "freedom." Her article "Nicaragua: Revolution and/or Democracy?" appeared in *Christianity and Crisis*, December 26, 1983. She has also authored a report on her experience as an observer of the elections in Nicaragua on November 4, 1984. Both are available through Food First.

results not from a scarcity of resources but from a scarcity of democracy—if by democracy we mean the wide distribution of decision-making power.

Unfortunately, this truth is not obvious. For power is invisible. People find it much easier to focus on the tangibles— acres of land, tons of grain, or numbers of tractors. Even well-intentioned aid programs designed to provide "inputs" for increasing food production ignore the fundamental question: development by whom and for whom? This is the question of power, the question that determines whether any so-called advance benefits the hungry or further enriches and entrenches the established economic and political elites.

Our findings have forced us to several broad conclusions concerning the responsibility of Americans.

Most fundamental, if hunger is rooted in antidemocratic relationships, in which a minority deprive the majority of their very right to a livelihood, then no amount of food aid, new production technology or any other transfer of resources from the industrial countries to the "poor countries" will eradicate hunger. Government-to-government aid channeled through elites unaccountable to the poor only bolsters the elites whose stranglehold over productive resources generates poverty and hunger in the first place. Nothing less is required than a fundamental shift in power from a privileged elite to leadership accountable to the majority. Such a genuine shift in power is properly called a "revolution" and is very distinct from a "coup," in which a new elite simply comes to power.

A revolution entails a fundamental shift in the very definition of economic development. Development means different things to different people. In the eyes of the privileged few, development means growth in GNP, opportunities to get rich, U.S.-style farms and factories, highways, fancy hotels and clubs, hospitals with the latest medical technology, shopping centers selling imported goods. In the eyes of the poor majority, it is land in their hands to grow food, freedom from peonage to moneylenders through inexpensive credit and crop insurance, affordable and accessible health care, schools for themselves and their children, higher wages, the nation's foreign exchange used to import the basics, and capital goods to help produce the basics.

The only hope to end hunger lies in the emergence of leadership whose definition of development is the same as that of the impoverished majority. Decision-making power from the village to the national level must be placed in the hands of those who feel themselves accountable to the poor and hungry and act accordingly.

Can this ever happen? The answer is yes. But it has occurred only when the poor themselves have acted on their own behalf. We cannot bring about such a shift in decision-making power for other people.

But most Americans recoil from these profound shifts of power, from revolutions. In this century, Americans have been taught to believe that *all* revolutions result in something as bad or worse than they replaced. For many of us, this has led to a cynical and despairing dead end: Disgust at the callous greed of privileged elites is nullified by the fear that revolutions always lead to totalitarianism.

The inevitable question is: Couldn't Nicaragua turn out the same way? Couldn't all of the revolutionary differences documented in this book eventually turn against the poor?

Yes, that possibility will always exist. But we believe that, while history has shown humanity's capacity for unspeakable cruelty and deadening tyranny in the name of popular ideals, in every era there are surprises, fresh initiatives reflecting humanity's unquellable urge for fairness, freedom, and dignity. No initiative is automatically guaranteed to fulfill its mandate successfully—but often, and certainly in Nicaragua today, there are excellent grounds for hope.

Nor do we believe that the existence of counterrevolutionary efforts proves that a revolution is flawed. On the contrary, any genuine revolution is almost certain to be attacked by deposed local elites and their foreign allies in an attempt to restore the old order.

Perhaps as much as any other people on earth we Americans should be able to acknowledge the possibility of creating something genuinely new. When our own nation was founded, many supposedly wise people thought its very principles to be madness. A high-ranking British officer said of the Declaration of Independence: "A more impudent, false and atrocious proclamation was never fabricated by the hands of man." James Madison observed that the founding of the United States was "useful in proving things before held impossible." Many American colonists—they were called Tories rather than contras—fought against the revolutionary break from the British Crown. Upon the defeat of the imperial forces, they exiled themselves to Canada and Britain, some to carry out counterrevolutionary designs.

It would seem that a people with such a history could not without great forgetfulness and loss of identity condemn the initiatives of others striving for self-determination.

What then is our responsibility as Americans? If we acknowledge that hunger is rooted in structures of control that deny the poor majority access to the resources they need, and if we acknowledge that the historical record demonstrates that unanticipated and remarkably creative societal change is ever possible, then the answer is clear:

We must give change a chance.

Change, deep structural change, is the only hope of the poor and hungry. We must not deny or allow anyone in our name to deny them that hope.

We are not called upon to go in and set things right "for them," to teach them democracy and fairness. No, these values have no meaning, indeed cannot exist, unless they are demands of a people themselves.

Our responsibility is simply to make sure that our nation's foreign policy does not stand in the way of the changes needed for the hungry to be able to *free themselves* from hunger. This means demanding that our government obey its own laws as well as international treaties to which it is party. It means insisting that our government end every form of shoring up governments that perpetuate political and economic exclusion of the majority of their citizens. And it means seeing that our government end all attempts to subvert and overthrow foreign governments, above all that of a country like Nicaragua where changes on behalf of the poor majority are under way.

We should work to create space, even enthusiasm, for fundamental shifts in power in the interests of the poor majority. Allowing our government to support dictatorships, even as people rise up against their tyranny—as we allowed our government to support the Somozas—increases the bloodshed in revolutionary change. The Somozas, just as those who hold power in El Salvador today, used our aid, weaponry, and diplomatic support to kill, torture, and even bomb their own people to protect the privileges of themselves and their clique.

We must see that new national leaders representing the interests of the poor need not feel threatened by external forces. If we allow our government to violate our laws by giving material and moral support to counterrevolution, as we are doing today in Nicaragua, we contribute not only to the killing of innocent people but to the creation of a siege mentality. Whenever a government feels threatened for its survival, it is likely to restrict civil and political liberties and violate civil rights. The U.S. government, for example, shamefully interned one-half million of its own citizens after the attack on Pearl Harbor and censored the media.

To make ourselves absolutely clear, we add one final point: What we believe is *not* required of us. Nothing that we have said should suggest that we think North Americans need to give their "approval" to the Nicaraguan government. In order to fulfill our moral responsibility to the poor, we need not decide whether it is a "democratic" or "totalitarian" government. Only the Nicaraguan people can decide that and act accordingly. It is *their* government, *their* revolution.

Our responsibility is more limited and within our power. It is to take the pressure off. It is to respect the sovereign right to self-determination. Only then do we give the hopes and aspirations of the poor and hungry in Nicaragua and around the world the best chance possible, unfettered by outside hostility.

SOCIAL INDICATORS

	1978	1984
Illiteracy Rate	50%	13%
Education Expenditures (millions of córdobas)	341	1,484
Percentage of GNP for Education	1.32	5.01
Total Students	501,660	1,127,428
Adult education enrollment	none	194,800
Preschool enrollment	9,000	70,000
Teachers	12,706	53,398
Persons covered by Social Security	460,000†	930,000*
Infant Mortality (per 1000 births)	121	72
Vaccinations	923,000†	2,875,015*
Health Budget (millions of córdobas)	373	1,528*
Physicians	1,309†	2172
Clinics	177†	487
Hospitals	40	46
Medical Consultations	2,400,000†	6,045,541*
Children receiving oral rehydration	N/A	173,081*
Population	2,545,000	3,110,000
Polio	101●	0
Measles	1,270●	153
Malaria	18,418●	12,907*

*1983.
●1979.
†1977.

Sources: Ministry of Health (for health figures), Ministry of Education (for education figures).

AGRICULTURAL POPULATION OF NICARAGUA (1978)

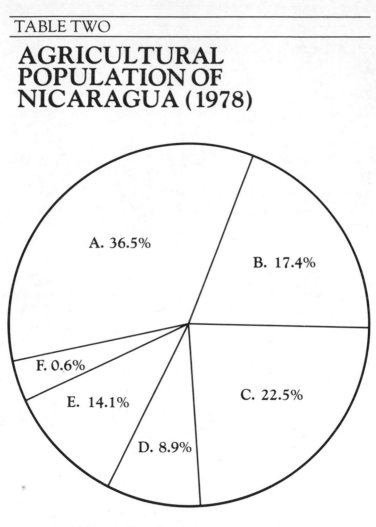

A. Holders of less than subsistence parcels
B. Seasonal farm laborers
C. Holders of subsistence parcels
D. Holders of medium-size parcels
E. Full-time salaried workers
F. Owners and managers of large landholdings

Source: CIERA

DISTRIBUTION OF RURAL INCOME (1972)

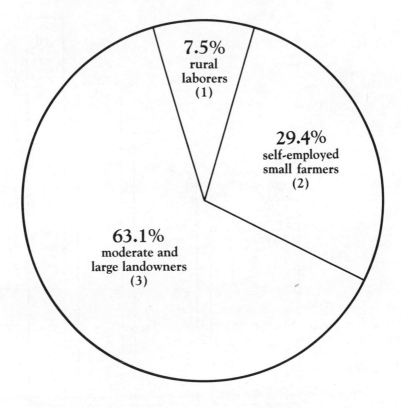

7.5%
rural
laborers
(1)

29.4%
self-employed
small farmers
(2)

63.1%
moderate and
large landowners
(3)

(1) 51% of economically active rural population
(2) 45.5% of economically active rural population
(3) 3.5% of economically active rural population

Source: *Unidad de Analisis Sectorial*, FAO Informe, 1979.

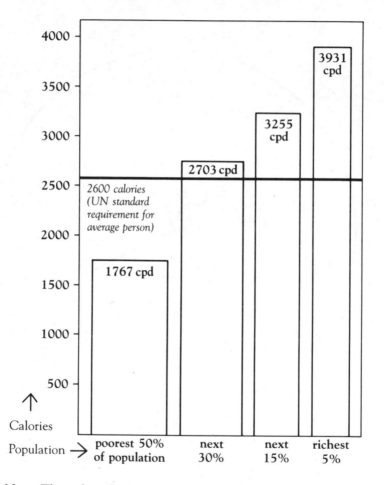

TABLE FOUR

NUTRITIONAL INTAKE BY INCOME GROUP (1971)

Note: The richest 5 percent of the population consumed 2.2 times more calories than the poorest 50 percent; 2.5 times more protein; and 3.5 times more fats.

Source: Fondo Internacional de Desarrollo Agricola, *Informe de la Mision Especial de Programacion a Nicaragua*, 1981, p. 54.

TABLE FIVE

CHANGES IN LAND OWNERSHIP (PERCENT)

	1978	1980	1985*
1. Individual owners (unorganized)			
over 850 acres	36.2	21.5	11.9
345 to 850 acres	16.2	13.4	11.6
86 to 345 acres	30.1	30.1	29.9
17 to 86 acres	15.4	13.0	7.7
less than 17 acres	2.1	2.5	1.8
2. Individual owners of less than 345 acres organized in credit and service associations (CCS)	–	0.4	11.2
3. Production cooperatives (CAS)	–	1.0	8.8
4. State farms (APP)	–	18.0	17.0

The state farm sector (APP) in 1980 was 2,580,000 acres. By July 1982 it had risen to 2,830,000 acres. By September 1985 it had fallen back down to 2,490,000 acres or around 17 percent of total area. In February 1986, a ranking MIDINRA official projected that the state sector would "probably go down to about 10 percent in the next few years."

Total area in farms and ranches: 13,886,000

*September 1985
Source: Ministry of Agriculture and Agrarian Reform (MIDINRA).

ACREAGE FOR MAJOR CROPS, 1948–1985

Export Crops	1948–52†	1974–76†	% change 48–52 to 74–76
Cotton	51,870	427,310	+724*
Coffee	138,320	207,480	+50
Sugar cane	37,050	98,800	+166
Sesame	51,870	19,760	−62
Bananas	N/A	5,636	–
Domestic Crops			
Rice	44,460	69,160	+56
Corn	251,940	573,140	+127
Beans	64,220	163,020	+154
Sorghum	81,510	130,910	+61
Total	721,240	1,695,216	+135

Source: International Fund for Agricultural Development (FIDA), columns 1 and 3; FAO, column 3; Tres Años de Reforma Agraria, Ministry of Agriculture and Agrarian Reform (MIDINRA); 1979–80 and 1983–85 MIDINRA.

1979–80††	1981–82††	1984–85††	% change 74–76 to 84-85
110,080	231,285	282,596	−33
240,800	259,906	216,032	+4
91,332	109,749	104,232	+5
19,608	35,711	37,840	+91
6,192	NA	6,536	+15
88,408	103,474	94,084	+36
412,800	497,863	464,400	−18
131,064	221,582	206,400	+26
120,916	138,140	127,108	−2
1,222,060	1,597,710	1,539,228	−9

†Multiyear average

††One-crop cycle

*Research suggests cotton acreage before revolution might have been somewhat exaggerated. Some large growers, especially close associates of Somoza, had "phantom acreage" in order to secure bank loans that they seldom repaid.

TABLE SEVEN

AGRICULTURAL PRODUCTION
(VOLUME) (1977–78 = 100)

	48–52[1]	61–65[1]	1970[2]	77–78[3]	79–80[3]	81–82[3]	82–83[3]	83–84[3]	84–85[3]	85–86†
Export Products*										
Raw Cotton	6	61	55	100	15[4]	45	55	62	50	39
Sesame	217	109	146	100	90	128	93	210	188	91
Bananas	11	193	187	100	95	104	74	113	99	100
Coffee	32	50	68	100	98	110	125	85	89	89
Sugar cane	22	39	63	100	87	119	112	115	95	109
Tobacco[5]	22	27	80	100	96	104	NA	170	138	145
Domestic products**										
Rice	46	112	226	100	132	193	204	213	185	202
Beans	46	102	129	100	71	101	115	137	144	140
Corn	58	94	124	100	80	107	102	121	119	131
Sorghum	84	108	146	100	148	225	123	239	265	457

Livestock Products

Beef	37	65	115	100	111	67	NA	85	98††	99††
Pork	59	148	267	100	111	168	NA	196	258††	264††
Chicken	16	37	51	100	50	125	NA	184	161	148
Eggs	NA	NA	39	100	99	384	NA	464	435	393
Milk[6]	NA	NA	66	100	57	65	NA	45	41	39

*Primarily for export

**Primarily for domestic consumption

†Projection (January 1986)

††Includes unlicensed slaughtering (equals 25% of beef and 33% of pork output).

1. Multiyear average. 2. Calendar year. 3. One crop cycle; in many cases crop seasons overlap the calendar year. 4. Reflects low acreage planted due to civil war. 5. Includes rubio and havana. 6. Includes only milk sent to processing plants. 7. Preliminary (January 1985) figures.

Sources: 1948 – 52 to 1970, FAO yearbooks; 1977 – 78, Information and Analysis Branch, Office of Agricultural Production (export and livestock figures based on 1980 Statistical Yearbook of Nicaragua (INEC); 1979 – 80 to 1984 – 86, the Ministry of Agriculture and Agrarian Reform (MIDINRA).

PER-CAPITA FOOD AVAILABILITY
(FROM NATIONAL PRODUCTION AND IMPORTS)

Products	Units	1976–78	1980–82	1983	1984
Corn	pounds	181.0	174.0	192.0	165.0
Beans	"	39.7	46.0	38.8	49.1
Rice	"	40.3	65.1	70.5	80.8
Flour	"	31.4	39.2	38.4	37.2
Sugar	"	98.1	91.9	102.0	104.0
Chicken	"	4.6	9.0	8.1	6.7
Pork	"	5.2	6.9	4.8	4.6
Beef	"	30.4	20.3	18.2	18.9
Cooking Oil	liters	17.1	23.7	26.6	22.7
Eggs	dozens	5.0	6.4	6.7	6.3
Milk	gallons	10.8	9.1	9.0	NA
Onions	pounds	NA	8.2	12.1	NA
Casava	"	NA	27.6	52.5	NA
Cabbage	"	NA	18.8	24.0	NA
Plantain	"	NA	48.9	45.0	NA
Potatoes	"	NA	11.3	11.0	NA
Tomatoes	"	NA	13.3	26.0	NA

Source: Center for Investigation and Studies of Agrarian Reform (CIERA); Ministry of Planning (MIPLAN).

MAJOR AGRICULTURAL EXPORTS
(THOUSANDS OF TONS, 1 TON = 2000 POUNDS)

	1948–52	1956	1969	1978	1979	1980	1981	1982	1983	1984
Sugar	6.3	4.4	62.9	104.9	89.4	67.4	111.6	103.3	118.8	111.0
Coffee	15.8	17.2	30.4	51.3	54.5	50.0	56.6	50.6	70.9	46.6
Cotton	3.6	36.9	68.8	131.7	111.8	21.4[1]	81.4	67.6	86.3	90.5
Bananas	13.0	4.4	22.4	136.1	117.3	119.6	103.1	47.8	89.9	87.5
Beef	NA	NA	20.2	36.7	37.0	22.5	10.4	16.0	15.7	9.9
Sesame	12.7	3.6	6.0	5.2	4.8	5.9	9.2	5.4	5.0	7.4
Tobacco	–	–	0.6	1.6	0.9	0.5	1.1	1.0	0.7	1.0

1. Reflects low acreage planted due to civil war.

Sources: FAO Yearbooks; 1980–84 from Ministry of Agriculture and Agrarian Reform (MIDINRA); Ministry of External Trade (MICE).

TABLE TEN

PRICES OF PRINCIPAL EXPORT CROPS
(IN DOLLARS PER POUND)

	1978	1979	1980–82	1983	1984	1985*
Cotton	.50	.55	.71	.64	.74	.65
Sugar, raw	.09	.10	.18	.15	.06	.04
Coffee	1.68	1.32	1.36	1.08	1.35	1.39
Beef	.90	1.20	1.18	1.00	.90	.92
Tobacco	NA	NA	NA	2.27	2.40	NA

*January–June average

Sources: 1978–80, World Bank Report on Nicaragua, 1981; 1981–85, Ministry of Agriculture and Agrarian Reform (MIDINRA).

278

TABLE ELEVEN

PURCHASING POWER OF NICARAGUA'S EXPORTS
(CHANGES IN PRICE OF IMPORT PACKAGE RELATIVE TO CHANGES IN PRICES OF NICARAGUA'S EXPORTS)

1972 = 100
1978 = 97
1979 = 81.5
1980 = 78.7
1981 = 69.5
1982 = 62.3
1983 = 54.4
1984 = 58.8
1985 = 51.9

Source: U.N. Economic Commission on Latin America Report, 1985.

TABLE TWELVE

FOREIGN TRADE AND DEBT
(IN MILLIONS OF U.S. DOLLARS)

	Imports	Exports	Trade Deficit	Debt	Debt Service	Debt Service as Percent of Exports
1973–77 (annual average)	539.9	442.4	97.5	899[1]	76.3	17.2
1980	930.0	503.0	427.0	1579	60.0	11.9
1981	999.0	500.0	499.0	2163	171.0	34.2%
1982	776.0	408.0	368.0	2797	196.0	48.0%
1983	806.9	431.3	375.6	3385	89.0[2]	23.7%
1984	826.2	384.8	441.4	3901	110.0	24.9%
1985[3]	832.4	310.0	522.4	4563	120.0[4]	38.7%

1. 1978
2. The 1983 and 1984 debt service was reduced through a renegotiation process in which the payment of the short-term debt was rescheduled on medium- and long-term bases.
3. Government projections made in November 1985.
4. June 1985: one month after U.S. trade embargo—international banks reschedule Nicaragua's debt, giving Nicaragua a 2-year grace period.

Sources: Central Bank of Nicaragua and ECLA (Economic Commission for Latin America).

ANNUAL INFLATION
(PERCENT)

	1981	1982	1983	1984
Basic Items	10	13	30	44
All Consumer Items[1]	23	22	33	50
Minimum Wage[2]	18	16	20	16

ANNUAL OVERALL INFLATION
(PERCENT)

1979	1980	1981	1982	1983	1984	1985
80	35.4	23.9	29	40	50	250 (proj.)

1. Defined as general price index, December–December.
2. Defined as average manufacturing worker's wage.

Source: Nicaraguan Statistics and Census Institute (INEC).

TABLE FOURTEEN

DESTRUCTION OF INFRASTRUCTURE AND PRODUCTION (1978–1984)
(IN MILLIONS OF U.S. DOLLARS)

	Insurrection 1978–79	Floods 1982	Military Aggression 1980–84	Financial War* 1981–84
Infrastructure	78	224	97	
Production (Agricultural, Industrial and Commercial)	402	132	283	
TOTAL	480	356	380	481
GRAND TOTAL	1,697			

Above figures do not include decapitalization (see chapter 5) estimated during this period to be over $800 million.

*Includes suspended U.S. loans and blocked or canceled loans from World Bank and the Inter-American Development Bank.

The human cost of the war 1980 through June 1985:

Deaths:	11,251	Kidnapped:	5,232
Wounded:	5,365	Displaced:	250,000
		War orphans:	7,582

Sources: U.N. Economic Commission for Latin America (ECLA); for human costs, President Ortega's speech to the U.N. General Assembly, October 1985.

TABLE FIFTEEN

NICARAGUA'S TRADING PARTNERS

	Exports by %				Imports by %			
	1970	1980	1983	1984	1970	1980	1983	1984
TOTAL	100.0	100.0	100.0	100.0	100.0	100.0	100.0	100.0
Central America	25.8	16.8	7.8	9.6	25.2	33.9	15.3	9.0
European Common Market	18.6	28.7	25.7	29.2	14.2	7.8	9.7	12.4
U.S.S.R., Cuba, Eastern Europe	—	2.7	12.7	6.2	0.1	0.2	16.6	25.7
United States	31.3	36.0	18.1	12.3	36.2	27.4	19.4	16.1
Japan	13.8	2.9	15.3	24.8	6.4	3.2	2.4	2.9
Mexico	0.5	—	2.1	1.7	1.3	2.2	19.8	9.7
Venezuela	—	—	—	—	4.1	16.8	0.6	0.6
Others	10.0	13.1	18.3	16.2	12.5	8.5	16.2	23.6

Source: ECLA report, 1983 (United Nations Economic Council for Latin America); Ministry of External Trade (MICE), 1984.

LAND DISTRIBUTED IN 1985: PROJECTED AND ACTUAL

Form of Ownership	1985 Projections		1985 Actual Distribution	
	Area*	Beneficiaries (# of Families)	Area*	Beneficiaries (# of Families)
Individual	189,000	3,774	328,582	11,764
Cooperative	18,000	392	269,602	5,636
Indigenous Communities	103,500	2,727	140,648	316
Total	310,500	6,893	738,832	17,616

*acres

Source: MIDINRA 1986.

FORM OF OWNERSHIP OF LAND DISTRIBUTED UNDER AGRARIAN REFORM LAW (1981–1985)

Period	Small-Medium Producers and Cooperatives	State Farms
1981–1982	30%	70%
1983	35%	65%
1984	43%	57%
1985	95%	5%

Source: MIDINRA 1986.

Nicaraguan
Political Chronology

1821 Nicaragua and rest of Central America declare independence from Spain and form a federation known as United Provinces of Central America.

1838 The Central American union is dissolved and Nicaragua becomes a republic.

1848 Lake Nicaragua is a major route for prospectors on their way to California Gold Rush. Travel across Nicaragua is under control of a company belonging to Cornelius Vanderbilt.

1850 The United States and Great Britain sign Clayton-Bulwer Treaty, which declares that both nations shall share rights to a trans-Nicaragua canal. The Nicaraguan government was not consulted.

1855 William Walker and 58 other American adventurers arrive in Nicaragua, having been given free passage on Vanderbilt's ships. Walker declares himself president, reestablishes slavery, and is recognized by U.S. President Pierce.

1857 Walker is defeated by a combined Central American force, which fears he will try to impose U.S. rule throughout the area. He takes refuge on a U.S. Navy ship.

1909 President Zelaya resigns in the face of open U.S. hostility after he canceled U.S. concessions in Nicaragua, borrowed money from Great Britain, and appeared to favor granting Great Britain or Japan rights to a canal across Nicaragua.

1912 U.S. troops arrive to end the political turmoil that followed Zelaya's resignation. They meet armed resistance from a small group organized by Benjamin Zeladon.

1914 Nicaraguan government signs Bryan-Chamorro treaty giving exclusive canal rights to U.S.

1925 Marines leave, feeling incumbent government is sufficiently pro-U.S. and stable.

1926 American troops return as attempts are made to oust pro-U.S. government.

1927 General Moncada, leader of forces opposing incumbent government, agrees to a peace treaty. One of his generals, Augusto César Sandino, rejects peace pact as a perpetuation of U.S.-imposed government. Sandino organizes guerrilla force to oppose American occupation troops.

1933 U.S. troops leave without defeating Sandino. Their role is assumed by the U.S.-created National Guard, headed by Anastasio Somoza García.

1934 Sandino is assassinated on orders of Somoza after attending peace talks with President Sacasa.

1936 Somoza forces President Sacasa from office and assumes presidency after fraudulent elections.

1954 Somoza permits Nicaragua to be used as staging area for CIA-sponsored coup against democratically elected Guatemalan President Arbenz.

1956 Somoza is assassinated by poet Rigoberto López Pérez at party celebrating Somoza's "renomination." He is succeeded by his eldest son, Luis Somoza.

1961 President Luis Somoza permits Nicaragua to be used as staging area for CIA-sponsored Bay of Pigs, Cuba invasion.

Frente Sandinista de Liberación Nacional (FSLN) founded.

1963 Somoza family confidant René Schick assumes presidency. Anastasio Somoza Debayle, brother of Luis, serves as head of National Guard.

1967 Anastasio Somoza Debayle assumes presidency.

1972 Earthquake destroys much of Managua. President Somoza's profiteering from international aid alienates business elite.

1974 FSLN offensive builds momentum after taking hostages at party for Managua's elite and exchanging them for ransom and freedom of political prisoners.

1978 **January.** Pedro Joaquín Chamorro, editor of opposition paper *La Prensa,* is assassinated, further isolating Somoza regime.

    August. FSLN seizes National Palace, taking dozens of congressmen hostage and exchanging them for ransom, freedom of political prisoners, and safe conduct to Panama.

1979 **July 19.** FSLN forces triumphantly enter Managua after flight of Somoza.

    July. Confiscation decree nationalizes Somocista property, including approximately 20 percent of the nation's total agricultural land.

1980 **March–August.** Literacy Campaign. Illiteracy reduced from 50 percent to 13 percent.

    May. Council of State inaugurated. Council members selected by popular organizations, unions, political parties, private business organizations, professional organizations, and agricultural unions.

    August. Elections announced for 1985.

1981 Rural Health Campaign begins. Rural clinics formed, polio vaccinations, malaria controlled.

    January–April. Ronald Reagan inaugurated as U.S. President; suspends aid to Nicaragua, including credits for wheat.

    April. Formation of UNAG (Unión Nacíonal de Agricultores y Ganaderos), small- and medium-farmers' association.

PAN, national food program, initiated. Top priority assigned to improving production and distribution of foodstuffs.

August. Agrarian Reform Law ratified by Council of State.

October. Ex-National Guard activity in Honduras increases. United States and Honduras begin joint military maneuvers.

The first land titling in Wiwilí.

December. Reagan authorizes $19 million in CIA funds for counterrevolutionaries ("contras").

"Red Christmas" contra attack on northern Atlantic coast. Full-scale attacks and economic sabotage begin.

1982 Severalfold increase in U.S. military and economic aid to Honduras.

January. Miskitu relocation. 18,000 evacuated from war zone along Río Coco border with Honduras.

February–April. U.S. blocks loans to Nicaragua from World Bank, Inter-American Development Bank, and United Nations Development Program. Inflation increases and foreign exchange becomes scarce.

March. Contra commandos, CIA-trained and equipped, bomb vital bridges. National Emergency goes into effect. Nicaragua protests U.S.-backed aggression before UN Security Council.

April. Alfonso Robelo and Eden Pastora form counterrevolutionary alliance (ARDE) in Costa Rica and open southern front in war.

May. Floods cause $350 million in agricultural damage. Followed by three months of drought.

June. Congress approves $5.1 million Reagan administration request for aid to business sector and Archbishop of Managua. Nicaragua rejects aid in August on grounds that the aid was intended to undermine the Sandinista government.

1983 Agrarian reform accelerates.

January. Formation of Contadora Group by Venezuela, Columbia, Mexico, and Panama.

February. First "Big Pine" U.S.-Honduran joint military maneuvers are carried out less than ten miles from Nicaraguan border.

March. Pope John Paul II visits Nicaragua. The Sandinista government facilitates transportation of hundreds of thousands to the Pope's outdoor masses. Pope's mass in Managua becomes highly charged when grieving Nicaraguan mothers confront Pope on his omission of a prayer for their dead.

May. Reagan administration eliminates Nicaragua's share in U.S. preferential price for imported sugar.

Alfonso Robelo of ARDE and Adolfo Calero of the FDN meet in Washington to discuss coordination of military activities against the Nicaraguan government. U.S. government refuses to grant a visa to Nicaraguan Interior Minister Tomas Borge to speak at Johns Hopkins and Harvard universities.

Midyear. First serious spot shortages of gasoline, toothpaste, toilet paper, rice, and cooking oil.

June. Nicaraguan government expels three U.S. diplomats, accusing them of involvement in CIA plot to kill Nicaraguan Foreign Minister Miguel D'Escoto. Reagan administration responds by closing all six Nicaraguan consulates in the U.S. and expelling 21 consular officials.

August. "Big Pine II" joint U.S.-Honduran military maneuvers (through February 1984), involving 4,000 U.S. soldiers and 19 warships off the coast of Nicaragua. Pentagon begins construction of eight new airfields in Honduras. FDN contra attacks from Honduras escalate.

September. Contadora Group 21-point Document of Objectives. Terms include withdrawal of all foreign military forces in Central America and a reduction in arms. Nicaragua agrees to terms.

Military Service Law. The draft applies to all men 17 to 65 years of age; men 26 to 50 and women 18 to 24 are subject to reserve duty.

October. Contras launch attack on Nicaragua's most important port, Corinto, from CIA ship offshore. Much of oil reserves destroyed.

Military leaders of Guatemala, El Salvador, and Honduras meet in Guatemala to reactivate the Central American Defense Council (CONDECA). Also present is General Paul Gorman, of the U.S. Army Southern Command.

November. U.S. Congress approves another $24 million in aid to counterrevolutionary groups fighting against the Nicaraguan government.

December. Amnesty is decreed for Miskitu Indians imprisoned for counterrevolutionary activities and any Nicaraguan, with the exception of contra leaders, who left Nicaragua after July 19, 1979.

1984   January. Kissinger Commission on Central America calls for continued military pressure on Nicaragua. Advocates stepped up economic aid for region, except Nicaragua.

February. National multiparty elections announced for November 1984.

February–March. Nicaraguan ports mined by CIA. U.S. refuses to recognize World Court rulings on Central America for two years.

March. Electoral law approved by Council of State.

April. Renewed U.S. naval and land maneuvers in region, involving 30,000 U.S. soldiers and two naval fleets.

June. Law of Consumer Protection is ratified by the Council of State. Provides for greater government control over food distribution and an "all-out war against speculation."

July–August. Partial lifting of state of emergency. Press censorship limited to military matters. Seven political parties register for November elections. More than 91 percent of the eligible electorate register to vote.

September. Contra planes and helicopter attack military school in Santa Clara, northern Nicaragua. Helicopter is shot down, two U.S. mercenaries die in crash.

Nicaragua announces unconditional acceptance of proposed Contadora peace treaty.

November. Nicaraguan elections. With 75 percent voter turnout, Sandinistas win 67 percent of the vote. Daniel Ortega is elected president, Sergio Ramirez vice president, and the six opposition parties share one-third of 96 National Assembly seats.

World Court provisional ruling calls on the U.S. to stop mining Nicaragua's harbors, and states that Nicaragua should not be subjected to "military and para-military actions since they are prohibited by the principles of international law."

1985   January   10.   Daniel   Ortega   inaugurated   as President.

January.   U.S. breaks off U.S.-Nicaragua ("Man-zanillo") talks.

U.S. withdraws from the World Court.

Secretary of State Shultz threatens to withdraw U.S. support for the Inter-American Development Bank if it grants a $58 million agricultural loan to Nicaragua.

February.   President Reagan publicly states that his policy objective is "to remove the present structure of the Sandinista government."

Nicaragua withdraws 100 Cuban military advisors.

April.   U.S. Congress votes to prohibit funds to the contras.

Obando y Bravo, Archbishop of Managua, is named a cardinal, Nicaragua's first, by Pope John Paul II.

Nicaragua submits a 250-page brief to the World Court outlining its case against U.S. aggression.

President Ortega makes a state visit to the USSR, Eastern Europe, and Western Europe. Receives aid and credits valued at $202 million from the Eastern bloc; $200 million in aid guarantees from France, Spain, Italy, and Finland.

May.   President Reagan declares a national emer-gency and imposes a trade embargo against Nicaragua.

Nicaraguan government, in a change of policy, announces that the Miskitus are free to return to the Río Coco.

A partial ceasefire declared between govern-ment forces and Miskitu fighters on the Atlantic coast.

June.   U.S. Congress approves $27 million in "humanitarian" aid to the contras.

A "Special Agricultural Zone" declared in Masaya Department, legalizing the expropriation of 80,000 acres from large cotton estates for distribution to land-poor campesinos.

Cardinal Obando y Bravo celebrates first mass as a cardinal in Miami; present are top contra leaders.

July. Contadora support group formed consisting of Peru, Argentina, Uruguay, and Brazil.

August. Seven political parties in the National Assembly present proposals on Nicaragua's future constitution.

September. Elliott Abrams, the U.S. State Department official, holds a meeting for U.S. ambassadors to Central American nations and other U.S. officials. Leaked minutes of meeting report him favoring the collapse of Contadora.

New Contadora peace treaty for Central America is proposed by the four Contadora nations (Mexico, Venezuela, Panama, and Colombia).

October. President Ortega addresses the U.N. General Assembly, making a peace proposal.

Nicaragua re-establishes a state of emergency. Catholic hierarchy's publication shut down.

November. Nicaragua rejects the September 1985 Contadora proposal, citing the lack of a mechanism to involve the U.S. in the peace process.

December. Contras use SA-7 missile to shoot down a Nicaraguan government MI-8 helicopter.

President Reagan signs a law reducing restrictions on aid to the contras by allowing for land vehicles, aircraft, and communications equipment.

1986   January. Agrarian Reform Law modified. Minimum acreage requirement eliminated for abandoned, idle, or otherwise unproductive properties to be subject to agrarian reform.

Reagan administration officials say the administration will propose to Congress 100 million dollars in military and "humanitarian" aid to the contras.

February Foreign ministers of eight Latin American nations meet with Secretary of State Shultz regarding the stalled Contadora peace process. They urge that the U.S. cease support of "irregular forces" in Central America.

Glossary

ATC: Asociación de Trabajadores del Campo.
Sandinista-affiliated farmworkers organizations.

CAS: Cooperativas Agrícolas Sandinistas.
Jointly owned and worked farm cooperatives.

CCS: Cooperativas de Crédito y Servicio.
Credit and service associations for individual small and medium farmers.

CDS: Comité de Defensa Sandinista.
Neighborhood organizations.

CIERA: Centro de Investigaciones y Estudios de la Reforma Agraria. Policy research center of the Ministry of Agricultural Development and Agrarian Reform.

COSEP: Consejo Superior de la Empresa Privada.
Higher Council of Private Enterprise.

ENABAS: Empresa Nacional de Alimentos Básicos.
National Basic Foods Corporation.

FAO: Food and Agriculture Organization of the United Nations.

FIDA: Fondo Internacional de Desarrollo
Agrícola. International Fund for Agricultural
Development.

IBRD: International Bank of Reconstruction and
Development (World Bank).

INCAE: Instituto Centroamericano de
Administracion de Empresas.

INRA: Instituto Nacional de Reforma Agraria.
Agrarian Reform Institute.

MICOIN: Ministerio de Comercio Interior. Ministry
of Internal Commerce.

MIDINRA: Ministerio de Desarrollo Agropecuario e
Instituto Nacional de Reforma Agraria.
The Ministry of Agricultural
Development and Agrarian Reform
Institute.

PAN: Programa Alimentario Nacional. National
food plan to achieve food self-sufficiency.

UNAG: Unión Nacional de Agricultores y
Ganaderos. Sandinista-affiliated union
of small and medium farmers and
ranchers.

UPANIC: Unión de Productores Agrícolas
de Nicaragua.
Union of Agricultural Producers of Nicaragua.
Association of large landowners and ranchers.

Sources Consulted

Much of the data for this book was gathered through personal interviews with farmers, ranchers, and farm laborers in Nicaragua; from officials and advisors in the Ministry of Agricultural Development and Agrarian Reform (MIDINRA), the Ministry of Planning, and the Casa de Gobierno; and from officials and activists of the ATC and UNAG. CIERA, the Center for Research and Investigation on Agrarian Reform, was my most important single source of information and statistics.

In place of footnotes, I have listed particular sources—many difficult to find outside Nicaragua. Excluded are the hundreds of conversations and informal interviews mentioned above.

Asociación de Trabajadores del Campo (ATC). *El Machete.* February, 1980.

Belli, Pedro. "Growth of Cotton Farming in Nicaragua." Ph.D. dissertation, University of California, Berkeley, 1968.

Barraclough, Solon, and Marchetti, Peter. *A Preliminary Analysis of the Nicaraguan Food System.* Geneva and Managua: United Nations Research Institute for Social Development and CIERA, June 1982.

Barricada. 30 May; 10, 11, 14, 20, 25, 29 June; 9, 30 July 1981. 28, 30 April; 8, 14, 17 May 1980. 16, 17 February 1981. 2, 4, 5, 15 June 1980.

297

Barricada. Lunes Socio-Económico, 1983–1984 collection. Compiled and published by CIERA.
"Las Hortalizas y la Lucha por el Auto-abastecimiento," 31 October 1983.
"Reforma Agraria: Esta es la Democracía," December 1983.
"El Consumo Básico del Pueblo Aquí y en Centroamerica," 6 February 1984.
"Los Problemas de la Distribución en la Region V," 6 February, 18 June 1984.
"Los Problemas de la Producción de Granos Básicos," 25 June 1984.
"La Revolución del Maiz en la Region II: el Plan Contingente de Granos Básicos," 19 July 1984.
"En Defensa del Consumidor," 6 August 1984.
"Qué Pasa con las Divisas?" 3 September 1984.
"Avanzamos Contruyendo los Suenos: Los Principales Proyectos de Inversión," 5 December 1984.

Bendaña, Alejandro. "Crisis in Nicaragua." NACLA, 12 (1980):6.

Benjamin, Medea; Collins, Joseph; and Scott, Michael. *No Free Lunch: Food and Revolution in Cuba Today.* San Francisco: Institute for Food and Development Policy, 1984.

Biderman, Jaime. "Class Structure, the State and Capitalist Development in Nicaraguan Agriculture." Ph.D. dissertation, University of California, Berkeley, 1982.

Black, George. *Triumph of the People: The Sandinista Revolution in Nicaragua.* London: Zed Press, 1981.

Central American Historical Institute (Instituto Historico Centroamericano).
Envío, June 1981, August 1981, October 1981, March 1982, September 1983, September 1985, October 1985.
Update, vol. 3, no. 36, 1 November 1984.
Update, vol. 3, no. 22, 16 July 1984.
Update, "Masaya Peasants Prompt Land Expropriations," vol. 4, no. 23, 12 July 1985.

Central American Report, vol. 9, no. 25, 2 July 1982.

Centro de Investigación y Estudios de la Reforma Agraria (CIERA). *La Pequeña Producción: Estudios de Casas,* July 1980.

CIERA. *Informes Sobre Las Empresas de Servicios del Estado,* June 1980.

CIERA. *Informe del Ministerio de Desarrollo Agropecuario*, August 1980.

CIERA. *Evaluación de la Política Económica Sandinista en el Sector Agropecuario*, December 1980.

CIERA. *Informes para El Segundo Aniversario*, June 1981.

CIERA. *Datos Generales Sobre El Sector Campesino*, April 1982.

CIERA. *Managua Food System Study: Preliminary Report.*

CIERA, ATC, UNAG. *Producción y Organización en el Agro Nicaragüense*, August 1982.

CIERA. *La Situación del Abastecimiento*, 1983.

CIERA. *Distribución y Consumo Popular de Alimentos en Managua*, February 1983.

CIERA. *Informe del Primer Seminario Sobre Estrategia Alimentaria*, June 1983.

CIERA. MIDINRA. *Informe de Nicaragua a la FAO*, July 1983.

Comercio Exterior. Mexico: Banco Nacional de Comercio Exterior, S.A., April 1981.

Comisión de Propaganda Agropecuaria, *Propaganda del PAN.*

Coone, Tim. "On the Road to Energy Self-Sufficiency." *Science for the People,* November/December 1983.

Deere, Carmen D., and Marchetti, Peter. "The Worker-Peasant Alliance in the First Year of the Nicaraguan Agrarian Reform." *Latin American Perspectives,* vol. 13, no. 2.

Deere, Carmen D.; Marchetti, Peter; and Reinhardt, Nola. "From State Farms to Peasant Property: The Development of Sandinista Agrarian Policy, 1979–1984." April 1984.

Dodson, Michael, and Montgomery, T.S. "The Churches in the Nicaraguan Revolution." Paper presented at the Latin American Studies Association national meeting, October 1980, Bloomington, Indiana.

Dore, Elizabeth W. "Nicaragua: The Experience of the Mixed Economy and Current Political Realities." Center for Latin American and Iberian Studies, rev. March 1984, Vanderbilt University.

Empresa Nicaragüense de Alimentos Básicos (ENABAS). *Informe Anual, 1983*, February 1984.

EPICA Task Force. *Nicaragua: A People's Revolution, Part 2.* Washington: EPICA, 1980.

Fitzgerald, E.V.K. "Stabilization and Economic Justice: The Case of Nicaragua." Working Paper, no. 34. The Kellogg Institute for International Studies, University of Notre Dame, September 1984.

Fondo Internacional de Desarrollo Agricola (FIDA). *Informe de la Misión Especial de Programación a Nicaragua.* Rome, 1980.

Food and Agriculture Organization of the United Nations (FAO). *Mission Report: Nicaragua,* October 1979.

FAO. *Production Yearbook* and *Trade Yearbook* (various years).

Franco, Brother Luis. "The First Steps of the Nicaraguan Agrarian Reform in León: An Interview by Michael Scott." Oxfam America, 5 November 1980.

La Gaceta (diario oficial). Managua, 21 August 1981, 2 October 1981.

George, Susan. *Prospects for Nicaraguan Exports of Basic Grains in the Present World Agricultural and Political Context.* A report to INRA-CIERA, 18 March 1981.

Grossman, Karl. *Nicaragua: America's New Vietnam?* New York: Permanent Press, 1984.

INCAP, UNASEC, AID. Nutrition Sector Assessment. Cited in "A Rural Education Program for Nicaragua" by Practical Concepts, Inc., 17 September 1976.

INRA. *La Revolución en El Campo.*

Instituto Centroamericano de Administración de Empresas (INCAE). *Altamira: Empresa Lechera del Pueblo Roger Deshon Arguello, and Complejo Azucarero Julio Buitrago.*

Instituto del Estudio de Sandinismo (IES). "Precios, Abastecimiento y Control de la Economía," April 1984.

Intercontinental Press, 3 March 1981.

International Bank of Reconstruction and Development (IBRD). *The Economic Situation of Nicaragua,* WH-8, August 1953.

Kaimowitz, David, and Thorne, Joseph R. "Nicaragua's Agrarian Reform: The First Year (1979–80)." *Nicaragua in Revolution: An Anthology.* Edited by Thomas W. Walker. New York: Praeger, 1981.

————. "A Half-Decade of Agrarian Reform in Nicaragua." *Nicaragua: The First Five Years.* Edited by Thomas W. Walker. New York: Praeger, 1985.

Korten, Dr. David C. *Crecimiento de la Población y Calidad de la Vida en Nicaragua.* Paper prepared for INCAE, 1973.

Latin America Regional Reports: Mexico & Central America. RM–81–07, 14 August 1981.

Lappé, Frances Moore, and Collins, Joseph. Interview with Peter Marchetti. *Now We Can Speak: A Journey Through the New Nicaragua.* San Francisco: Institute for Food and Development Policy, 1982.

————. Interview with Salvador Mayorga. *Now We Can Speak.*

Marchetti, Peter. "Reforma Agraria y La Conversión Difícil: Republicación de Recuros, Redistribución de Poder, y Los Explotados del Campo en Chile y en Nicaragua." *Estudios Rurales Latin Americas,* vol. 4.

Ministerio de Comercio Interior (MICOIN). "El A.B.C. de Abastecimiento," July 1984.

Ministerio de Desarrollo Agropecuario e Instituto Nacional de Reforma Agraria (MIDINRA).
Tres Años de Reforma Agraria, 4, 5 May 1982.
Sector Agropecuario: Resultados 1983 y Plan de Trabajo 1984, February 1984.
"Indicadores Añuales de Producción Agropecuaria: 1983," May 1984.
"Informe Sobre Reforma Agraria." Dirección General de Reforma Agraria, no. 8, May 1984; no. 11, August 1984.
"Estudio de Factibilidad 'Ciclo Siete' Proyecto Lechero Chiltepe" Empresa de Desarrollo Ganadero, n.d.
Revolución y Desarrollo, no. 1, June 1984; no. 3, 1985.
"Plan de Reforma Agraria y Producción Agropecuaria," 1985–86.
Informaciónes Agropecuarias, October 1985.

Ministerio de Planificación, *Determinación y Análisis de la Satisfacción de las Necesidades Básicas en los Sectores Urbanos de Nicaragua,* May 1981.

Murray, Douglas L. "Social Problem-Solving in a Revolutionary Setting: Nicaragua's Pesticide Policy Reforms." *Nicaragua Perspectives,* 1984. Unpublished.

Nuevo Diario, 1, 4 July 1981.

Nuevo Diario. "Defensa del Consumidor." (Wednesday feature, various weeks).

Nuñez, Orlando S. *El Somocismo y El Modelo Capitalista Agro-Exportador.* Managua: UNAN, 1981.

Proceso (Mexico), 20 July 1981.

Programa Alimentario Nacional (PAN). "Report on the Popular Mobilization Program for Food Self-Sufficiency," May 1984.

Randall, Margaret. *Sandino's Daughters.* Vancouver, B.C. and Toronto: New Star Books, 1981.

Ryan, John. *Area Handbook for Nicaragua.* Washington, D.C.: U.S. Printing Office, 1956.

Secretaria Nacional de Propaganda y Educación Politica del FSLN. *Poder Sandinista,* 12 September 1980.

Selser, Gregorio. *Sandino.* New York: Monthly Review Press, 1981.

Simon, Laurence. "After the Revolution: An Interview with Jaime Wheelock." *Food Monitor,* July/August 1980.

Swezey, Sean L., and Daxl, Rainer. "Breaking the Circle of Poison: The IPM Revolution in Nicaragua." Food First Research Report. San Francisco: Institute for Food and Development Policy, 1983.

UNICEF. *Análisis de la Situación Económico-Social de Nicaragua,* July 1984.

United Nations. Economic Commission on Latin America. *1983 Economic Report on Nicaragua,* Mexico City, 1984.

"U.S. Blocking World Bank and Inter-American Bank Loan." *New York Times,* 22 October 1984.

Vergapopoulos, Kostas. "L'Agriculture Pérepherique dans le Nouvel Order International." Paper delivered at the Fifth World Congress of Rural Sociology. Mexico, D.F., August 1980.

Wainker, P.F. "The Agricultural Development of Nicaragua: An Analysis of the Production Sector." Ph.D. dissertation. University of Missouri, 1975.

Weeks, John. "The Central American Economics in 1983 and 1984." Washington, D.C.: American University, 2 April 1984.

Weir, David, and Schapiro, Mark. *Circle of Poison.* San Francisco: Institute for Food and Development Policy, 1981.

Wheelock, Jaime. *Imperialismo y Dictadura: Crisis de una Formación Social.* Mexico, D.F., Siglo XXI, 1975.

———. "No Hay Dos Reformas Iguales." *Nicarauac,* vol. 1, May/ June 1980.

———. Speech delivered in Managua, 14 July 1980.

Wheelock, Jaime, and Carrion, Luis. "Apuntos Sobre el Desarrollo Económico Político del FSLN," 1980.

Witness for Peace. *Bitter Witness: Nicaraguans and the "Covert" War.* Draft Report, no. 1, Santa Cruz, 1984.

Working Papers. Interview with Peter Marchetti, March/April, 1982.

Nicaragua Resource Guide

Books

Berryman, Philip. *What's Wrong in Central America.* New York: Pantheon Books, 1985.

Black, George. *Triumph of the People: The Sandinista Revolution in Nicaragua.* London: Zed Press, 1981.

Booth, John A. *The End and the Beginning: The Nicaraguan Revolution.* Boulder, CO: Westview Press, 1982.

Borge, Tómas, et al. *Sandinistas Speak.* New York: Pathfinder Press, 1982.

Brody, Reed. *Contra Terror in Nicaragua.* Boston: South End Press, 1985.

Cabestrero, Teófilo. *Blood of the Innocent.* Maryknoll, NY: Orbis Books, 1985.

Cardenal, Ernesto. *The Gospel in Solentiname.* Maryknoll, NY: Orbis Books, 1976.

Cardenal, Ernesto. *Zero Hour and Other Documentary Poems.* New York: New Direction Books, 1980.

Cardenal, Ernesto. *Flights of Victory.* Maryknoll, NY: Orbis Books, 1985.

Diskin, Martin. *Trouble in Our Backyard.* New York: Pantheon Books, 1983.

Dixon, Marlene, ed. *On Trial: Reagan's War Against Nicaragua.* San Francisco: Synthesis Publications, 1985. Testimony of the Permanent People's Tribunal.

Dixon, Marlene, and Jonas, Susanne, eds. *Nicaragua Under Siege.* San Francisco: Synthesis Publications, 1984.

Eich, Dieter, and Rincón, Carlos. *The Contras: Interviews with Anti-Sandinistas.* San Francisco: Synthesis Publications, 1984.

EPICA Task Force. *Nicaragua: A People's Revolution.* Washington, DC: EPICA, 1980. 100-page primer. From EPICA, 1470 Irving Street N.W., Washington, DC 20010.

Everett, Melissa. *Bearing Witness, Building Bridges.* Philadelphia: New Society Publishers, 1986. Interviews with North Americans living and working in Nicaragua.

Hirshon, Sheryl, with Butler, Judy. *And Also Teach Them to Read.* Westport, CT: Lawrence Hill and Company, 1983.

Lappé, Frances Moore, and Collins, Joseph. *Now We Can Speak: A Journey through the New Nicaragua.* San Francisco: Institute for Food and Development Policy, 1982. Interviews with many Nicaraguans. $4.95 from IFDP, 1885 Mission Street, San Francisco, CA 94103.

Levie, Alvin. *Nicaragua: The People Speak.* South Hadley, MA: Bergin and Garvey, 1985. Oral histories, photojournalism.

Marcus, Bruce, ed. *Nicaragua: The Sandinista People's Revolution.* New York: Pathfinder Press, 1985. Speeches by Sandinista leaders.

McGinnis, James. *Solidarity with the People of Nicaragua.* Maryknoll, NY: Orbis Books, 1985.

Meiselas, Susan. *Nicaragua June '78–July '79.* New York: Pantheon Books, 1981. Color photographs and chronology.

Millet, Richard. *Guardians of the Dynasty: A History of the U.S.-Created Guardia Nacional de Nicaragua and the Somoza Family.* Maryknoll, NY: Orbis Books, 1977.

PACCA (Policy Alternatives for the Caribbean and Central America). *Changing Course: Blueprint for Peace in Central America and the Caribbean.* Washington, DC: PACCA, 1984.

Pearce, Jenny. *Under the Eagle.* Boston: South End Press, 1984.

Randall, Margaret. *Sandino's Daughters*. Vancouver, BC and Toronto: New Star Books, 1981. From the Crossing Press, Trumansberg, NY 14886.

Randall, Margaret. *Christians in the Nicaraguan Revolution*. Vancouver, BC: New Star Books, 1983.

Randall, Margaret. *Risking a Somersault in the Air*. San Francisco: Solidarity Publications, 1984.

Rius (Eduardo del Rio). *Nicaragua for Beginners*. New York: Writers and Readers Publishing, 1984.

Rosset, Peter, and Vandermeer, John, eds. *The Nicaragua Reader*. New York: Grove Press, 1983.

SCAAN (Stanford Central America Action Network). *Revolution in Central America*. Boulder, CO: Westview Press, 1983.

Selser, Gregorio. *Sandino*. New York: Monthly Review Press, 1981.

Swezey, Sean L., and Rainer, Daxl. *Breaking the Circle of Poison: The IPM Revolution in Nicaragua*. San Francisco: Institute for Food and Development Policy. Nicaragua's efforts to implement a national, integrated pest management system. 24 pages, $4.00 from IFDP, 1885 Mission Street, San Francisco, CA 94103.

Walker, Thomas, ed. *Nicaragua: The First Five Years*. New York: Praeger, 1985.

Weber, Henri. *Nicaragua: The Sandinist Revolution*. London: New Left Review Editions, 1981.

Wheelock, Jaime. *Imperialismo y Dictadura: Crisis de una Formación Social*. Mexico City: Siglo XXI, 3rd edition, 1979.

Wheelock, Jaime. *Nicaragua: The Great Challenge*. Managua: Alternative Views, 1984.

Periodicals

Brigadista Bulletin. Newsletter for North Americans returned from the international work brigades in Nicaragua. Nicaragua Exchange, 239 Centre Street, New York, NY 10013, (212) 219-8620.

Envío. Monthly "newsletter" on political, economic, and social developments in Nicaragua from Jesuit-run Instituto Histórico Centroamericano. Available in English from Central American Historical Institute, Intercultural Center, Georgetown University, Washington, DC 20057 for $35 per year.

Indigenous World / El Mundo Indigena. Covers the indigenous peoples of North and South America and features comprehensive and well-documented coverage of Nicaragua's indigenous peoples. Available in English and Spanish from Indigenous World , 274 Grand View Avenue, San Francisco, CA 94114, (415) 647-1966.

Lasa-Nica Scholars News. Newsletter of the Latin American Studies Association Task Force, which focuses on education and research projects in Nicaragua. Available from Latin American Studies Association, Sid Richardson Hall, Unit 1, University of Texas, Austin, TX 78712.

Legislative Update. Coalition for a New Foreign and Military Policy, 712 G Street S.E., Washington, DC 20003, (202) 546-8400.

Nicaraguan Perspectives. Quarterly. Nicaragua Information Center, P.O. Box 1004, Berkeley, CA 94704, (415) 549-1387.

Nicaragua Through Our Eyes. Newsletter of CUSCLIN, the Committee of U.S. Citizens Living in Nicaragua. Distributed by the Austin Peace and Justice Coalition, 1022 West 6th Street, Austin, TX 78703.

Report on the Americas. Bimonthly publication of the North American Congress on Latin America (NACLA), focusing on the political economy of the Americas. 151 West 19th Street, 9th floor, New York, NY 10011.

Strategic Reports. Published by the Center for the Study of the Americas (CENSA), 2288 Fulton Street, #103, Berkeley, CA 94704.

Update. Covers current events in Nicaragua and other Central American countries. Central American Historical Institute, Intercultural Center, Georgetown University, Washington, DC 20057, (202) 625-8246.

Update. Bimonthly plus special reports. Washington Office on Latin America, 110 Maryland Avenue, N.E., Washington, DC 20002.

Films

Access to Films on Central America, c/o CISPES Northwest Regional Office, 5825 Telegraph Avenue #54, Oakland, CA 94609, (415) 486-1177. National listing of films and distributors.

From the Ashes, 16mm, color, 60 min, English subtitles. Available from Document Associates, 211 E. 43rd Street, New York, NY 10017, (212) 682-0730. The reconstruction of Nicaragua from the point of view of one family.

Living at Risk, 1985, color, 59 min. Available from New Yorker Films, 16 West 61st Street, New York, NY 10023, (212) 247-6110. A film depicting the Nicaraguan crisis through the daily lives of five brothers and sisters from a middle-class family.

Nicaragua: No Pasarán, 1984, 74 min. Available from New Yorker Films, 16 West 61st Street, New York, NY 10023, (212) 247-6110. Focuses on the Nicaraguan revolution and the people's struggle to survive in the face of massive U.S. economic and military pressure.

Sandino Hoy y Siempre, 16mm, color, 57 min, English subtitles. Available from Icarus Films, 200 Park Avenue South, Suite 1319, New York, NY 10003. A portrait of Nicaragua and its people during the reconstruction process.

Sandino Vive!, 16mm, color, 28 min, 1980, Spanish or English. Free loan from Maryknoll Fathers and Brothers, Maryknoll, NY 10545. The church's role in the overthrow of Somoza.

Thanks to God and the Revolution, 16mm, color, 30 min, English subtitles. Available from Icarus Films. An inquiry into the role of Christians in social change and armed struggle.

These Same Hands (Nicaragua: Las Mismas Manos), ¾ inch video-cassette format, 53 min. Available from World Focus Films, 2125 Russell Street, Berkeley, CA 94705, (415)848-8126.

The Uprising, 35mm, color, 96 min, Spanish or English. Available from Kino International, 250 West 57th Street, New York, NY 10019, (212) 586-8720. Director Peter Lilienthal's dramatization of events during the final period of fighting in 1979.

Women in Arms, 16mm, color, 59 min, Spanish or English. Available from Hudson River Productions, P.O. Box 515, Franklin Lakes, NJ 07417. Participation of women in the war and the transformation of society.

Tape and Slide Shows

"Born from the People." Available from the Office of World Service and World Hunger, Presbyterian Church (U.S.A.), 341 Ponce de León N.E., Atlanta, GA 30365.

"Central America: We Can Make a Difference." Institute for Food and Development Policy. Analyzes the roots of the conflict in Central America and ways we can work for change. Available from IFDP, 1885 Mission Street, San Francisco, CA 94103.

"Nicaragua: The Challenge of Revolution," 25 min, 139 slides/tape presentation with script and information packet. Available from the Nicaragua Network. Describes the most important development in the revolutionary process.

"Nicaragua Libre," 20 min, 80 b/w slides. Available from Jeanne Gallo, SND, 24 Curtis Avenue, Somerville, MA 02144. Social conditions and history of struggle plus the effort to build a new society.

"Now We're Awakened! Women in Nicaragua," 30 min, 80 color slides/tape and information packet. From PAN, 410 Merritt #7, Oakland, CA 94610. Women's participation in the overthrow of the dictatorship and the building of a new order in Nicaragua.

"Through Our Eyes: North Americans in Nicaragua," 22 min, filmstrip/slide/tape presentation. A project of the Committee on the Caribbean and Latin American, National Council of Churches.

Organizations

American Friends Service Committee, 1501 Cherry Street, Philadelphia, PA 19102, (215) 241-7000.

CENSA/CIERA Agricultural Exchange, 2288 Fulton Street #103, Berkeley, CA 94704. Promotes cooperation on agricultural projects between farmers and academics in Nicaragua and U.S.

Central America Health Rights Network, 853 Broadway #1105, New York, NY 10003, (212) 420-9635.

Council on Hemispheric Affairs, 1900 L Street, N.W., Room 201, Washington, DC 20036.

Environmental Project on Central America (EPOCA), c/o Earth Island Institute, 4089 26th Street, San Francisco, CA 94131, (415) 821-7625.

Faculty for Human Rights in Central America (FACHRESCA), 929 Fresno, Berkeley, CA 94707.

Humanitarian Assistance Project for Independent Agricultural Development in Nicaragua (HAP-NICA), 402 Monroe, Ann Arbor, MI 48104, (313) 761-7960.

Institute for Food and Development Policy (IFDP), 1885 Mission Street, San Francisco, CA 94103, (415) 864-8555.

MADRE, 853 Broadway, Room 301, New York, NY 10003, (212) 777-6470. In solidarity with mothers and children in Central America.

Nicaragua Exchange, 239 Centre Street, New York, NY 10013, (212) 219-8620. Coordinates harvest brigades to Nicaragua.

Nicaragua Network, 2025 I Street N.W., #1117, Washington, DC 20006, (202) 223-2328.

North American Congress on Latin America (NACLA), 151 West 19th Street, New York, NY 10011, (212) 989-8890.

Pledge of Resistance National Clearinghouse, 614 W. 114th Street, New York, NY 10025, (212) 870-3313. Broad-based movement of people pledging to commit acts of civil disobedience or legal protest to military action in Central America.

Quixote Center, 3311 Chauncey Place #301, Mt. Rainer, MD 20712, (301) 699-0042. Humanitarian aid to Nicaragua and educational information.

TecNica, 110 Berkside Drive, Berkeley, CA 94705, (415) 848-0292. Technical support group for Nicaragua.

Washington Office on Latin America (WOLA), 110 Maryland Avenue, N.E., Washington, DC 20002, (202) 544-8045.

Witness for Peace, P.O. Box 29497, Washington DC 20017, (202) 269-6316. Hotline: (202) 332-9230. Faith-based movement to change U.S. policy in Nicaragua through nonviolent action.

AUTHOR

Joseph Collins is an internationally recognized researcher, author, lecturer, and media consultant on third-world food and agricultural policies. Since 1979 he has visited Nicaragua regularly both to do research and to serve as an unpaid advisor on agrarian reform.

Among the books Dr. Collins has authored or co-authored are: *Food First: Beyond the Myth of Scarcity; Aid as Obstacle; Agrarian Reform and Counter-Reform in Chile; Now We Can Speak: A Journey Through the New Nicaragua;* and *No Free Lunch: Food and Revolution in Cuba Today.*
Currently he is collaborating on two books to be released in 1986: *World Hunger: Twelve Myths* and *Help That Hurts: Where Do Our Aid Dollars Go?*

He is co-founder of the Institute for Food and Development Policy, headquartered in San Francisco. He is also a founding board member of Policy Alternatives for the Caribbean and Central America (PACCA) and a member of the Commission on United States–Central American Relations.

CONTRIBUTING AUTHORS

Frances Moore Lappé, who with Joseph Collins founded the Institute for Food and Development Policy, is author of *Diet for a Small Planet.* A noted writer and lecturer on hunger and development issues, she is co-author of a number of books with Dr. Collins, including the two works in progress cited above.

Paul Rice is an economic planner and policy analyst with the Ministry of Agricultural Development and Agrarian Reform (MIDINRA) in the Estelí region of Nicaragua. He has lived in Nicaragua since 1983 and previously worked as a researcher on agrarian reform with the Nicaraguan Institute for Economic and Social Research (INIES).

Nick Allen is Executive Producer of *Faces of War*, a 30-minute television documentary on Central America, and Executive Director of Neighbor-To-Neighbor, the Central America television organizing project of the Institute for Food and Development Policy.